VIEWS OF THE BIBLICAL WORLD

VIEWS OF THE

BIBLICAL WORLD

1

THE LAW

First International Edition

Printed in Israel, 1959

Jordan Publications, Inc. Chicago — New York

Published in the United States of America by Jordan Publications Inc., 1959

Library of Congress Catalogue Card number 59—7767

PRINTED IN ISRAEL

Printing of colour plates, texts, cover and endpaper — E. Lewin-Epstein Ltd, Bat-Yam. Type-setting — Haaretz Press Ltd, Tel-Aviv. Photolito work — Clichés Schwitter A. G., Zürich; Omanim Meuchadim Ltd, Tel Aviv. Maps — E. Lewin-Epstein Ltd, Bat-Yam. Paper — Van Reekum Papier-Gepacy N. V., Netherlands. Design of cover, back and endpaper — Jacob Zim, Tel Aviv.

English Edition prepared under the Supervision of
Merton Dagut, Anne Katzenstein, Inna Pommerantz
Revised by
the Hon. Edwin H. Samuel

Maps — Eng. Pinhas Yoeli
Graphic Art and Lay-Out — Jacob Zim
Technical Adviser — Saul Golan
Photography — Zoltan Kluger

On the publication of the first volume — the volume of The Law — of "Views of the Biblical World", I welcome the initiative shown in this important cultural undertaking. It will throw fresh light on the biblical world and will, through its illustrations, bring it to life. The Editorial Committee has provided students of the Bible throughout the world with a clear picture, based on the most recent scientific conclusions, of the physical, ethnic and historical surroundings in which the heroes of the biblical stories lived and fought. This publication, with its vivid photographs, reveals to us the living treasures of the distant past. It brings us closer to the world of the Patriarchs, the Judges and the Prophets. It gives us a pictorial idea of the early days which we have been able to study till now from the literature alone. This deficiency has now been filled by this volume of pictures and drawings. They will serve as a new, live commentary on the world of the Bible. I have full confidence in the members of the Editorial Committee and in the publishers. Their names provide a guarantee that the book follows the highest scientific and artistic standards. I trust that it will serve all lovers of the Bible — both in Israel and among the other nations of the world — as a valuable aid in both study and education.

Izhak Ben-Zvi

PRESIDENT OF ISRAEL

INTRODUCTION

THE biblical period, from the migration of the Patriarchs until the establishment of the Second Temple, covers approximately a thousand years. Its cultural tradition, as expressed in the Bible, was part of the civilization of the ancient Middle East. This civilization ranged from the great cities in Mesopotamia and the valley of the Nile to the nomads in the desert bounded by the Fertile Crescent. In the midst of these ancient nations, Israel arose and grew strong.

The composition of the book we know as the Bible was still in process when the world which it described was already disappearing. For, after Alexander's conquest, the spiritual and material character of these Biblical lands was fundamentally changed under the pervasive influence of Hellenistic culture. It was during this period that attempts were begun to popularize the Bible among the nations. On both linguistic and interpretative levels, efforts were made to make the Bible accessible to the educated classes of the time. Most probably, drawings were appended to the Bible stories to bring that distant past vividly within the grasp of the contemporary reader. It is presumed that Jewish artists in Alexandria, the centre of Hellenistic culture, were the first to supplement the biblical text with pictures, although unfortunately none of them has been preserved. Other sequences of drawings on biblical subjects followed, each conceived in the taste of the period in which it was produced. An impressive example of one of these sequences was discovered in the synagogue of Dura-Europos (3rd cent. A.D.). The influence of this form of art may be seen in the murals in the Christian catacombs in and around Rome (3rd and 4th centuries); in the mosaic floors of various Palestinian synagogues (5th and 6th centuries); in wall mosaics in Italian churches (6th to 10th centuries) up to the Byzantine miniatures of the 9th to the 12th centuries.

During the Middle Ages and the Renaissance, the heroes and tales of the Scriptures were popular artistic subjects, the artists stressing the Bible's timeless and eternal values. Two distinct approaches to biblical art developed during this period: Romanesque and Gothic art depicted the biblical figures in medieval dress, presenting Joseph, Moses, Saul and David as nobles, ministers, scholars, kings and knights, garbed in the clothes and observing the usages of contemporary life. The representation of biblical scenes in contemporary garb, a relic of this medieval approach, is found even today. This is an expression of faith in the permanence of the ethics and wisdom of the Bible, which remain unaffected by the passage of centuries and the evolution of cultures, revealing human beings that come alive in every period, in every place and in every costume.

In contrast to this conception, the artists of the Renaissance, particularly Michelangelo and Raphael and their successors, imagined the biblical heroes in the light of early Christian tradition. They drew them as idealized immortals, dressed in the pallium of ancient Greece or in the toga of Rome. These figures were purposely set apart as the embodiment of spiritual truths, unconnected with any particular time or place.

A new approach made its appearance with the end of the Renaissance. It seemed to the artists that the special oriental atmosphere peculiar to the Scriptures was not authentically expressed in just any garb, and an attempt was made to get away from their occidental environment. In their search for suitable models, they turned sometimes to the Moslem East, the historic stage of biblical action; sometimes to the ghettoes of Europe, where the descendants of biblical Israel had made their homes. This was the attitude taken by Rembrandt and his successors.

Finally, in the wake of archaeological research begun in the first half of the nineteenth century, biblical illustrators adopted a new stylistic concept of their subject, based on scientific fact and deduction. One by one, the antique treasures of the East, saved from destruction during thousands of years of strife by their protective layers of debris, were brought to light and analysed. The hieroglyphics of Egypt and Babylonian-Assyrian cuneiform writings were deciphered and the accompanying reliefs and frescoes cleared. This opened up to the artist the wealth of the biblical and even pre-biblical lore contained in these ancient sources. The abundance of illustrative material uncovered not only served as a useful commentary on various texts but also shed considerable light on the life of the period in general. During the past 150 years, archaeological and historical research and biblical interpretation have produced a mass of material from which the life and culture of biblical times can be reconstructed with considerable accuracy. The picture that emerges, however, is quite different from the various artistic conceptions of the Scriptures fashionable at different periods during the past 2000 years.

Many pieces of the puzzle of this exotic and wonderful world, in which the Jews lived from the dawn of their existence until their exile, are still missing. Nevertheless, we do have sufficient evidence to reconstruct in a general way the life of biblical times. Whole passages of the Bible, verses and even single words which, till recently, had been unintelligible are now fully understood in the light of archaeological, epigraphic and literary research. An understanding of the Scriptures is thus more readily achieved. Modern Bible study has come to be a composite of several sciences — archaeology, history, geography and philology. Nevertheless, the eternal ethical and spiritual values of the Book of Books have not suffered by this research: on the contrary, they have been enhanced. In our own generation, we have seen their influence and prestige increase.

The amazing achievements of oriental studies, both in the deciphering of ancient tongues and in archaeology, have resulted in attempts to analyse this material as a whole. From the end of the 19th century up to the present day, several books have tried to bring the Bible home to the reader through illustrations based on the conclusions of archaeological and historical research in the lands of antiquity. Thus we have the works of H. Gressmann (in German), of J. B. Pritchard (in English) and the "Biblical Treasures" by M. Soloveitchik (in Hebrew and German). All these books, however, have arranged their material according to subject matter, a method appropriate to the research student interested in specific details of a certain aspect of life in the ancient East. This method, however, is hardly suited to the person who reads the Scriptures in the order in which they are composed and feels in need of a picture to illuminate the particular passage puzzling him. A pioneering attempt in this direction, dealing so far only with the Pentateuch, was made some years ago by P. Bonaventura Ubach of the Montserrat Monastery in Catalonia.

The increased interest in Israel's past, shown both in Israel and on the part of Jews and Christians alike abroad, has induced the initiators of the "Views of the Biblical World" to publish this illustrated commentary on the Bible. The project was conceived by the publisher, Mr. J. Makavy: it was planned and executed under the supervision of Professor Benjamin Mazar, President of the Hebrew University of Jerusalem. The pictures have been arranged according to chapter and verse, in order to ensure continuity. The biblical content has throughout been regarded as the principal aim of the project: the short commentaries appended serve mainly to explain and clarify the original text. If we had chosen to deal with every verse in the Bible, or even with only the important verses, we would never have been able to cope with the mass of material available. We have therefore limited ourselves to verses which we consider typical or of particular interest and capable of being illustrated.

The pictures we have selected include views of ruins on the surface as well as of those revealed through archaeological excavations; ancient cities, their fortifications, their public buildings and houses, temples and altars; tools, weapons, ornaments, ritual objects, musical instruments and household utensils; works of art recording acts of religious faith and spiritual vision; examples of the flora and fauna of the biblical lands; landscapes; and maps showing boundaries and explaining the migrations and military expeditions.

We have attempted to illustrate biblical life in all phases of its activity: at war and in peace; in the house and in the field: we have portrayed artisans and craftsmen, recreation and religious ceremonies. Emphasis has been placed on depicting man at work, in preference to pictures of inanimate artifacts. Material from the pagan world has been introduced to show the elements of that ancient culture against which the laws and prophets of the Bible warred and to provide the background to the moral and religious struggle of Israel.

In only very rare cases have proven relics of biblical events and personages been actually preserved from the ravages of time; and it goes without saying that these exhibits have been included in the "Views of the Biblical World", following the best available source.

The guiding principle in the selection of material has been its *authenticity*. To bring out in full the reality of the Bible stories, the editors have made every effort to find illustrations dating from the period dealt with by the text, or as close to it as possible. The commentaries identify the pictures as to time, place and their relation to the subject at hand; and, when necessary, provide an authoritative explanation of the biblical passage. We have tried to base our material on the results of the very latest biblical research, while presenting it in a form readily understood by the general reader. A bibliography arranged according to subject matter will be appended to the fourth volume for the benefit of those who wish to delve further into this matter.

CREDITS

Naturally, a work of this nature has involved the employment of a large staff. The advice of many institutions, scholars and private individuals has frequently been sought and every application was met courteously. Dr. M. Avi-Yonah started to gather the material in 1955: the following year, he and Dr. A. Malamat began editing the book itself. Apart from the editors, members of the editorial board, the editorial advisory council and the many assistants (the names of whom are given in the editorial list), we are grateful to many scholars and museum collections throughout the world. To those who helped us to gather the photographs or who supplied suggestions for the body of the text, we owe our sincere gratitude. Among them are Prof. W. F. Albright (who took the time to go over the pictorial material of this first volume); Dr. R. D. Barnett, London; Dean S. A. Callisen, New-York; Prof. N. Glueck, Cincinnati; R. W. Hamilton, Oxford; Prof. Seton Lloyd, Ankara; Dr. G. Neumann, Berlin; Prof. A. Parrot, Paris; Prof. G. E. Wright, Chicago; Father R. North, S.J., of the Pontifical Institute in Jerusalem; Dr. M. H. Ben-Shammai, M. Broshi, M. and Mrs. T. Dothan, H. Gevaryahu, B. Liphshitz, A. Reuveni, S.J. Schweig, Prof. M. Stekelis, Dr. D. Zaitschik and Dr. D. Zohary— all of Jerusalem.

We also wish to thank those members of the public in Israel and abroad who endorsed the project at its outset. At their head stand the President of Israel, Izhak Ben-Zvi, the Minister of Education and Culture, Z. Aranne, and the Minister for Religious Affairs, M. H. Shapira.

We have pleasure in thanking the Israel Ministry for Foreign Affairs, the Ministry of Education and Culture, the Ministry of Commerce and Industry, the Ministry of Finance and the Ministry of Defence as well as the Jewish Agency and 'Malben' for their encouragement and help.

Our thanks are also due to all the museums, collectors and photographers who helped to collect suitable photographs. Those in Israel include the Archaeology Department of the Hebrew University; the Antiquities Department (museum and library) of the Ministry of Education and Culture (directed by S. Yeivin); the Bezalel National Museum; the James de Rothschild Expedition at Hazor; the collection of the late Prof. A. Reifenberg; the collection of J. Leibovitch; the Clark collection at the Jerusalem Y.M.C.A.; the collection of Dr. Y. Yadin; the collection of K. Katz; the collection of Prof. S. F. Bodenheimer; the Schocken Library; the Pontifical Biblical Institute in Jerusalem; the Biological Institute in Tel Aviv (under the direction of Prof. H. Mendelsohn); the Geological Institute of the Ministry of Development (under Prof. Y. Ben-Tor); the Israel Aero Club; Dr. Y. Galili and Dr. P. Merom.

Contributors abroad include the Metropolitan Museum in New York; the Oriental Institute of the University of Chicago; the archives of Prof. N. Glueck; the Boston Art Museum and Mr. M. Davidson; the University of Pennsylvania Museum; the Brooklyn Museum; the Baltimore Museum; the Detroit Art Museum; the British Museum, London; the Ashmolean Museum, Oxford; the Bodleian Library, Oxford; the Louvre, Paris; the de Clercq collection, Paris; the Rijksmuseum, Leyden, and the Turin Museum.

The editorial board also wishes to thank the following authors, editors, and publishers for permission to use pictures included in books or articles by D. Baldi, (Marietti); A. M. Blackman (Egypt Exploration Fund); H. Bonnet (De Gruyter & Co.); E. Chiera (Harvard University Press); W. R. Dawson (Egypt Exploration Society); N. de G. Davies (Metropolitan Museum); E. Douglas van Buren (Yale University Press); C. S. Fisher (Harvard University Press); A. Furman; K. Galling (J. C. B. Mohr – Paul Siebeck); Sir A. Gardiner (Oriental Institute, University of Chicago); A. Gayet (Presses Universitaires de France); H. Grimme (Folkswang Verlag); P. Lemaire (Marietti); A. Lhote (Librairie Hachette); G. Loud (Oriental Institute, University of Chicago); D. G. Lyon (Harvard University Press); R. A. S. Macalister (Palestine Exploration Fund); A. Mechiterian (A. Skira); P. E. Newberry (Constable & Co. Ltd.); M. Pallottino (A. Skira); A. T. Peet (Egypt Exploration Society); W. Phillips (V. Gollancz); H. Rancke (J. C. B. Mohr – Paul Siebeck); G. A. Reisner (Harvard University Press); H. Schmöckel (G. Klipper); B. Ubach (Monestir de Montserrat); Sir L. Woolley (British Museum – University of Pennsylvania); and W. Wreszinski (J. C. Hinrichs).

In addition, we have made use of the comprehensive works composed by R. Lepsius and A. Ch. T. E. Prisse d'Avennes. Most of the photographs of Israel and of articles in Israel museums were taken by Z. Kluger. We also made use of pictures from the collections of the Marburg Photographical Institute, G. E. Matson of Los Angeles, B. Rotenberg, N. Tadmor, A. Volk, A. Allon, M. Bar-Am, I. Tal, Prof. D. Amiran, P. Merom and Dr. A. Heilbronner. We have used several photographs from the United States and Europe whose owners wish to remain anonymous.

We wish to thank the following for their devoted work: the management and staff of Schwitter A.G., Zürich; Omanim Meuchadim Ltd., Tel Aviv; the E. Lewin-Epstein Ltd. Press, Bat Yam; the Haaretz Press Ltd., Tel Aviv, and the Hakorech Binders' Cooperative, Holon.

Most of the pictures dealing with warfare, weapons and fortifications were prepared by Dr. Y. Yadin for his own book on these subjects, which is to appear shortly through the publisher of this work.

The English translation of the biblical text is based mainly on "The Holy Bible, Revised Standard Version," 1952, by kind permission of Thomas Nelson and Sons, Ltd., London & Edinburgh.

"Views of the Biblical World" will comprise, when completed, four volumes, one for each of the accepted divisions of the Bible: the Pentateuch, the Early and Late Prophets, and the Hagiographa.

                                                                    THE EDITORS

GENESIS

On the right – the title page of a Pentateuch manuscript, dating to the thirteenth century A.D.
On this page are represented the events from the Fall to Bileam's encounter with the angel.
(Photographed by kind permission of the Schocken Library, Jerusalem)

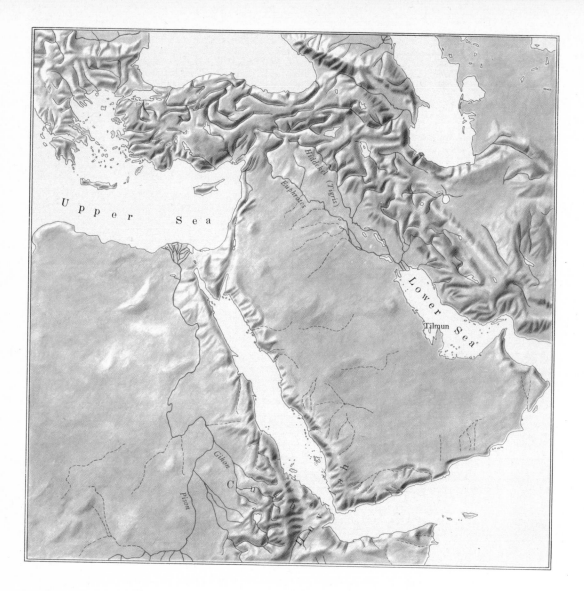

A river flowed out of Eden to water the garden, and there it divided and became four rivers. The name of the first is Pison; it is the one which flows around the whole land of Havilah, where there is gold; ... The name of the second river is Gihon; it is the one which flows around the whole land of Cush. And the name of the third river is Hiddekel, which flows east of Assyria. And the fourth river is the Euphrates.

(Gen. 2 : 10-14)

The Garden of Eden was created for man, so that his life should be happy and carefree. A similar tradition about a marvellous garden containing trees with fruits rich in vivifying juices is found in Sumer and Akkad. But there is an important difference between the Sumero-Akkadian story and that related in the Bible. The main purpose of the former is to describe the habitation of the gods in paradise; whereas the latter is essentially a lofty ethical parable about the knowledge of good and evil and about sin and its punishment.
God planted the Garden "in Eden to the east". The geographical description of the Garden of Eden is very vague and somewhat imaginary. As the early Rabbis said: "Eden ... is a special place and no mortal knows where it is" (*Midrash Haggadol, Bereshith*). Of the four rivers issuing from the main stream, only two — the Euphrates and the Hiddekel (Tigris) — are known. The other two appear to bear symbolical names: Pison from the Hebrew root *push* meaning "to spring forth", and Gihon from the root *giah* in the sense of "bursting forth". Some scholars identify them with the streams of the White and Blue Niles (according to the apocryphal commentary on the Book of Genesis found among the Dead Sea Scrolls, the Gihon is in the region of the Red Sea). Possibly the four rivers refer to the two great centres of ancient civilization: the Nile Valley and Mesopotamia. Mesopotamian tradition places paradise in the region of the Persian Gulf; to be exact, at Dilmun, probably the modern Bahrein.

Now the serpent was more subtle than any other wild creature . . .   (Gen. 3 : 1)

In the ancient world, the snake was the symbol of cunning and the incarnation of evil. In talmudic legend, the snake primevally had the same upright stance and ate the same foods as man; and only after man's sin was it punished with the curse of "upon your belly you shall go, and dust you shall eat all the days of your life" (Gen. 3 : 14). Later Jewish traditions depicted the snake as a demon or a fabulous monster, as in Babylonian mythology. In ancient Mesopotamian art, various kinds of legendary snakes are portrayed: body and forelegs are those of a lion, while the hind-legs resemble the feet of an eagle.

Above — a legendary dragon represented in glazed brick on the Gate of Ishtar in Babylon dating from the reign of Nebuchadnezzar II (6th cent. B.C.).

Below — a seal from approximately the same period, showing a man and woman sitting under a Tree of Life while a snake rears itself up beside them. This scene has been interpreted in two opposite ways. One view is that it depicts the story of the Garden of Eden. This is contested by those who hold that the similarity of the details is pure coincidence, and that the figures on the seal are merely symbols of fertility (the snake) and of long life (the tree).

HE drove out the man; and at the east of the garden of Eden He placed the cherubim and a flaming sword which turned every way, to guard the way to the tree of life.   (Gen. 3 : 24)

In the Bible, as in oriental tradition generally, the Tree of Life symbolizes man's yearning for eternal life. When the first man sinned, he was debarred by divine decree from eating of the Tree of Life; and the cherubim were stationed to guard every approach to it "lest he put forth his hand . . . and eat, and live for ever" (Gen. 3 : 22).

The Tree of Life, flanked by its guardian cherubim, is a frequent motif in Mesopotamian art. The figure below shows the drawing (restored) of a side of an ivory casket from Nimrud on the Tigris dating to the 8th cent. B.C. The Tree of Life is depicted as a date-palm, economically the most important of the trees grown in Mesopotamia. Beside it stand two legendary creatures, each having a human head, a lion's body, and wings. The style is Assyro-Phoenician.

The upper figure shows a bone handle from Hazor of approximately the same period. This is a Palestinian version of the Mesopotamian motif. Here, too, the Tree of Life is depicted as a young date-palm protected by a four-winged seraph, of whom only the wing-tips are visible here.

Now Abel was a keeper of sheep and Cain a tiller of the ground. In the course of time Cain brought to the LORD an offering of the fruit of the ground, and Abel brought of the firstlings of his flock and of their fat portions... (Gen. 4 : 2-4)

Cattle-rearing and tilling the soil — two of the great fundamentals of human existence — were practised by man as early as the Mesolithic Age. The primeval hatred between the farmer and the nomad finds expression in the story of Cain and Abel, the two elder sons of Adam. This conflict is also reflected in Sumerian literature: one of their myths stresses the hostility between the shepherd-god and the farmer-god. But, whereas the Sumerian myth is concerned principally with the material advantage of the farmer and the shepherd, the story of Cain and Abel lays stress on divine justice and the heinousness of murder.

The cylinder seal of the second half of the fourth millennium B.C. shown here depicts the presentation of animal and vegetable offerings to the Sumerian goddess Inanna (Ashtoreth). The symbol of the goddess are gateposts with a streamer, visible on the right of the seal. The bearded figure clothed in a lozenge-patterned garment, who is offering an animal-shaped vessel to the goddess, is evidently Tammuz, the shepherd-god of Sumero-Akkadian mythology.

ᴀɴᴅ he built a city and
called the name of the city
after the name of his son,
Enoch.　(Gen. 4 : 17)

Cain, the first tiller of the soil, founded the first city (called "Enoch" perhaps with etymological reference to its
inauguration — Hebrew *hanokh* means "to inaugurate"). It was agriculture, especially irrigation, that made
possible the permanent human settlements from which large cities subsequently developed. This brief verse thus
sums up a most important chapter in the history of human progress.
The excavations at Jericho have brought to light a walled city of the Neolithic Age (seventh to fifth millennium
B.C.; see illustration). It is no mere chance that the oldest known city in the world was founded here: the desert
oasis, well suited to the raising of irrigated crops, drew the nomad tribes to Jericho.

ADAH bore Jabal; he was the father of those who dwell in tents and have cattle. (Gen. 4: 20)

The Hebrew word "father" *(ab)* has two different shades of meaning: (a) the head of the family; (b) the leader and mentor of a given human group. In this verse, it means both the progenitor and the chief of the shepherds and cattle-owners. Some ancient peoples believed that the various crafts practised by humanity were of divine provenance. In the Bible, on the other hand, they are of human origin, and are traced back to the descendants of Adam. In the earliest times, as in our own day, the tent was the emblem of nomad shepherd tribes wandering over the desert and the sown in search of pasture. At a later period, the tent acquired the extended metaphorical meaning of house, family, family tradition: "Each of you to your tents, O Israel" (2 Chron. 10 : 16). The tent became a symbol of guileless, peaceful and carefree life, as in the description of Jacob as "a quiet man, dwelling in tents" (Gen. 25 : 27). The beduin tent of our own day differs but little from the tent of biblical times. It is divided into compartments, one of which is reserved for the entertainment of guests. The size of the tent depends on the size of the beduin's family and his wealth. While the ordinary tent contains two or three compartments, that of a senior, influential sheikh may have as many as seven. Sometimes the sheikh has a special tent for guests where public prayers are held.

The illustration shows a beduin tent in the vicinity of Beersheba.

HIS brother's name was Jubal;
he was the father of all those who
play the lyre and pipe.

(Gen. 4 : 21)

Music, one of the earliest of the human arts, has always
been held in high esteem in the East, both by the settled
inhabitants and by the nomad tribes. Among the oldest
known musical instruments are the *kinnor* — the lyre,
and the *'ugab,* apparently a kind of pipe the strains of
which, as its name in Hebrew indicates, stirred the hearer
with passionate longing. The upper figure shows a
steatite bas-relief from the early third millennium B.C.,
which was brought to light in the excavation of Adab
(Bismaya) in Sumer. On it we see the orchestral use of
instruments. The conductor(?), holding a leafy baton,
stands on the left; while two harpists, one with a five-
stringed, the other with a seven-stringed, harp march
towards him, followed by a drummer and a trumpeter.
The figures above are apparently dancers. The lower
illustration shows a West Semitic nomad plucking a
seven-stringed harp. The scene is taken from a wall-
painting at Beni Hasan from the 19th century B.C. (for
the whole picture, see p. 114).

ZILLAH bore Tubal-cain; he was the forger of all instruments of bronze and iron.   (Gen. 4 : 22)

The art of working copper was known in various parts of the Orient as early as the fourth millennium B.C.; for example, in Persia and Armenia, as well as in Sinai and Palestine. The illustrations show the earliest copper objects yet discovered in Western Palestine, dating to the end of the fourth millennium B.C. Below we see copper adzes that were unearthed in 1956 at Metser, near the entrance to the Pass of Megiddo. The copper mace-heads shown above were found at Beer-Matar, near Beersheba. Not far from these mace-heads were discovered fragments of crucibles for smelting and refining. From this we may infer that Beersheba was one of those early and important metal-working centres that used ores brought from Edom and the Arabah. This district was the roving-ground of the well-known ancient smiths, the nomad Kenites. Indeed, one of the basic meanings of the Hebrew root *qyn* — as in Kenites and in the name Tubal-cain — is 'smith' or 'metal-worker'.

27

THIS is the book of the generations of Adam. When God created man, He made him in the likeness of God... When Adam had lived a hundred and thirty years, he became the father of a son in his own likeness, after his image, and named him Seth ... Thus all the days that Adam lived were nine hundred and thirty years; and he died. (Gen. 5 : 1-5)

The ancient world had traditions similar to 'The Book of the Generations of Adam' which also told of the remarkable age to which the earliest generations lived. The oldest of these inscribed traditions is the Sumerian list of kings (see the clay prism shown above) compiled early in the second millennium B.C., which in outline resembles the biblical 'Book of the Generations of Adam'. All these ancient traditions divided human history into two eras: a) the generations before the Flood; b) the generations after the Flood. Both generations alike lived preternaturally long lives. There is, however, a profound difference between the biblical story and the Sumerian conception of the world. In Sumerian tradition, the earliest generations of man constitute a line of kings, some of them mythological and even semi-divine figures; whereas, in the Bible, these first ancestors of humanity are ordinary mortals and heads of families. Moreover, the biblical life-span is far shorter than the fantastic ages attributed to the Sumerian kings. In comparison with them, even Methuselah, the longest-lived biblical character with his "nine hundred and sixty-nine years", was relatively short-lived.

ENOCH walked with God; and he was not, for God took him.   (Gen. 5 : 24)

Embedded in the dry genealogical lists of the 'Book of the Generations of Adam' there are also relics of stories about the lives and deeds of the earliest heroes. One of these tells that Enoch, a seventh generation descendant of Adam, did not die a natural death; but, like the prophet Elijah (2 Kings 2), was taken by God. The many legends that later grew up around the figure of Enoch were collected in the apocryphal 'Book of Enoch'. The king Etana, who is mentioned in the Sumerian king list, was also said to have been carried up to heaven.

The cylinder-seal from the end of the third millennium B.C. illustrates one of these legends. Etana is trying to rise skywards on eagle's wings, while both men and beasts look on in amazement. All fix their stupefied gaze on the ascending figure, and one of the men holds his hand to his gaping mouth. The Sumerian myth relates that Etana tried to reach the upper heavens against the will of the gods, and failed miserably.

So the LORD said, "I will blot out man whom I have created from the face of the ground . . ."

(Gen. 6 : 7)

The traditions of many peoples have preserved recollections of a flood which overwhelmed the earth and wiped out the primeval race of men. Of these, the closest to the biblical story is the Mesopotamian tradition which has been best preserved in the well-known Gilgamesh epic. The resemblance between this epic and the biblical story of the Flood, however astonishing in detail, is more apparent than real. In the Mesopotamian tradition, no ethical reason is given either for the decree of destruction or for the saving of the hero: both alike are simply the result of the arbitrary decision of the gods. The Bible, on the contrary, gives a moral reason for the extermination of humanity — "for the earth is filled with violence" (Gen. 6 : 13), and Noah is saved from the Flood because he "was a righteous man, blameless in his generations" (ibid., 9).

The reproduction shows tablet XI of the Gilgamesh epic which contains a late Babylonian version of the flood story discovered in Nineveh. In the beginning of the tablet, Gilgamesh asks Utnapishtim, the hero of the Babylonian story, how he won everlasting life. In reply, Utnapishtim relates in detail how the flood came upon the earth and how he was saved.

MAKE yourself an ark of gopher wood; make rooms in the ark, and cover it inside and out with pitch. This is how you are to make it: the length of the ark three hundred cubits, its breadth fifty cubits and its height thirty cubits.

(Gen. 6 : 14–15)

Both Noah's ark and the boat in the Gilgamesh epic are described as unusually large vessels.

According to the figures given in the Bible, the ark was about 500 feet long, 80 feet wide and 50 feet high, which would mean that its overall displacement was approximately 43,000 tons. The boat of Mesopotamian tradition was a gigantic cube with sides of about 200 feet each, i.e. a displacement of over 200,000 tons. The details given in the description of these vessels — in spite of the exaggerated figures — point to a fairly high standard in the craft of boat-building. (Cf. also the description of the construction of the ark in which Moses was placed, Exod. 2 : 3 and p. 131).

The seal reproduced here shows a wooden craft manned by two sailors with the figure of a bearded man standing before a shrine. This scene is reminiscent of several characteristic features of the Gilgamesh epic.

FOR behold, I will bring a flood of waters upon the earth . . .   (Gen. 6 : 17)

The flood waters were fed from two sources: a) "all the fountains of the great deep burst forth"; b) "and the windows of heaven were opened" (Gen. 7 : 11). The torrent of waters rose ever higher and higher till "all the high mountains . . . were covered" (ibid., 19). Animal life was blotted out (ibid., 21-23), and God is revealed in all His incomparable might. "The voice of the LORD is upon the waters: the God of glory thunders: the LORD, upon many waters" (Ps. 29 : 3). The world seemed to be returning to its primeval chaos. The flood lasted one hundred and fifty days (Gen. 7 : 24), while Noah's ark was borne ever upwards on enormous breakers, carrying within it the sparks of life which were the hope of the world's renewal.

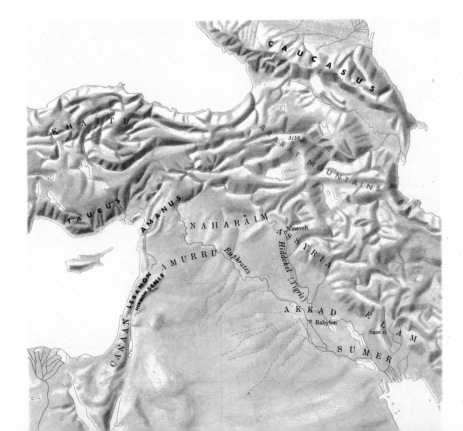

The Bible relates that, at the end of the Flood, the ark came to rest on the mountains of Ararat, i.e. one of the mountain ridges in the land of Ararat which is known to us, both from the Bible (Isa. 37 : 38) and from Assyrian sources. In the Babylonian story of the flood, as related in the Gilgamesh epic, we are told that the boat came to rest on Mount Nisir, apparently south of Ararat. A later Babylonian tradition (quoted by Berosus) locates the resting-place in Armenia, i.e. Ararat. According to the Book of Jubilees, the ark came to rest on Mount Lubar, one of the mountains of Ararat. The same is implied by the apocryphal Dead Sea scroll commenting on the Book of Genesis. Later Jewish, and likewise Christian and Moslem, traditions place the site in the Kurdish mountains of Armenia. Two mountains in the north-eastern corner of Turkey are today called Great Ararat and Little Ararat (see map and photograph), one of them the highest peak in Armenia (17,000 ft.).

AND in the seventh month, on the seventeenth day of the month, the ark came to rest upon the mountains of Ararat.   (Gen. 8 : 4)

I set My bow in the cloud, and it shall be a sign of
the covenant between Me and the earth. (Gen. 9 : 13)

God promises His creatures that life shall never again be destroyed by a great flood. Even if the skies are clouded
and the rain falls, man need never again have fear of extinction; for there is a sign of God's covenant with man —
"When the bow is in the clouds, I will look upon it and remember the everlasting covenant" (Gen. 9 : 16).
The rainbow is seen here in the sky above the Dead Sea while drops of rain are still falling and the sun gradually
prevails against the clouds. The occasional appearance of the rainbow after thunderstorms makes it a harbinger
of fine weather.
From the earliest times, man, awe-struck by the rainbow's gorgeous hues, has regarded it as a manifestation of
God's might. Babylonian, Arab and Indian legends all relate that the gods hung their bow in the sky or on a cloud
after victory over their foes: it thus became a symbol of the heavenly host.
In Israelite tradition, the rainbow mainly symbolizes not God's power, but His covenant — His loving-kindness
and His mercy towards His creatures. The orthodox Jew, on seeing a rainbow, blesses Him "who remembers
His covenant, is faithful to it, and keeps His word".

NOAH was the first tiller of the soil. He planted a vineyard. (Gen. 9 : 20)

Noah's first action after the Flood was to plant a vineyard. This tradition suggests that the first vineyards in the world were planted in the region of Ararat. And, in fact, modern scientific investigation would seem to confirm that viticulture started in Anatolia, close to Ararat, and from there spread to East and West. The ancient inhabitants of Anatolia, the Hittites, prized the vine highly, as we may see from the specific protection afforded to vineyards by the Hittite Code of Law (sec. 101).

The figure shows a relief hewn in the rock near Ivriz, in the Taurus mountains (southern Asia Minor). The king Warpalawa of Tubal (Gen. 10 : 2) is shown praying to Tarhund, the god of fertility. The god is girded with vine-clusters and holds wheat stalks and a bunch of grapes in his hands as symbols of plenty. Though the relief dates only from the 8th cent. B.C., the veneration of the grape expressed in it goes back even further into the dim past in this part of the world.

THE sons of Japheth: Gomer, Magog, Madai, Javan, Tubal, Meshech, and Tiras. The sons of Gomer: Ashkenaz, Riphath, and Togarmah. The sons of Javan: Elishah, Tarshish, Kittim, and Dodanim. From these the coastland peoples spread . . .

(Gen. 10 : 2-5)

The 'Table of the Nations', which lists 70 (or 71) nations of the world, is unique in ancient literature. Its purpose is to show how, after the flood, the world was peopled again by the descendants of Noah. The peoples listed are not classified by race; instead there appear to be several principles underlying the division "by their families, their languages, their lands, and in their nations" (Gen. 10 : 31, cf. also vv. 5, 20, 32). Historical and political considerations, as well as racial, linguistic and geographical groupings, were no doubt responsible for the genealogical relationships between the nations given here and the tracing back of their origin to one of the sons of Noah. The identification of the peoples mentioned in this chapter presents a difficult problem.

The reproductions show peoples whose identity can be definitely established or reasonably conjectured (following the biblical order):

P. 36, upper right: Madai — A late Median type on a relief from Persepolis (5th cent. B.C.).

Upper left: Yavan — An ancient Attic head (7th cent. B.C.).
Below: Tiras — identified by some scholars with the Etruscans. Couple in a tomb-fresco from Tarquinii (3rd cent. B.C.).

P. 37, middle: Ashkenaz — apparently identical with the Scythian tribes. A figure on a gold vase from Kul Oba (Crimea, 4th cent. B.C. or earlier).

P. 36, middle left: Elishah — apparently Cyprus. A head from Aya Irini (6th cent. B.C.).

P. 37, above: Dodanim (in the 'table' of 1 Chron. 1 : 7 — Rodanim) — are perhaps the Rhodians. Painted plate representing fighting warriors from Rhodes (6th cent. B.C.).

It would appear that the sons of Japheth dwelt principally in the countries to the north of Palestine on the Mediterranean islands and coasts (see map).

THE sons of Ham: Cush, Egypt, Put, and Canaan . . . Egypt became the father of Ludim, Anamim, Lehabim, Naphtuhim, Pathrusim, Casluhim (whence came the Philistines), and Caphtorim. Canaan became the father of Sidon his first-born, and Heth, and . . .   (Gen. 10 : 6-16)

The art of antiquity emphasizes the special characteristics of every people. This differentiation was carried to the greatest lengths by the Egyptians who, for this purpose, used a different colour for the skin of each people.

The representation below (wall painting from the tomb of Seti, c. 1300 B.C.) shows from right to left: Libyans (white), Nubians (black), Asiatics, i.e. Canaanites (dark brown), and the Egyptians themselves (red-skinned). They are distinguished not only by the colour of their skin, but also by their different dress, features and coiffure. The four sons of Ham, represented in this painting, may have been intended to demonstrate the wide extent of the Egyptian empire which was made up of four territories — Egypt itself; Cush, i.e. Nubia, to the south; Put, i.e. Libya, to the west; and Canaan to the east. The sons of Mizraim (Egypt) include the Philistines and inhabitants of the island Caphtor (Crete) (Deut. 2 : 23).

The representations opposite show:

Upper right: a Philistine wearing the characteristic feathered headdress, from Medinet Habu in Egypt (early 12th cent. B.C.).

Upper left: a Caphtorite, from a fresco in the Palace of Knossos in Crete (14th cent. B.C.).

Lower right: a Canaanite, a painting on a potsherd from Beth-shean (14th cent. B.C.).

Lower left: a Hittite soldier from a relief on a city gate of Boghazköy, the Anatolian capital of the Hittite kingdom (14th or 13th cent. B.C.).

THEREFORE it is said, "Like Nimrod a mighty hunter before the LORD." (Gen. 10 : 9)

Nimrod was a primeval hero who, like other great figures known to us from the Babylonian epics (Gilgamesh and Enkidu), performed such marvels of valour in the hunting of wild beasts that his name became proverbial to his contemporaries. On a basalt stele from the end of the fourth millennium B.C., unearthed on the site of Erech (Uruk), we see the figure of a bearded hero with a chaplet on his head. In the upper part of the picture, the hero is spearing a lion that is attacking him: in the lower part, he shoots at two lions with his bow and wounds them. Nimrod must have been an ancient hero of this type. Josephus says that Nimrod incited the generation of dissension to build the Tower of Babel (*Antiquities* I, 4, 2 — § 113-114).

THE beginning of his kingdom was Babel, Erech, and Akkad, all of them in the land of Shinar.

(Gen. 10 : 10)

Nimrod, the hero, was also a warrior and conqueror who ruled over a large kingdom in the land of Shinar containing some of the greatest and most famous cities of Mesopotamia. Thus, one of the cities of his realm was Erech (the modern Warka) with its magnificent towering temples, about 120 miles south of Babylon. Situated on the banks of the Euphrates, Erech was one of the oldest centres of Sumerian culture. This had reached a high level as early as the middle of the fourth millennium B.C., as witness its cylinder seals and the invention of writing. It is, therefore, not surprising that this city was frequently mentioned in the early legends of Mesopotamia. The Gilgamesh epic, for example, relates that its hero built a magnificent wall round the city and erected temples in it.

The view of the city's remains shows the precincts of the temple of Anu, the god of heaven and the chief deity of the Sumerian pantheon. On the right, there is an inner court containing an altar. In the background, another temple precinct can be seen.

THE sons of Shem: Elam, Asshur, Arpachshad, Lud, and Aram ... Arpachshad became the father of Shelah; and Shelah became the father of Eber. To Eber were born two sons: the name of the one was Peleg ... and his brother's name was Joktan.

(Gen. 10 : 22–25)

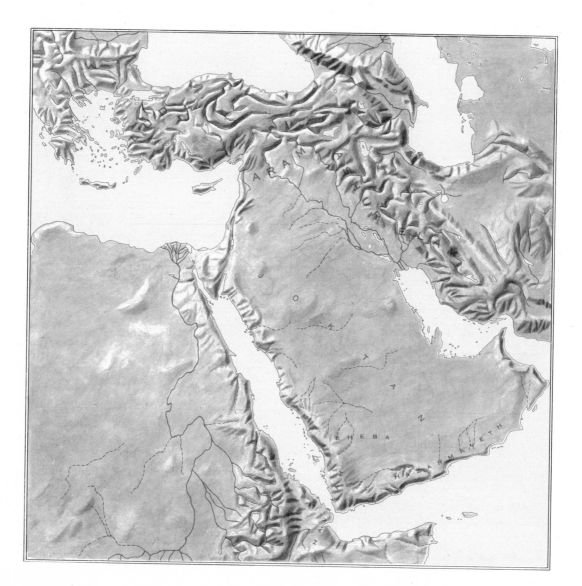

Shem, "the father of all the children of Eber" (Gen. 10 : 21), i.e. the ancestor of the Hebrews, is mentioned last in the list only to emphasize his importance. The modern scientific term 'Semitic' is not identical with the sons of Shem. Peoples speaking a Semitic tongue are found among the sons of Ham, e.g. Cush and his sons, and some of the sons of Canaan; while Elam (see below) is not considered a Semitic people in the modern sense. Still, most of the sons of Shem did speak a Semitic language and were related to the Hebrews (see map).

We see above, from right to left:

a) Shem — the head is that of an East Semitic ruler of the city of Adab (from the end of the third millennium B.C.).

b) Elam — a people that lived to the east of Babylonia The picture shows an Elamite soldier from the 'Frieze of the Archers' in the Palace of Susa (5th cent. B.C.).

c) Ashhur — one of the chief peoples of Mesopotamia which reached its apogee in the 8th and 7th cent. B.C. The picture shows the head of an Assyrian on a relief of this period.

d) Aram — a people that, at the end of the second millennium B.C., spread as far as Syria and Palestine. The relief is from Zinjirli and portrays the Aramean king, Bar-Rakab, of the 8th cent. B.C.

e) Eber — the people to which the Children of Israel belonged and which included West — and South — Semitic tribes. The reproduction is of a wall painting from Mari, depicting an inhabitant of the middle Euphrates region from the patriarchal period (18th cent. B.C.).

f) Joktan — the father of the South Arabian tribes — is represented on the lower right by a bronze statue of Maadkarib, a ruler from southern Arabia (6th cent. B.C.). The statue was discovered at Marib, the ancient capital of Sheba, which is the name of one of Joktan's sons.

And they said to one another, "Come, let us make bricks, and burn them thoroughly." And they had brick for stone, and bitumen for mortar.

(Gen. 11 : 3)

As there is no stone in the broad plains of Mesopotamia, bricks made of clay were usually used for building. The malleable clay was pressed into moulds and then baked in special ovens. Sometimes pitch (above: "bitumen") was also used as a kind of mortar between the bricks.

The builders, mainly kings, had foundation bricks stamped to perpetuate their memory. Thus, King Esarhaddon of Assyria (first half of the 7th cent. B.C.) had an inscription stamped on several bricks used in his restoration of the Temple of Marduk in Babylon. The words inscribed on the brick above record the making of new burnt bricks for the repair of the sanctuaries Esagila ("the house which lifts its head") and Etemenanki ("the house of the foundation of heaven and earth") which were included in the precincts of the temple of the god Marduk. The story of the Tower of Babel partly reflects the Babylonian names of these sanctuaries.

THEN they said, "Come, let us build ourselves a city and a tower with its top in the heavens, and let us make a name for ourselves, lest we be scattered abroad upon the face of the whole earth."

(Gen. 11 : 4)

From as early as the third millennium B.C., a feature of the cities of southern Mesopotamia was their gigantic towers. Called *ziggurat*, these 'skyscrapers' rose storey above storey in the temple precincts, with the abode of the god perched aloft on "their top in heaven".

The picture above shows a reconstructed model of one of these buildings of the 7th cent. B.C. Reconstructions of the towers can be pieced together from, among other things, pictures on cylinder seals portraying them in the various stages of their erection.

The picture below shows an Assyrian seal from the latter half of the second millennium B.C., portraying a priest building a *ziggurat* on the river-bank.

Another seal (in the lower picture opposite) from the end of the third millennium B.C., illustrates the method employed in building the towers, including the making of bricks and carrying them up on ladders.

TERAH took Abram his son and Lot the son of Haran, his grandson, and Sarai his daughter-in-law, his son Abram's wife, and they went forth together from Ur of the Chaldeans to go into the land of Canaan . . . (Gen. 11 : 31)

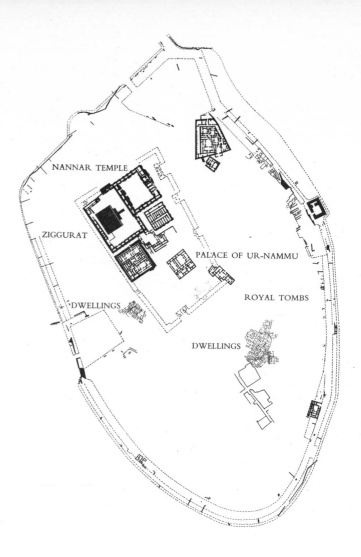

Ur of the Chaldees, from which Abram's family migrated to Haran, was an important Sumerian centre which reached its political apogee at the end of the third millennium B.C. It is not surprising that the family of Terah, like other clans of West Semitic nomads, were attracted to this urban centre of civilization and settled in its neighbourhood. The name of the city was Ur, the further specification "of the Chaldees" being a reference to the Semitic tribes of that name *(Chasdim* in Hebrew) that roved in this district. It is noteworthy that, according to the genealogical table given in the Bible, the family of Terah was related by blood to the Chasdim: Chesed was the son of Nahor, Abraham's brother (Gen. 22 : 22). The migration of Terah and his family to Haran may have been connected with the decline of Ur in the first century of the second millennium B.C. However, the Bible several times emphasizes that in Abram's case, the departure from Ur was by command of God (Gen. 15 : 7).

The figures depict Ur of the Chaldees just before the patriarchal period:

Above — plan of Ur in the year 2000 B.C. as revealed in Sir Leonard Woolley's excavations (1931).

Middle — remains of a street, named 'Quiet Street' by the excavators.

Below — the temple area with the *ziggurat* tower of Nannar, the moon god, rising high above the other buildings of the city. This view illustrates the cultic buildings of the city.

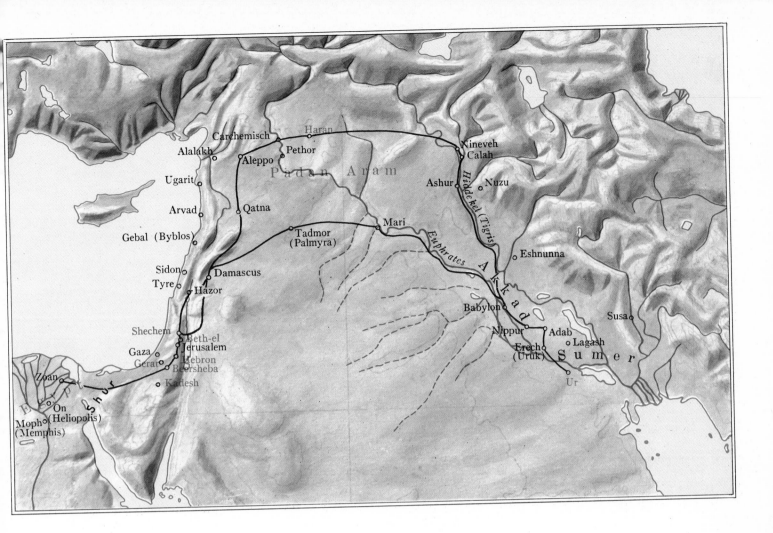

G O from your country and your kindred and your father's house . . .   (Gen. 12 : 1)

The migration of Abram and his family from Ur of the Chaldees, by way of Haran, to Canaan (Gen. 11 : 31) followed an ancient route linking the centres of civilization, from Mesopotamia to Egypt. The fertile countries of the region stretch in the form of a crescent from the Persian Gulf, along the Tigris and Euphrates, down to the Mediterranean and the River of Egypt. This is the so-called 'Fertile Crescent'. The migration of the Patriarchs was part of a vast movement of peoples that passed across the Fertile Crescent at the beginning of the second millennium B.C. In extant itineraries of Babylonian travellers of the same period, we find precise descriptions of the stopping-places from southern Babylonia to the region of the upper Euphrates. The letters found at Mari, from the patriarchal period, also enable us to follow the caravan routes from Babylon to Canaan.
The lines on the map, reconstructed from the sources mentioned above, mark the ancient international arteries of communication. As can be seen, they pass through the main cities, from southern Babylonia to Egypt.
There is an echo of the wanderings of the Patriarchs around Haran in the place-names in this vicinity — such as Serug, Nahor and Terah — which recall the family tree of Abram.

AND he journeyed on from the Negeb as far as Bethel, to the place where his tent had been at the beginning...
(Gen. 13 : 3)

When Abram and his family reached the land of Canaan, they began to wander about the hill region and the Negeb — the sparsely populated areas of the country — where they found pasturage for their cattle. The Patriarchs would pitch their tents near the few urban settlements and enter into economic and social relations with the local inhabitants (such as Ephron the Hittite, see Gen. 23; and the people of Shechem, ibid., 34). This way of life is characteristic of semi-nomads, in contrast to the wholly nomadic beduin tribes of the desert who regard permanent settlements with a mixture of disgust and contempt.

The two views illustrate the topographical background to the wanderings of Abram in the hill region and in the Negeb.

Above — The hill region in the centre of Palestine, scene of the temporary encampments set up by the Patriarchs in their wanderings.

Below — tents pitched in a Negeb landscape near Beersheba. This is a scene that has not changed from ancient times to the present day. Such beduin tents, easy to strike, fold, load on camels and carry from place to place, are used now, as then, by nomad tribes going south to Sinai and Egypt or returning northwards.

AND Lot lifted up his eyes, and saw that the Jordan valley was well watered everywhere like the garden of the LORD, like the land of Egypt in the direction of Zoar.

(Gen. 13 : 10)

While the general meaning of the "Jordan valley" apparently refers to the floor of the rift valley along which the river winds its course from the Sea of Chinnereth to the Dead Sea, it is impossible, from the biblical references, to fix its exact limits. Here the fertile region to the south of the Dead Sea seems to be meant. But, according to another verse (1 Kings 7 : 46) it is the country on either side of the Jordan some distance to the north of the Dead Sea to which the term should be applied. The view of the Jordan plain as spread out from the vicinity of Beth-el (see figure), is one of the most beautiful landscapes in Palestine. It is, therefore, not surprising that Lot at once chose the plain for his habitation.

The oases in the lower part of the Jordan and on the plains of Moab had a flourishing population at the beginning of the second millennium B.C. It was these oases that gave the whole plain the appearance of "the garden of the LORD"

So Abram moved his tent, and came and dwelt by the oaks of Mamre, which are at Hebron; and there he built an altar to the LORD.

(Gen. 13 : 18)

The 'Oaks of Mamre' were an oak grove near to Hebron. The place was named after Mamre who was one of Abram's allies, like Aner and Eshcol (Gen. 14 : 13, 24). The Bible actually identifies Mamre with Hebron (Gen. 23 : 19; 35 : 27), apparently meaning one of the outlying quarters of the city.

At the time of the Second Temple, there were traditions about an ancient grove in the neighbourhood of Hebron. The huge tree mentioned by Josephus as having stood in the vicinity since the foundation of the city was apparently at a spot known as Botnah (Terebinth), today called by the Arabs Ramet el-Khalil, about two miles north of Hebron. In the Roman-Byzantine period, the site was sacred to both pagans and Christians, and its sanctuary became the scene of one of the most important fairs in Palestine. Excavation of the site has revealed the foundations of a wall from the time of Herod (see figure above).

AND all these joined forces in the Valley of Siddim (that is the Salt Sea)... After the return from the defeat of Chedorlaomer and the kings who were with him, the king of Sodom went out to meet him... And Melchizedek King of Salem brought out bread and wine; he was priest of God most high.   (Gen. 14 : 3, 17-18)

Chapter 14 of the Book of Genesis has preserved memories of an extensive campaign undertaken by the four northern kings against five kings in Southern Canaan: the Kings of Sodom and Gomorrah, Admah, Zeboiim and Zoar. The mention of Zoar suggests that the battle was joined somewhere near the south end of the Dead Sea. After the defeat of the Canaanite kings, the remnants of their forces fled to the mountains encircling the Dead Sea (Gen. 14 : 10 — see illustration below). Abraham, who came to the assistance of the Canaanites and expelled the invaders, was honoured by the King of Sodom and by Melchizedek, King of Salem i.e. Jerusalem.

Melchizedek is the perfect type of ancient oriental priest-king. He is the god's personal representative and the priest who officiates in his shrine. The god whom he serves was known in Canaan as *El elyon* (God Most High). In later times, Melchizedek became the prototype of the ancient ruler of Jerusalem and even the Davidic kings considered themselves his legal heirs: "The LORD hath sworn and will not change his mind, You are a priest for ever after the order of Melchizedek" (Ps. 110 : 4).

The statue above represents a north-Canaanite monarch of the first part of the 14th cent. B.C., Idrimi, King of Alalakh, "the servant of the god". He is sitting on his throne, wearing a headdress, encircled by a fillet. The hem of his garment seems to be rolled into the likeness of a snake entwined around the king's body, as if to emphasize the divine power which protects him.

AND HE brought him outside and said, "Look toward heaven and number the stars, if you are able to number them." Then HE said to him, "So shall your descendants be."

(Gen. 15 : 5)

The star-studded night sky of Canaan is a breath-taking and soul-stirring spectacle, which uplifts the heart of man and fills him with a mysterious enchantment. Primitive man of the ancient world was drawn to the stars, finding his way by them, dreaming by their light and yearning for them when he was shut in by city walls. The clear air of the Palestinian hills heightens the brilliance of the stars, revealing the host of heaven in all its splendour. This sublime spectacle is as old as the creation: "When the morning stars sang together, and all the sons of God shouted for joy" (Job 38 : 7).
Such a sight it was that banished Abram's gloomy thoughts about his future and filled his heart with faith in the Creator who had promised to give him offspring and to bless them.
The picture shows the brightest part of the Milky Way between the constellation of the Archer (top left) and the Scorpion (bottom right).

THEN the LORD said to Abram, "Know of a surety that your descendants will be sojourners in a land that is not theirs, and will be slaves there, and they will be oppressed for four hundred years." (Gen. 15 : 13)

The prophecy about the servitude of Abram's seed "in a land not theirs" is shrouded in mystery. No name is even given to the land in which Abram's descendants are to live as foreigners. But the land itself was well known to Abram: Egypt, the land of the Nile, the land of plenty, had always attracted the nomad tribes. In the time of the Patriarchs, the connections between the inhabitants of Canaan and Egypt had become still closer; Canaanites used to enter Egypt and settle there temporarily or even permanently.

The Egyptians put the Semitic tribesmen, including the Canaanites, to work at building and agriculture, in the same way as they exploited other foreigners, such as the Nubians and Libyans, and even native Egyptians. The prophecy about the sojourn in Egypt faithfully reflects the conditions of the time.

The illustration shows a typical landscape in Lower Egypt. Above the plain rise the Pyramids, the eternal symbol of the exploitation and enslavement of humanity for the greater glory of kings.

Now Sarai, Abram's wife, bore him no children. She had an Egyptian maid whose name was Hagar.

(Gen. 16 : 1)

According to the usage of the time, Abram had no claim to Sarai's handmaid, Hagar, except with his wife's permission. So the Rabbinical interpretation: "She had a handmaid, not he — since Abraham had no rights over her" (*Midrash Leqah Tob*). The Bible stresses that Hagar was Egyptian (cf. Gen. 21 : 9) and that she took an Egyptian wife for her son Ishmael (ibid., 21). In view of the great demand amongst Canaanite notables for handmaids from Egypt, with its advanced civilization, Sarai may have purchased Hagar during Abram's sojourn with her in Egypt.

The figure shows a statue of a typical Egyptian handmaid from the end of the third millennium B.C. She is wearing a wig, as customary in ancient Egypt, and carrying a basket of fruit on her head and a fowl in her right hand: on her neck there is a bead necklace. The model was found in the Tomb of Meketre at Thebes.

THE angel of the LORD found her
by a spring of water in the wilderness, the spring on the way to Shur.
(Gen. 16 : 7)

Wandering in the desert, Hagar came upon a spring of water. In the almost waterless Negeb, such oases form natural resting-places for wayfarers. Indeed, the very existence of the nomads depends on the springs which supply them with water for their flocks and serve as camping-places on the desert tracks. In her flight, Hagar followed one of the tracks leading to her native Egypt, the way to Shur, which is mentioned again in the story of the Exodus (see p. 147 below).
The picture shows a spring and palms in the desert of the southern Negeb.

HE shall be a wild ass of a man, his hand against every man and every man's hand against him; and he shall dwell over against all his kinsmen.

(Gen. 16 : 12)

Ishmael, Abram's first-born son, did not inherit his father's estate, but led a nomad life in the desert. Ishmael is a "wild ass" of a man (Hebrew: *pere adam*), i.e. a man or a tribe who cannot adjust themselves to communal life, like the intractable wild ass that cannot be trained to live with other animals. Even so, Ishmael does not dwell in the midst of his brethren, but "over against them" and is constantly at war with them. The Ishmaelite is thus the eternal desert robber. The Bible elsewhere relates that Ishmael lived as an archer in the wilderness of Paran (Gen. 21 : 20-21). The descendants of Ishmael were nomad tribes in northern Arabia such as the Nebaioth, Kedar, Dumah and Tema (Gen. 25 : 13-15).

The figure reproduces a section of a relief of Ashurbanipal, King of Assyria (middle of the 7th cent. B.C.), portraying a fight between Assyrians and desert raiders. Two half-naked Arabs are seen astride a fleeing camel: one of them is urging on the camel while the other draws his bow.

THEN Abraham took Ishmael his son and all the slaves born in his house or bought with his money, every male among the men of Abraham's house, and he circumcised the flesh of their foreskins . . .   (Gen. 17 : 23)

Circumcision is the visible sign of God's covenant with Israel: "so shall my covenant be in your flesh an everlasting covenant" (Gen. 17 : 13). God commanded Abraham to circumcise every male eight days old, both those born in his house and those bought with money (ibid., 12), including Ishmael and his household. From non-biblical sources we know that circumcision was also practised by the Egyptian priesthood, who used flint knives for the purpose.

A relief from the tomb of Ankhmahor at Sakkarah, belonging to the Sixth Dynasty (second half of the third millennium B.C.), depicts the circumcision of thirteen-year old youths (roughly of Ishmael's age at the time of his circumcision). The operation is performed by a priest who is here shown circumcising the youth on the left with the help of another man to whom he says: "Hold him so that he cannot move". The instruments used are made of flint. So Zipporah circumcised her son with a flint (Exod. 4 : 25), and Joshua circumcised the Children of Israel with "flint knives" (Josh. 5 : 3). The ancients continued to use flint knives following ritual tradition, even after the introduction of metal instruments.

AND Abraham hastened to the tent to Sarah, and said, "Make ready quickly three measures of fine meal, knead it, and make cakes." (Gen. 18 : 6)

Abraham provided for his guests a repast of the best that semi-nomads can offer: fine meal, calf's meat, butter and milk. The absence of wine is explained by its being customary only among the settled inhabitants of Palestine. On Abraham's orders, Sarah makes the guests cakes of the finest flour-meal. These were evidently a kind of thin flat cake which required very little baking, similar to the *matzah* cakes baked for the Exodus from Egypt by the Israelites who "could not tarry" (Exod. 12 : 39).

The pottery figurine reproduced here in its actual size portrays a woman bent over a three-legged kneading-trough. In the trough there are two lumps of dough, one of which is being kneaded by the woman. The figurine was found in one of the graves at Achzib (c. 8th cent. B.C.). Although the workmanship is primitive, the artist's eye for detail is striking.

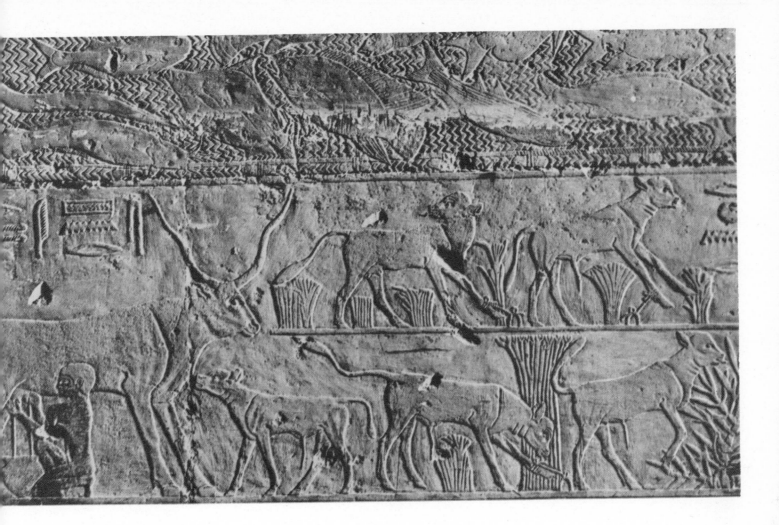

AND Abraham ran to the herd and took a calf, tender and good, and gave it to the servant, who hastened to prepare it. (Gen. 18:7)

The finest food of all, fit to be set before the most honoured guest, was 'a tender calf'. The picture, reproduced from the tomb of a landowner named Tiy who lived during the Fifth Dynasty (second half of the third millennium B.C.), shows a cow and several calves standing in a field of pasture. The cattle have long, thin horns, a type that was also common in Canaan. In the lower register, on the left, a calf is held by a man.

THEN the LORD rained on Sodom and Gomorrah brimstone and fire from the LORD out of heaven; and HE overthrew those cities, and all the valley, and all the inhabitants of the cities, and what grew on the ground. (Gen. 19 : 24-25)

The overthrow of the Cities of the Plain, though only briefly described in the Book of Genesis, became, with the passage of generations, a terrible symbol of fiery devastation. The verses above mention only two cities: Sodom and Gomorrah. Elsewhere in the Bible (Deut. 29 : 23), the number is given as four: Sodom, Gomorrah, Admah and Zeboiim; while Josephus, the Midrash, and the early Christian writings add a fifth.
The biblical statement that Sodom and Gomorrah were near to Zoar (Gen. 13 : 10; 19 : 15-23) implies that they were situated not far from the south-eastern corner of the Dead Sea. This region is a barren waste relieved only by a few starkly contrasting spots of vegetation; "unsown, and growing nothing, where no grass can sprout" (Deut. 29 : 23). Hence the deep and lasting impression made on the local population by the biblical story of the punishment from heaven which blotted out the sinful cities and turned them into an everlasting desolation (Isa. 13 : 19-20). Later writers — no doubt influenced by observation of the hot springs in the region — held that, deep in the brimstone-saturated ground under Sodom, the fires sent down from heaven were still blazing. "Vestiges of the divine fire and faint traces of five cities are still visible" (Josephus, *Jewish Wars*, IV, 8, 4 — § 483).

BUT Lot's wife behind him looked back, and she became a pillar of salt.   (Gen. 19 : 26)

From ancient times right down to the present day, popular imagination has been fascinated by the figure of Lot's thoughtless and inquisitive wife who, for disregarding God's command, was turned into a pillar of salt. As early as the time of the Second Temple, the pillar of salt was thought to be in the region of Mount Sodom. Thus Josephus writes: "I saw the pillar of salt on my travels, for it exists to this day" (*Antiquities*, I, 11, 4 — § 203).

Mount Sodom, at the south-western corner of the Dead Sea, is remarkable for its sharp pinnacles, the lower parts of which consist of salt layers and the upper of salt and marl columns. One or another of these pinnacles which look like a human shape is regarded by popular tradition as the wife of Lot (see picture). However, as a result of climatic and geological factors the 'pillars' are in a constant state of formation and disintegration. This has given rise to various legends about the transformation of Lot's wife.

FROM there Abraham journeyed toward the territory of
the Negeb . . . and he sojourned in Gerar.   (Gen. 20 : 1)

From time to time, Abraham and Isaac pitched their tents in the neighbourhood of Gerar where the rich soil was
suitable both for pasturage and tillage. While there, they enjoyed the protection of Abimelech, king of Gerar.
The geographical position of Gerar — between Beersheba and Gaza — and historical evidence support the
identification of the Gerar valley with Wadi esh-Sheria. Gerar itself is nowadays usually identified with Tell Abu
Hureira on the banks of this wadi (see illustration). Above the large mound, which covers an area of about 40
acres, rises the still higher acropolis, surrounded by a wall of *terre pisée,* descending in four spurs towards the
valley.
On the higher part of the tell and the area around were found many potsherds from the Middle Bronze Age —
the period of the Patriarchs.

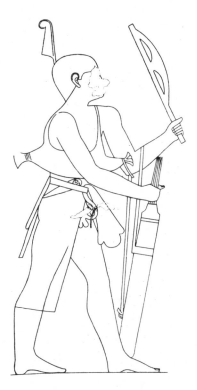

So Abraham rose early in the morning, and took bread and a skin of water, and gave it to Hagar, putting it on her shoulder . . . (Gen. 21 : 14)

Before going out into the waterless desert, Hagar is provided by Abraham with a skin water-bottle of the kind habitually carried by desert nomads from ancient times down to the present day. This bottle, made of goat- or sheep-skin, cannot be broken like earthenware, and can be folded up when empty.

In the picture on the left, reproduced from a tomb at Meir in Egypt dating to the Twelfth Dynasty (the patriarchal age), we see a heavily armed man with a water-bottle strapped on his left shoulder and held under his right arm. The bottle is fastened at both ends: the fastenings can be loosened for drinking or filling.

The other picture, from Beni Hasan, shows Semitic nomads, also from the patriarchal age, on their way to Egypt. One of them carries a water-bottle on his shoulder (for the whole picture, see p. 114).

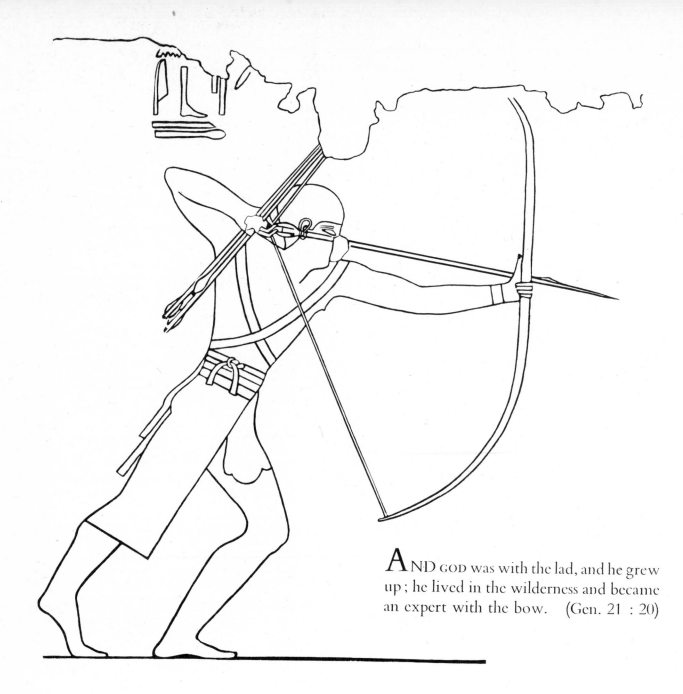

A ND GOD was with the lad, and he grew
up; he lived in the wilderness and became
an expert with the bow.   (Gen. 21 : 20)

Ishmael's survival in the desert against great odds is regarded by the Bible as a sign of divine providence; for, in contrast with the peaceful existence of the Patriarchs, Ishmael led the typical life of a desert nomad who lived by hunting and raiding with his trusty weapon — the bow. Until the discovery of gunpowder, the bow was the most important long-range weapon, both in war and in hunting. At an early period, the peoples of the Orient learnt how to make bows from wood, animal sinews and pieces of bone (the 'composite' bow). Such a bow was extremely flexible and could shoot to great distances.

A painting on the walls of a tomb from the Middle Kingdom at Meir in Egypt gives a clear indication of how the long-range hunting bow was used. The archer holds the bow in his left hand and stretches the bowstring with his right hand in which he also holds a number of arrows ready for immediate use. The rest of the arrows were kept in a special quiver, particularly during the battle (cf. also p. 75).

ABRAHAM planted a tamarisk tree in Beersheba and called there on the name of the LORD, the Everlasting God. (Gen. 21 : 33)

At least five kinds of tamarisk are found in Palestine, growing wild in sandy or saline soils. Presumably Abraham's tamarisk is one of the two kinds found in the Negeb. The tamarisk, with its sturdy trunk and evergreen leaves, was considered to be a symbol of eternity. In Beersheba, there was an ancient tamarisk which, a hundred and fifty years ago, was still associated with Abraham by popular tradition. The local inhabitants used also to show the visitor an ancient well, said to date from the time of Abraham, with a tamarisk beside it.
The picture shows tamarisks near modern Beersheba, which can be seen in the background.

So Abraham . . . saddled his ass, and took two of his young men with him and his son Isaac. (Gen. 22 : 3)

Abraham follows the customs of Semitic dignitaries: he rides on his ass, while his son and his servants walk beside him. Among the reliefs discovered in the Sinai peninsula is this illustration of the same travelling etiquette as practised by the local Semites. The reproduction is taken from a stele in Serabit el-Khadim in the Sinai mines, from the reign of Amenemhet III (about the end of the 19th century B.C.).

In the reproduction, we see a man riding on an ass which is led on a halter by a servant, while a second follows behind with a stick. Both servants are carrying spears. At the end of the halter there is a round, red object — perhaps the bridle-ring. The rider is carrying an axe in his left hand and a staff in his right. In another scene, the rider's son is seen behind the ass. The rider is probably a Semitic dignitary, "the brother of the ruler of the land of Retenu", the latter being the Egyptian name for Canaan in the patriarchal age. Possibly the term "brother of" also indicates a high social standing (cf. Gen. 13 : 8).

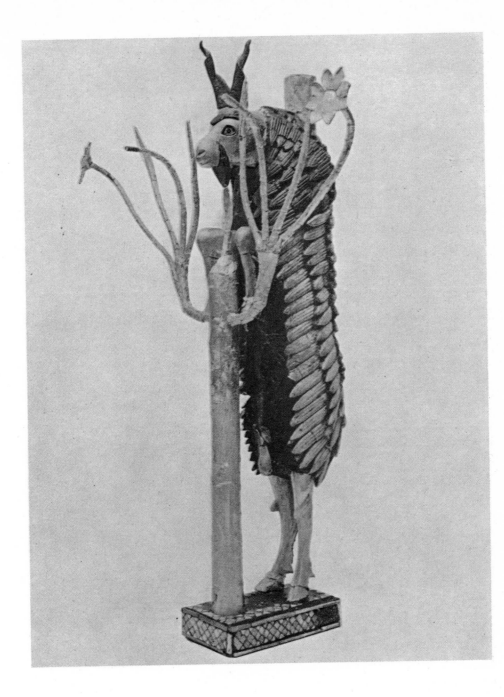

AND Abraham lifted up his eyes and looked,
and behold, behind him was a ram, caught in a
thicket by his horns . . .   (Gen. 22 : 13)

The ram, which has already been mentioned in connection with the sacrifice of the Covenant (Gen. 15 : 9),
played an important part in the sacrificial ritual. Here, in the story of the sacrifice of Isaac, the ram is offered up
in place of Abraham's only son. The ram often gets caught by its horns while nibbling at thickets.
In Sumer, the ritual use of the ram goes back to the proto-historic period. A pair of figurines found in the royal
tombs of Ur from the middle of the third millennium B.C. (one of which is reproduced here) represent a ram
caught in a thicket. The thicket in the picture branches out into leaves and two flowers of symbolic significance.
The ram is resting its two forelegs on the main branch and looking out through the thicket. Its body is made of
wood, its head and feet of gold, its belly of silver, its beard and the hair on its shoulders of lapis lazuli and its
fleece of seashells set in bitumen. The ram figurines apparently served as stands for libation vessels.

ABRAHAM rose and bowed to the Hittites, the people of the land . . .   (Gen. 23 : 7)

Abraham, who was "a stranger and a sojourner" (Gen. 23 : 4 : i.e. one who owned no land) in the land of Canaan, took up his abode in a settled community, one of whose early constituents were the Hittites. In the 15th century B.C., the Hittite empire began to expand from its centre in Anatolia and extended its dominion into Syria. Here it came into conflict with Egypt, which also sought to dominate large areas of Asia. The struggle between these two empires for the control of Syria and Canaan reached its climax at the battle of Kadesh on the Orontes, in northern Syria (c. 1286 B.C.).

The relief shows Hittite prisoners-of-war taken at the battle of Kadesh and portrayed with great accuracy by the Egyptian artist. They all display the typically Hittite features — shaven face (unlike the Semitic Canaanites), prominent nose, sloping forehead and receding chin.

The Hittites who lived in Hebron at the time of the Patriarchs were presumably settlers who came from the north and established themselves in Canaan at an early date.

ABRAHAM agreed with Ephron; and Abraham weighed out for Ephron the silver which he had named in the hearing of the Hittites, four hundred shekels of silver, according to the weights current among the merchants.   (Gen. 23 : 16)

The children of Heth at first pressed Abraham to accept the cave of Machpelah as a gift. Perhaps this should be regarded as a custom of the period, connected with the prohibition of the sale of land; or again, it may be no more than a typically oriental form of bargaining. Abraham's insistence on buying the burying-place for "the full price" (Gen. 23 : 9) was no doubt intended to establish his legal right to the property.
Payment was made in silver bars or silver rings, the value of which was fixed by weighing. (Coins were not in use until the 7th cent. B.C.).
The reproduction shows us how silver and gold rings were accurately weighed on scales. An ox-weight is laid on the left-hand scale, while other weights are kept at hand in a metal basket. The scribe is recording the weight of the rings. The picture is taken from the tomb of Rekhmire at Thebes, from the time of the Eighteenth Dynasty.

AFTER this, Abraham buried Sarah his wife in the cave of the field of Machpelah east of Mamre (that is, Hebron) in the land of Canaan.

(Gen. 23 : 19)

The purchase of the cave of Machpelah was Abraham's first step towards the realization of the promise given by God that he would inherit the land (Gen. 15 : 7). The cave became the family burial vault of all the Patriarchs and their wives, except Rachel. A tradition going back to the time of the Second Temple locates the cave of Machpelah at the foot of Jebel el-Jaabira, east of old Hebron. In the mosque built above this cave there are cenotaphs which are said to mark the position of the tombs in the cave below (in the centre, Abraham and Sarah; to the south-east, Isaac and Rebekah; to the north-west, Jacob and Leah). The lower part of the wall round the mosque, up to the battlements, is from the time of Herod the Great.

THEN the servant took ten of his master's camels and departed ... And he made the camels kneel down outside the city by the well of water ...

(Gen. 24 : 10-11)

The one-humped and two-humped camels are known for their stamina and sturdiness in the harsh conditions of the desert. The use of the camel as a domestic animal apparently goes back to prehistoric times (Mesolithic Age), as witnessed by a rock-engraving at Kilwa in south-east Trans-Jordan. However, the use of the camel did not become common till the 12th century B.C. While camels are occasionally mentioned in the patri-archal stories, the usual beast of burden then was the ass. Camels were used only on long journeys, such as to Mesopotamia — a distance of about 600 miles.

The picture shows camels beside a well.

So I put the ring on her nose, and the bracelets on her arms.   (Gen. 24 : 47)

The servant's aim is to win Rebekah's heart by gifts and jewels, as customary in the East. The Bible preserves many references to feminine jewellery, including two kinds of ring: a nose-ring (Isa. 3 : 21; Ezek. 16: 12) and an ear-ring (Gen. 35 : 4; Exod. 32 : 2-3). In our passage, the exact weight of the golden ring is given as half a shekel (*beqa'*), or roughly six grammes (Gen. 24 : 22). It is noteworthy that gold jewellery was widely used in the patriarchal period, i.e. the Middle Bronze Age, which archaeological finds show to have been a time of material prosperity in Canaan. Gold rings were especially characteristic of the Ishmaelites (Judges 8 : 24). To this day, the beduin girls wear jewels of the kind shown in the accompanying photograph which was taken in the tents of a beduin tribe in southern Israel.

Below is a nose-ring similar to that worn by the beduin girl.

AND Rebekah said to the servant, "Who is the man yonder, walking in the field to meet us?" The servant said, "It is my master." So she took her veil and covered herself.   (Gen. 24 : 64-65)

The meeting of Isaac and Rebekah took place near Beer-lahai-roi in the Negeb. Rebekah descends from her camel in honour of the man who was "walking in the field": on learning that he is Isaac, she covers her face with her veil. The womenfolk of the Canaanite nomads were not generally in the habit of veiling themselves: even in Assyria only noble women used to cover their faces. Rebekah came from Aram–Naharaim, and her action is thus a sign of her aristocratic origin. In the Arab countries, this custom has lasted down to the present day.

The relief from Palmyra reproduced here shows a group of veiled women from the first cent. A.D.

Esau was a skilful hunter, a man of the field, while Jacob was a quiet man, dwelling in tents.

(Gen. 25 : 27)

The Bible lays special emphasis on the utterly different characters of Esau, the warlike hunter who roams far and wide, armed with his special weapon, and of Jacob, the peaceful, innocent shepherd. This contrast between two brothers — emphasized both by their different occupations and by their different characters — occurs more than once in the biblical stories.

The art of the ancient East also brings out, in its own way, the differences between the hunter and the shepherd. The statue from Mari on the right, dating to the patriarchal period (the beginning of the second millennium B.C.), portrays a bearded shepherd, wearing a hairy cloak with a band round his head. He is holding a kid in his arms and pressing it against his chest. This portrayal recalls Rebekah's words to her son Jacob: "Go to the flock, and fetch me two good kids" (Gen. 27 : 9). The shepherd's face wears an expression of calm nobility, as befits a patriarchal cattle-owner.

The second picture (from an Assyrian relief of the 8th cent. B.C.) puts us in mind of Esau when he "came in from his hunting" (Gen. 27 : 30). The bearded hunter is holding a hare in his hand and carrying a ram across his shoulder.

N<small>OW</small> then, take
your weapons, your
quiver and your bow...
(Gen. 27 : 3)

Esau, the hunter, arms himself for the chase. Of the weapons mentioned in this verse, only the bow is known. The exact meaning of the words translated here as "weapon" *(keli)* and "quiver" *(teli)* is not clear.

Ancient pictures can perhaps help us to identify these weapons. The painting reproduced here from the tomb of Kenamun at Thebes in Egypt (15th cent. B.C.) shows three armed men. One is holding in his left hand a triangular shaped bow (a composite bow made of wood, sinews and bone; see also p. 64). The bow is in a magnificent case which protects it from damp and desiccation. In his right hand he is holding a boomerang for hunting birds, and it is not impossible that this is the sort of weapon meant by *keli* in our verse. On the hunter's back there is a quiver, which is perhaps the meaning of *teli,* since the quiver was usually hung on the back (the Hebrew word *taloh* means 'to hang').

B<small>Y</small> your sword you
shall live ...

(Gen. 27 : 40)

The blessing here given by Isaac to Esau refers to the warlike character of the Edomites who lived by the sword and were constantly at war with their neighbours, especially Israel. It is remarkable that the sword, unlike the dagger, was only introduced into warfare at a relatively late date, mainly from the time of the Patriarchs (first half of the second millennium B.C.). The type of sword most commonly used in this period and during the occupation of Canaan, especially by the aristocracy and the charioteers, was the curved sword which served principally as a slashing instrument. A typical example is the sword reproduced here from the excavations at Gebal (Byblos, 18th cent. B.C.). Similar specimens have been unearthed at Shechem, Ugarit, Beth-shean and Gezer. The long handle (providing a good leverage), and the sharp edge (on the convex side of the blade), made the sword specially suitable for slashing and cutting in contrast to the straight two-edged sword which was used for thrusting.

THEN Rebekah said to Isaac, "I am weary of my life because of the Hittite women. If Jacob marries one of the Hittite women, such as these, one of the women of the land, what good will my life be to me?"
(Gen. 27 : 46)

Fearing that Jacob will take a wife from the daughters of Heth, Rebekah asks Isaac to send him to Paddan-aram (Gen. 28 : 2). The biblical story twice mentions that Esau actually did take Hittite wives who "made life bitter for Isaac and Rebekah" (Gen. 26 : 34-35; 36 : 2). We have already mentioned the Hittite settlers in southern Palestine (see p. 68).
Reproduced here is a relief from Carchemish of Hittite priestesses holding ritual vessels. The Hittite style is clearly seen in the typically large Hittite nose and the full-length cloak worn by Hittite women over their undergarment as a protection against dust and wind.

THUS Isaac sent Jacob away; and he went to Paddan-aram to Laban, the son of Bethuel the Aramean, the brother of Rebekah, Jacob's and Esau's mother.   (Gen. 28 : 5)

The Patriarchs formed marriage connections with the family of their kinsman Nahor in Aram Naharaim (here called Paddan-aram), the country from which they came. The meaning of the word Paddan is obscure. In the Assyrian language it means 'road': however, according to a parallel passage in Hosea 12 : 12, it means 'field'. The region in question is the wide plain stretching between the Euphrates and the river Khabur, the modern el-Jezireh. Everywhere in this plain there are mounds which mark the sites of ancient settlements. The one shown in the picture is Tell Hajjab to the west of the river Balikh. Beside it, there is a village of domed clay huts, like bee-hives, and the tents of beduin who periodically attach themselves to the outskirts of the settled community. This was probably the way in which the shepherd clans of Bethuel and Laban pitched their tents on the outskirts of the ancient cities.

H E called the name of that place Beth-el;
but the name of the city was Luz at the first.
(Gen. 28 : 19)

On his way to Paddan-Aram, Jacob passed by Bethel, already sanctified in Abraham's time, when he built there an altar to the Lord (Gen. 12 : 8; 13 : 3). Here, God appeared to Jacob in a dream ("there was a ladder set up on the earth") and renewed the promise made to Abraham that he and his seed after him should inherit the land. Hence, to Jacob, the place seemed to be "the house of God" and "the gate of heaven" (Gen. 28 : 17). The ancient city of Beth-el was situated near the modern Arab village of Beitin, north of Ramallah. The excavations of the site have brought to light a settlement from the beginning of the 21st century B.C. In the patriarchal period (Middle Bronze Age) the site was occupied by a fortified city which reached the height of its power in the Late Bronze Age. The archaeological finds from this period show that the place was an important Canaanite centre up to its destruction at the time of Joshua's conquest of Canaan. The well-built walls shown in the picture are later than the patriarchal period. When ,in the time of the Monarchy, Jeroboam the son of Nebat made Beth-el into one of the two main centres of worship in Israel, his choice was presumably determined by the ancient sanctity of the place (1 Kings 12 : 29).

16) Furthermore, Kelim-ninu as wife
17) to Shennima has been given; if Kelim-ninu bears (children)
18) Shennima shall not take another wife;
19) but if Kelim-ninu does not bear,
20) Kelim-ninu a woman of the land of Lullu (i.e. 'a foreign handmaid')
21) as wife for Shennima shall take;
22) as for the (concubine's) off-spring, Kelim-ninu shall not send (them) away.
23) Any sons that out of the womb of Kelim-ninu
24) to Shennima may be born,
25) all the lands, buildings, whatever
26) their description, to (these) sons are given.
27) In case she does not bear a son, then
28) the daughter of Kelim-ninu of
29) the lands and buildings one (portion of inheritance) shall take.

The social customs found in the stories of the Patriarchs reflect the practices and laws which prevailed at that time in the countries from which they came. In the archives discovered in the city of Nuzu to the east of the river Tigris (near the modern oil-town of Kirkuk), we find many parallels to the patriarchal way of life. Especially instructive is a marriage clause in an adoption agreement witnessed by the mayor of Nuzu, a fragment of which (lines 16-29) is shown above (including translation).

This document throws light on several aspects of Jacob's family status in the household of Laban: a) Shennima, who was a slave in his master's house, like Jacob in Laban's house, marries his master's daughter. If this wife bears him sons, he is not free to take other wives (cf. Laban's words to Jacob in Gen. 31 : 50). b) If she does not bear children, she is obliged to provide her husband with a handmaid that she may obtain children by her, as did Rachel and Sarah (Gen. 16 : 2-3; cf. Laws of Hammurabi, sect. 144-146; 168-171). c) In contrast to Sarah's treatment of Hagar (Gen. 21 : 9-10), the mistress here has no right to drive out the handmaid and her children. Sarah's conduct may, indeed, have been a departure from custom, which would explain why the Bible states: "and the thing was very displeasing to Abraham on account of his son" (Gen. 21 : 11). d) The last lines translated here show that daughters can inherit from their father no less than sons, as Leah and Rachel claimed: "All the property, which God has taken away from our father, belongs to us and to our children" (Gen. 31 : 16).

WHEN Rachel saw that she bore Jacob no children . . . she said, "Here is my maid Bilhah; go in to her, that she may bear upon my knees, and even I may have children through her." So she gave him her maid Bilhah as a wife; and Jacob went in to her.   (Gen. 30 : 1-4)

IN the days of wheat harvest Reuben went and found mandrakes in the field and brought them to his mother Leah. Then Rachel said to Leah, "Give me, I pray, some of your son's mandrakes."

(Gen. 30 : 14)

The mandrake *(Mandragora officinalis)* is a stemless perennial plant common in Israel. Its crumpled dark green leaves are arranged in the form of a rosette with the stalks of the flowers rising from its centre. It has purplish-blue flowers and small, yellow, tomato-shaped fruit with a pleasant scent to which reference is made in the Song of Solomon: "the mandrakes give forth fragrance" (7 : 13). The thick proliferating root goes deep into the ground, making the plant very difficult to pull out. According to Josephus, anyone who does this will die.

There was a widespread popular belief current among many nations in the medicinal properties of this plant, especially in its value as an aphrodisiac and cure for barrenness. Scientific investigation has shown the mandrake to contain nothing more than a few mild stimulants; nor, indeed, does a literal rendering of the biblical text suggest that it has any connection with love and fertility In return for the mandrakes, Rachel permits Jacob to lie with Leah, so that the fifth son is born, not by the wife who obtained the fruit — Rachel — but by the one who forwent it — Leah.

THEN Jacob took fresh rods of birch and almond and plane, and peeled white streaks in them . . . (Gen. 30 : 37)

Jacob set peeled sticks in the watering troughs, so that the sheep should look at them while in heat and mistake them for spotted and speckled rams (see below p. 84). The trees used for this purpose by Jacob are found in the Middle East and were known to the ancient inhabitants of Canaan. The *libneh* (storax-tree: *Styrax officinalis*) is a small tree which grows in the copses and is so called because its flower and the underside of its leaves are white (in Hebrew *laban* means white). Ancient translators and commentators also connected the name of the tree with its white colour. The *luz* cannot be a walnut-tree as is usually assumed, since there are no wild walnut-trees in Palestine. What is meant is probably the almond *(Amygdalus officinalis)* which is called *loz* in Arabic and which has grown in Palestine since time immemorial, sometimes close to the storax-tree *(libneh)*. The oriental plane *(Platanus orientalis)* is a large, handsome tree that grows wild in the northern of the part country, on the banks of wadis and in damp places.

The photographs were taken in Western Galilee. On the left we see the storax-tree, in the centre the almond, on the right the plane.

HE set the rods which he had peeled in the front of the flocks in the runnels, that is, the watering troughs, where the flocks came to drink.   (Gen. 30 : 38)

The runnels and drinking-troughs beside springs and wells were than as today places where the shepherds met and "the animals ... gathered together" (Gen. 29 : 7). The runnels are long, narrow channels dug in the ground, in order to provide enough drinking-space when the cattle come crowding to the water. The troughs are mostly hollowed out of stones, though occasionally they are made from rows of stones held together by clay. Their shape may be elongated, rectangular or round.

The picture is of a drinking-trough of the patriarchal period found in the excavation of Hazor, next to one of the gates of the lower (Canaanite) city. It consists of a row of grooved stones into which the water was channelled.

The water was drawn from the wells in various containers and then emptied either into the trough, as was done by Rebekah (Gen. 24 : 20), or into the runnels (Hebrew *rehatim*) as was done by the daughters of Jethro (Exod. 2 : 16).

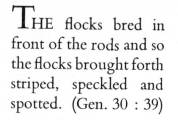

THE flocks bred in front of the rods and so the flocks brought forth striped, speckled and spotted. (Gen. 30 : 39)

The payment requested by Jacob seems small enough; the speckled, spotted and black of the sheep, and the spotted and speckled of the goats. Most sheep are white and most goats black, very few of them being of mixed colour, i.e. speckled and spotted. Laban segregated this minority to prevent it from mating with the rest of the flock and thus increasing its number. But Jacob fixed peeled sticks in the water-troughs (Gen. 30 : 38). By this ruse Jacob succeeded in multiplying the offspring of the striped, speckled and spotted animals and thus increased his own flock.

Egyptian paintings give us detailed portrayals of scenes from shepherd life. The one reproduced here from the tomb of the sculptor Api at Thebes (Nineteenth Dynasty) shows a flock of goats going out to pasture at the end of the harvest. The shepherd in the top row is carrying a staff in his right hand and a wooden pole with a water bottle hung at its front end in his left. At the other end of the pole there is a bread-sack and in front of it what looks like a shepherd's pipe in a case. He is followed by his dog. The shepherd in the bottom row, right, is following his flock: with his right hand he is playing on his pipe, while in his left he holds a shepherd's crook with a sack hung on it. Most of the goats grazing in the field and nibbling at the branches of trees are black, white or red, while a few are of a mixed colour which might be described as 'spotted' and 'speckled'.

AND Rachel stole her father's household gods . . . Now Rachel had taken the household gods and put them in the camel's saddle, and sat upon them.

(Gen. 31 : 19, 34)

Light is thrown on the story of Rachel's theft of the *teraphim* by the documents discovered in the ancient city of Nuzu (see p. 80). These documents show that the *teraphim*—which were household gods (cf. Laban's words to Jacob in Gen. 31 : 30: "But why did you steal my gods") — carried with them the right of inheritance. Thus Rachel was perhaps endeavouring to preserve this right for herself at the moment of Jacob's final departure from Laban's household, on the eve of his return to Canaan.

Excavations in Mesopotamia have brought to light small domestic idols which may be similar to the *teraphim* mentioned in the biblical story (v. figure below, on the right).

The stolen *teraphim* were hidden under the camel-saddle. In a relief from Gozan (Tell Halaf) (see figure above) belonging to the 9th cent. B.C., the rider is shown seated on a saddle secured to the camel's back by crossed girths. His hair is bound by a fillet and he holds a stick in his hand.

The saddle is placed on the camel's hump for the comfort of the rider. In ancient times, as still today, it was usually decorated with large, coloured beads and the neck of the camel was sometimes hung with crescents and pendants (Judges 8 : 21, 26) (v. figure below, on the left). To this day, the beduin are in the habit of smuggling contraband goods in the saddles of their camels, just as in ancient times.

AND Jacob said to his kinsmen, "Gather stones," and they took stones, and made a heap; and they ate there by the heap. Laban called it Jegar-sahadutha: but Jacob called it Galeed.

(Gen. 31 : 46-47)

The dispute between Laban and Jacob about the right to the family inheritance (see preceding page) ended in the 'making of a covenant' between them. Such covenants were usually accompanied by special ceremonies and were recorded in tangible form, as by the erection of cairns and pillars, the partaking of a joint repast and the swearing of a solemn oath. The cairn here simply marked the boundary between the territory of Abraham's family and that of Nahor's family: "I will not pass over this heap to you, and you will not pass over this heap and this pillar to me" (Gen. 31 : 52).
Such cairns are particularly numerous in Trans-Jordan, in the district where Jacob and Laban set up their memorial stone. Hence the popular etymology of the name Gilead as "heap of witness" (Hebrew *gal 'ed*). To this day, the Arabs erect cairns to mark a spot as sacred, or as a memorial of a peace-pact between hostile tribes.
The picture shows a typical heap of stones used as a memorial cairn.

A<small>ND</small> crossed the ford of the Jabbok.
(Gen. 32 : 22)

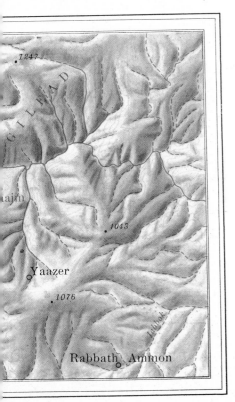

The Jabbok (called in Arabic Nahr ez-Zerqa) is one of the important rivers of Trans-Jordan and one of the two chief tributaries of the Jordan, the other being the Yarmuk. It rises near Rabbath Ammon (Amman) and follows a crescent-shaped course (see map), first northwards and then westwards, to join the Jordan about 25 miles north of the Dead Sea: it is about 40 miles long. The deep cleft of the Jabbok was an international boundary; first between Ammon and the kingdom of Sihon the Amorite, and later between Ammon and Israel.

In the picture, the twisting course of the Jordan is seen on the left and the Jabbok with its green fields on the right, with the rugged mass of the mountains of Gilead between them. Travellers going from north to south in Trans-Jordan used either to make a detour round the Jabbok by the edge of the desert to the east, or to cross the river by one of its fords. In spite of the difficulties of the latter route, Jacob chose it as being shorter and offering better pastures for his cattle.

THEN he said, "Your name shall no more be called Jacob, but Israel, for you have striven with God and with men and have prevailed." (Gen. 32:28)

After the wrestling at Penuel, God bestowed on Jacob the name Israel. Hence the Children of Israel were so called after their great ancestor, Jacob. The name Israel, which occurs 2,355 times in the Old Testament, designates first of all the descendants of Jacob before the conquest of Canaan, then all the nation and its whole territory, or only the northern part of it — the kingdom of Israel as distinct from the kingdom of Judah. Other peoples, too, call the Hebrew tribes by this name. The first mention of the name Israel outside the Bible occurs on the victory stele of Pharaoh Merneptah in c. 1220 B.C. (see top figure). In the list of enemies conquered by him in Canaan, the Pharaoh mentions that "Israel is laid waste, it has no seed". Hundreds of years later we find on the stele of Mesha, King of Moab, the words: "Israel has perished utterly".

In the middle: the name *isr'l* in hieroglyphic writing as it appears in line 27 of the inscription of Merneptah.

Below: tracing of a section of the Mesha stele containing the name "Israel" (marked in red) written in ancient Hebrew script (which was also the Moabite script).

BUT Jacob journey-
ed to Succoth, and built
himself a house, and
made booths for his
cattle; therefore the
name of the place is
called Succoth.

(Gen. 33 : 17)

After the wrestling with the man of God at Penuel, and after the meeting with Esau on the far side of the Jordan,
Jacob continued on his way to Succoth. The Bible connects the name of the place with the booths (Hebrew *succoth*)
built there by Jacob. Succoth, one of the cities of the Jordan plain, was an important centre controlling the fertile
valley formed by the junction of the Jabbok and Jordan rivers, which was consequently called "the Vale of
Succoth" (Ps. 60 : 6; 108 : 7).
At a later period, the city is mentioned as part of the inheritance of Gad (Josh. 13 : 27). Still later, in Solomon's
reign, the Temple vessels were cast between Succoth and Zarethan (1 Kings 7 : 46).
The Talmud identifies Succoth with Der'alla *(Jerusalem Talmud, Shebiith,* IX, 2), and to this day the largest tell
in the area is called Tell Deir'alla. On the surface of the mound were found many potsherds dating from the
patriarchal age to the end of the Israelite period. The figure above shows the mound (in the background) and
its vicinity.

H AMOR and his son Shechem came to the gate of their city and spoke to the men of their city . . .   (Gen. 34 : 20)

Shechem is situated in the centre of Palestine in a fertile, well-watered valley between Mount Ebal and Mount Gerizim (see p. 289). This is the point at which the road following the north-south watershed of the country crosses the valley-road which connects the coastal plain with the Jordan valley. The settlement of ancient Shechem goes back to the remotest past. By the beginning of the second millennium B.C., it was a flourishing city (it is mentioned in the Egyptian documents of this period) and, as such, attracted the attention of the Patriarchs. The excavation of ancient Shechem (Tell Balata, at the entrance to the modern town of Nablus) has uncovered the remains of a large wall from the Middle Bronze Age. These remains enable us to reconstruct the appearance of the ancient Canaanite city (see upper figure). In the wall a gateway was found, divided into several bays, as usual at that time (see lower figure). The gateway was the most convenient place for public business, such as law-suits (Deut. 21 : 19) or buying and selling (2 Kings 7 : 1). The gateway of Shechem was thus the natural place for Hamor and his son Shechem to consult the city notables on the question of their relations with the family of Jacob.

S O they gave to Jacob all the foreign gods . . . ; and Jacob hid them under the oak which
was near Shechem. (Gen. 35 : 4)

Jacob purifies all the members of his household, including the menservants and handmaids, and consecrates them to the
worship of God by changing their garments (Gen. 35 : 2) and removing the strange gods from their midst. It will be
remembered that Rachel had brought *teraphim* with her from her father's house in Paddan-Aram (see note to Gen.
31 : 19, 34): there may have been similar objects in the possession of other members of Jacob's household as well. So
now, after what happened at Shechem, the time had come to purify his whole household.

Canaanite idols of the patriarchal period (Middle Bronze Age) have been found in various excavations in Palestine.
Those shown in the reproductions above are made of bronze and pottery. Presumably, it was idols like these that Jacob
buried under "the oak which was near Shechem". An oak also features in the story of the covenant which Joshua made
with the people before his death. On that occasion, Joshua addressed the people in words similar to Jacob's here: "Then
put away the foreign gods which are among you" (Josh. 24 : 23).

AND Deborah, Rebekah's nurse, died, and she was buried under an oak below Bethel; so the name of it was called Allon-bacuth.

(Gen. 35 : 8)

There are three kinds of oak in Palestine: 1) the common ever-green oak *(Quercus calliprinos);* 2) the deciduous oak of Tabor *(Quercus ithaburensis),* found in the Sharon, on the Carmel and in Galilee; and, 3) the somewhat rare deciduous *Quercus infectoria.* The oak mentioned in this verse is apparently the common oak, since the other two kinds are not found in the region of Beth-el. This species, when protected from the depredations of man and beast, grows into a tall, sturdy tree. The majestic leafy specimens found in the hills of Judah and Benjamin are landmarks visible for miles around.

In the Bible, the oak is a symbol of sturdiness and longevity (Amos 2 : 9; Isa. 6 : 13). It sometimes also marks an important spot. The oak below Beth-el, beneath which Rebekah's nurse, Deborah, was buried, was called "the Oak of Weeping" *Allon-bacuth* (from the Hebrew *bakhoh* "to weep"). Possibly there is some connection between this *Allon-bacuth* and the place Bochim mentioned in Judges 2 : 1, 5.

SO Rachel died, and she was buried on the way to Ephrath (that is, Bethlehem), and Jacob set up a pillar upon her grave, it is the pillar of Rachel's tomb, which is there to this day.

(Gen. 35 : 19-20)

There were two traditions in Israel about the location of Rachel's tomb. According to the first (which has been preserved to this day), it is near Bethlehem, as stated in Genesis 35 : 19-20; 48 : 7. According to the other, it is somewhere in the territory of Benjamin, north of Jerusalem, as stated in 1 Samuel 10 : 2: "you will meet two men by Rachel's tomb in the territory of Benjamin at Zelzah" (cf. the possible reference in Jeremiah 31 : 15). Since the time of the Tannaites (first and second centuries A.D.) Biblical commentators have wrestled with the problem of reconciling these contradictory statements.

The modern visitor is shown the Tomb of Rachel to the north of Bethlehem. The first explicit location of the grave in this spot occurs in the writings of Origen, one of the Church Fathers, in the first half of the 3rd century A.D. The tomb has undergone many changes in the course of generations. Two famous Jewish travellers, Rabbi Benjamin of Tudela and Rabbi Petahia of Regensburg, who visited the site in the 12th century, say that the tomb consisted of eleven stones, covered by a dome built on four pillars. Petahia gives a characteristic explanation of the design: "On the tomb of Rachel there are eleven stones, one for each of the eleven tribes; there is no stone for Benjamin, since his mother died in giving birth to him". The present edifice was erected in 1841 (see illustration).

Now Israel loved Joseph...; and he made him a long robe with sleeves. (Gen. 37 : 3)

The high destiny of Joseph, the son of Jacob's old age, as the future ruler of Egypt was presaged in the special regard shown him by his father from a very early age and in the divine omens vouchsafed to him in his youthful dreams. The long robe with sleeves that Joseph's father so lovingly made for him, was a costly garment usually worn by great kings (see 2 Sam. 13 : 18). High-ranking and wealthy Canaanites are often portrayed in Egyptian paintings from the second millennium B.C. wearing magnificent garments like that mentioned in our verse. This "coat of many colours" (as it is usually translated) was made of pieces of cloth stitched together with embroidery that emphasized the lines of the garment. The sleeves were unusually long, reaching to the elbow and sometimes even as far as the wrist. Usually a scarf of the same cloth was worn with the coat, being wound in a spiral round the waist. Sometimes the cloth was of a different colour inside and out and therefore had a multi-coloured appearance when worn in folds and wound round the body: the lower edge of the garment was hemmed.

The lower picture shows a Canaanite coat, without scarf, from a wall painting dating to the reign of Amenhotep III.

In the other illustration, we see two Canaanite tribute-bearers wearing coats with scarves of the same material wound about them (end of 15th cent. B.C.; detail from illustration on p. 110).

Now Joseph had a dream... "Behold, we were binding sheaves
in the field, and lo, my sheaf arose and stood upright; and behold,
your sheaves gathered round it and bowed down to my sheaf."

(Gen. 37 : 5-7)

Joseph's first dream shows us that the sons of Jacob, though primarily cattle-breeders, also tried their hand at
farming. Canaan had a highly developed agriculture even before the patriarchal period.
The setting of Joseph's dream is the farmer's most important season of the year — the harvest. The relief reproduced here depicts peasants harvesting their crop. The peasant standing on the right is piling the sheaves in a
large stack prior to their being loaded on to asses and carried to the threshing-floor. The picture is taken from
the tomb of Akhhotep at Sakkarah (second half of the third millennium B.C.).

So Joseph went after his brothers, and found them at Dothan.   (Gen. 37 : 17)

Joseph's brethren left the Valley of Hebron to pasture their flocks at Shechem (Gen. 37 : 12). Thence they went on to Dothan, the northern limit of the wanderings of the Patriarchs in Canaan. From the earliest times down to the present day, the shepherds of Palestine have been accustomed to go through the country from south to north in search of food for their cattle. The region around Dothan affords good pasturage, hence the word *midbar* applied to it in Gen. 37 : 22, meaning a place where flocks are driven (from the Hebrew root *dabor*; cf. Exod. 3 : 1). The name of Dothan is preserved in the modern Arabic Tell Duthan, which is a large, high mound at the northern end of the mountains of Ephraim, overlooking a broad valley. Two roads, one from the valley to the mountains and the other from the north through the Plain of Sharon to Egypt, cross near the tell. Dothan was on the highway from Hebron via Jerusalem and Shechem to the Valley of Jezreel, which was the route followed by Joseph's brethren. In the time of the Kingdom of Israel, Dothan, then a fortified city, was besieged by the Aramaean armies in their attempt to capture the prophet Elisha (2 Kings 6 : 13-14).
The excavations carried out on the tell, from 1953 onwards, have shown that the site was continuously occupied from the beginning of the Canaanite age to the end of the Israelite period (from c. 3000 B.C. to c. 600 B.C.).

AND looking up they saw a caravan of Ishmaelites coming from Gilead, with their camels bearing gum, balm and myrrh, on their way to carry it down to Egypt.   (Gen. 37 : 25)

From ancient times until very recently, the trade between Asia and Egypt was carried on by nomadic tribes whose possession of camels gave them control of the trade routes. The use of the camel and its conquest of the desert opened the way to trade on an international scale. It is thus not surprising that such experienced camel-drivers as the Ishmaelites, roaming in the Egyptian border region, were able to monopolize the trade between Canaan and Egypt. In David's reign, the supervisor of the royal camels was Obil, the Ishmaelite (1 Chron. 27 : 30). A pack-camel can carry 5-6 cwt.; and a riding-camel can cover up to 100 miles a day. The camel in the desert requires little food or water since its hump and stomach are capable of storing all the water, food and fat it requires for many days. Camel's milk is the main drink of desert tribes. All this explains the adornments lavished on the animal, the hundreds of names that it has in Arabic and the praises sung to it by the Arabs, the successors of the Ishmaelites.

A wild beast has devoured him; Joseph is without doubt torn in pieces.   (Gen. 37 : 33)

Jacob naturally believed the story made up by his sons, since he knew that shepherds were in constant danger from wild beasts which were much more common in ancient Palestine than in our day. The people of that time were vividly aware of what it meant to be torn to pieces by a wild beast, and this motif is represented in a number of their works of art.

Here, for example, is an ivory relief from Nimrud on the Tigris (8th cent. B.C.), on which the following scene is portrayed: in front of a stylized forest, a lioness is pouncing upon a negro who falls with his head thrown back as the beast sinks its teeth in his throat. The man's clothes and hair are decorated with gold-leaf. The background consists of stylized papyrus and lotus plants with golden outlines and stems, the papyrus flowers being inlaid with carnelian, the lotus flowers with lapis lazuli. The relief is the work of Phoenician artists whose compositions are a blend of Egyptian and Assyrian styles.

MEANWHILE the Midianites had sold him in Egypt to Potiphar, an officer of Pharaoh, the captain of the guard. (Gen. 37 : 36)

Potiphar was a high official in the royal court. The 'captain of the guard' (in Hebrew *sar hatabbahim,* lit. 'overseer of the cooks') was originally in charge of the king's kitchen; but the official designated by this title became ultimately also responsible for internal security and for the royal prisons (cf. Gen. 40 : 3). Nebuchadnezzar's 'captain of the bodyguard' also bears a similar title (2 Kings 25 : 8).

The picture shows a wooden statue of an Egyptian army officer with a necklace and armlets of gilded plaster. He wears a wig and he has a short garment, fastened in front, round his waist. The statue is from Thebes and dates from the Eighteenth Dynasty (15 cent. B.C.).

So Joseph found favour in his sight and attended him, and he made him overseer of his house ... The blessing of the LORD was upon all that he had, in house and field.

(Gen. 39 : 4-5)

Joseph rises step by step through the various offices in the household of Potiphar, Pharaoh's minister. He starts as a slave; then he becomes "a successful man" (Gen. 39 : 2); he rises to be overseer of the estate (ibid., vv. 4-5); and finally he is given absolute control of the whole household: "so he left all that he had in Joseph's charge; and having him he had no concern for anything but the food which he ate" (ibid., v. 6). The Bible lays special stress on Joseph's jurisdiction over the house and the estate, since these constituted the main property of an Egyptian noble.

The lower figure shows the house of a high Egyptian official who was in charge of the royal treasury in the reign of Amenhotep II in the second half of the 15th century B.C. This wall-painting (from el-Amarna) depicts the structure and management of a typical Egyptian nobleman's house. Under the ground floor there is a spinning and weaving workshop; on the ground floor there is a reception hall; on the first floor there are offices; and under the roof there is a granary. To the right we see the staircase and vestibules supported by two pillars.

The upper picture — from the tomb of Nakht (15th cent. B.C.) — depicts the work done in the fields every year after the inundation of the Nile. The lord of the estate sits in a booth supervising the ploughing and sowing. Where the soil is still moist, the work is done by hand with a hoe; where it is already dry, teams of oxen are used for ploughing. Signs of the inundation are clearly seen. Beside the booth stand vessels containing food and drink for the lord. At the left side of the lower register there is food and drink for the workers.

WE have had dreams, and there is no one to interpret them...

(Gen. 40 : 8)

In the ancient East, various methods were employed in the interpretation of dreams, such as allusion, etymology of words, association of ideas, magic numbers and the like. These different methods were developed into an occult science by the sages of Egypt and Babylonia and recorded in special 'dream-books'. One of these 'dream books' is extant in a copy made in the 13th cent. B.C. in the hieratic Egyptian script: the original may be as early as the beginning of the second millennium (patriarchal period). We reproduce here a section from this book. Under the heading "If a man sees himself in a dream" there are descriptions of various dreams, some good, some bad. The word for "bad" is written in red, the colour of blood.

Joseph must have known the Egyptian methods of dream-interpretation; and his wisdom helped him to succeed even where the Egyptian magicians failed (Gen. 41 : 8): thus he was able to interpret the dreams of the chief butler and chief baker. According to the book of dreams reproduced here, wine usually has a good meaning, while birds are apparently a bad omen. So, in Joseph's interpretation, a good end is foretold for the chief butler who, in the dream, squeezes the grapes into Pharaoh's cup, and a bad end for the chief baker who saw the birds eating Pharaoh's meal from the basket on his head. Joseph also attaches great significance to the number 'three' which recurs in both dreams (see Gen. 41 : 12-13; 18-19).

So the chief butler told his dream to Joseph... "In my dream there was a vine before me, and on the vine there were three branches; as soon as it budded, its blossoms shot forth, and the clusters ripened into grapes." (Gen. 40:9-10)

At the beginning of his dream, the chief butler sees a vine ripening rapidly before his eyes: its tendrils burst into leaf and, forthwith, clusters of grapes ripen upon it. The second part of the dream has, by contrast, a slow, measured rhythm: the minister holds the king's cup in his hand, takes the grapes, squeezes them into the cup and gives it "into Pharaoh's hand" (Gen. 40:11 — see next page). The minister performs his task with the care and precision that befit attendance on a king.

The dream is based on first-hand knowledge of Egyptian viticulture which was practised as early as the first dynasties, having been introduced from Asia. The Egyptians became expert vine-growers: they were acquainted with different species of vine and classified their wines accordingly. Vintage scenes are common in the tomb-paintings of the third and second millennia B.C. One of the loveliest is that from the tomb of Nakht at Thebes (middle of the second millennium) reproduced here. It gives a detailed picture of the rich harvest garnered from a thick-tendrilled, heavy-clustered vine. Two men are seen picking the clusters.

102

ON the third day, which was Pharaoh's birthday, he made a feast for all his servants, ... He restored the chief butler to his butlership, and he placed the cup in Pharaoh's hand.

(Gen. 40 : 20-21)

From later Ptolemaic records we know that the Pharaohs used to commemorate their birthdays with a court celebration and a general amnesty. The chief butler was amongst those pardoned while the banquet was in progress, as foretold in the dream interpreted by Joseph. The high eminence of the post of chief butler is strikingly illustrated by the fact that the Pharaoh Eye (middle 14th cent. B.C.) was chief butler at the court of Akhenaton before his own ascension to the throne. In the reliefs made for his tomb, he boasts of having held this post and describes the honours and favours that he received from the Pharaoh.

The unfinished relief reproduced on the left shows Akhenaton seated at the left, while Eye stands before him pouring wine into his cup.

The picture on the right is of a banquet at which the two Pharaohs are feasting together like friends. Various kinds of food are heaped up before the banqueters.

AND behold, there came up out of the Nile seven cows sleek and fat, and they fed in the reed grass.   (Gen. 41 : 2)

Some of the basic features of life in ancient Egypt are reflected in Pharaoh's dream. Pharaoh stands on the bank of the Nile, the source of fertility and plenty in Egypt. Some scholars hold that the god of the Nile in Egyptian religion is Osiris, whose boat is sometimes accompanied by seven cows (cf. the seven cows of Pharaoh's dreams). According to the Greek historian Diodorus Siculus, the symbol of the Nile is actually the bull sacred to Osiris, the founder of agriculture. The picture, which is taken from the tomb of Nefertari, wife of Ramses II (13th cent. B.C.) shows seven fine, fat cows. In front of every cow there is a manger with its the cow's name above it. One such name is "the big, the beloved, the red one". The cows' udders are bursting with milk. Behind them walks a large, powerful bull.

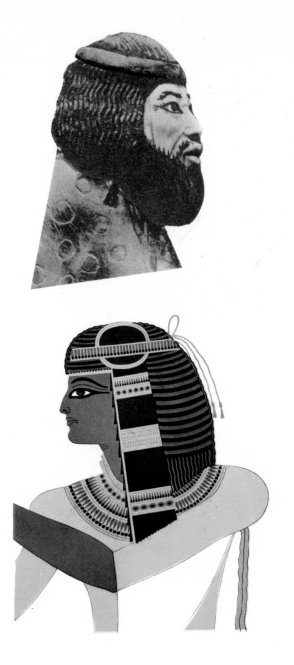

AND they brought him hastily out of the dungeon; and when he had shaved himself and changed his clothes, he came in before Pharaoh. (Gen. 41 : 14)

Upon learning of Joseph's skill in the interpretation of dreams, Pharaoh ordered Joseph to be brought before him. The short, clipped style of the verse indicates the urgency of the command and the suddenness of the change in Joseph's fortunes. In their treatment of Joseph, Pharaoh's servants display that scrupulous regard for cleanliness of person and dress which was characteristic of the ancient Egyptians, especially when commanded to appear before Pharaoh. The shaving of Joseph is in accordance with the custom of the aristocracy and middle-class in Egypt, who used to shave their faces, unlike the bearded Semitic Canaanites. This contrast is conspicuous in Egyptian art.

The reproduction on the right is of a painting from the tomb of Userhet from the reign of Amenhotep II (15th cent. B.C.). A barber is shown combing and setting the hair of a recruit to Pharaoh's army. He first ties back the hair into a single coil, then divides it into separate strands and finally fixes it with grease from the bowl.

The figure on the upper left shows a typical, heavily-bearded Canaanite (carved wooden head of a walking-stick from the tomb of Tutankhamon).

The figure on the lower left (painting from Thebes) shows a shaven Egyptian notable of the New Kingdom.

THEN Pharaoh took his signet ring from his hand and put it on Joseph's hand, and arrayed him in garments of fine linen, and put a gold chain about his neck.   (Gen. 41 : 42)

The manner of Joseph's appointment to his high office is illustrated by various Egyptian paintings which portray such ceremonies in detail. The signet ring and gold chain were characteristic Egyptian symbols of royalty, and their possession invested Joseph the Hebrew with viceregal powers.

The lower picture shows a gold signet ring being conferred by the Pharaoh Tutankhamon on the prince Huy, on the latter's becoming the king's regent in Nubia (wall-painting from the tomb of the prince at Thebes).

Above is depicted the appointment of Horemheb as one of Pharaoh's generals. Horemheb is raising his hands in delight and gratitude for the gifts bestowed upon him by Pharaoh. His neck is hung with a gold chain which he has just received from the king. Two of his children are embracing him, while another two are bringing a royal gift of necklaces. Horemheb himself subsequently became king of Egypt. (Reproduction of a relief from the tomb of Horemheb, second half of the 14th cent. B.C.).

AND Joseph stored up grain in great abundance, like the sand of the sea, until he ceased to measure it, for it could not be measured.
(Gen. 41 : 49)

Acting on the advice which he himself had given to Pharaoh, Joseph began to organize the storing of surplus corn from the years of plenty on a nation-wide scale: "and stored up food in the cities: he stored up in every city the food from the fields around it" (Gen. 41 : 48). When the famine years came and the people cried to Pharaoh for bread, Joseph threw open the royal granaries and "he it was that sold to all the people of the land" (Gen. 42 : 6). These activities are in accord with the Egyptian custom of storing up the surpluses of the seasonal produce in royal storehouses. Such storehouses are portrayed in many Egyptian pictures, with scribes listing the amount of grain in them.

The lower picture, from the period of the Twelfth Dynasty (patriarchal age), shows the governor's house in the sixteenth district of Upper Egypt. The corn has just arrived from the fields; porters are pouring it into sacks under the watchful eyes of an overseer and then carrying the full sacks up to the loft; two scribes are listing the sacks as they are filled. In the loft, the sacks are received by a special overseer and recorded a second time by the scribe beside him. To the left there is a treasury. The same elaborate system of checks and counter-checks was no doubt employed by Joseph's officials when they laid in the corn (Gen. 41 : 48).

In the upper picture is a model of a set of granaries from the tomb of Kamena (Fourth Dynasty, middle of the third millennium B.C.).

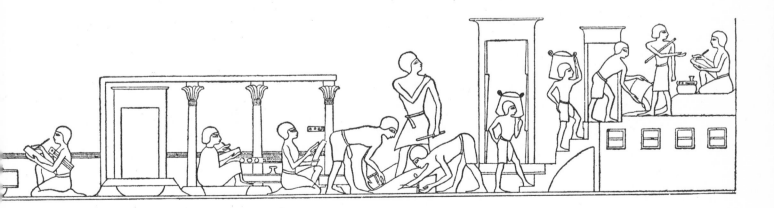

AND the seven years of famine began to come, as Joseph had said. There was famine in all lands; but in the land of Egypt there was bread. (Gen. 41 : 54)

In the course of its history, Egypt, being dependent on the vagaries of the Nile for its food-supply, has known years of famine. A text attributed to the time of Pharaoh Djoser, the founder of the Third Dynasty, who reigned about one thousand years before Joseph, tells of a famine that afflicted the country in his reign, as a result of the Nile's failure to overflow its banks for seven successive years (cf. the seven lean years in the time of Joseph). In tombs of the Twelfth and Thirteenth Dynasties (roughly contemporary with Joseph), Egyptian notables refer to a famine that occurred in their lifetime and to the distribution of food to the starving population. One of these nobles says: "In the time of the famine, which prevailed for many years in the land, I sold corn to the city". The accompanying relief, which once adorned the walls of an Egyptian temple at Sakkarah (in the second half of the third millennium), artistically portrays people dying from starvation.

AND Joseph gave orders to fill their bags with grain, and to replace every man's money in his sack, and to give them provisions for the journey. This was done for them. Then they loaded their asses with their grain and departed.

(Gen. 42 : 25-26)

When the sons of Jacob went down to Egypt to buy corn, they rode on asses which they loaded for the journey back to Canaan with "the good things of Egypt" (Gen. 45 : 23). They put the corn and the asses' fodder in sacks (cf. Gen. 42 : 27).
The picture shows a donkey carrying a large sack followed by an Egyptian who is belabouring the donkey with a stick held in his right hand. In his left hand there is another stick. The relief is from the wall of the tomb of the prince Reemkuy (Sakkarah, c. 2500 B.C.).

THEN their father Israel said to them, "If it must be so, then do this: take some of the choice fruits of the land in your bags and carry down to the man a present..."

(Gen. 43 : 11)

Jacob, knowing that the Egyptians were extremely fond of the fruits of Canaan, sends some with his sons as a gift for the ruler of Egypt. It was a common occurrence for delegations of the inhabitants of Canaan to bring the kings and nobles of Egypt gift-offerings, such as precious vessels, perfumes and cosmetics, wine, honey and so on (see also p. 114). There are many Egyptian pictorial records of such delegations (see p. 116).

In this picture (from a tomb at Thebes dating to the 15th cent. B.C.), we see bearded Semites, wearing the characteristic long Canaanite gown (see p. 94) and carrying gifts in various vessels (including an ointment horn). The tribute is proffered from a posture of humble submission. The first men in each row perform a lowly obeisance before the ruler, as did the sons of Jacob: "and Joseph's brothers came, and bowed themselves before him with their faces to the ground" (Gen. 42 : 6).

SLAUGHTER an animal and make ready, for the men are to dine with me at noon. (Gen. 43 : 16)

The chief food that Joseph's steward was ordered to prepare for the honoured guests was meat. Greek authors attest that meat was served every day in Egypt at the meals of kings and priests. The Egyptians ate apart from the Hebrews, "because the Egyptians might not eat bread with the Hebrews; for that is an abomination to the Egyptians" (Gen. 43 : 32). This isolationism of the Egyptians is also evident in Herodotus' statement that an Egyptian will not touch the knife of a Greek, nor will he eat the flesh of a ritually pure ox that has been cut by the knife of a Greek.

The model shown here portrays: 1) The slaughtering of an ox: the man standing to the left of the animal is cutting its jugular vein, while the man on the right stoops to catch the blood in a container. 2) In the centre of the model we see the preparation of beer: a man is pouring the beer through a sieve into a jar, while a woman appears to be sealing the jars that have been filled. 3) On the left, a woman is grinding corn. The model was found in an Egyptian tomb of the Ninth Dynasty, from the end of the third millennium B.C.

My cup, the silver cup...
Is it not from this that my lord
drinks, and by this that he
divines?... (Gen. 44 : 2, 5)

The Bible states that Joseph used the cup for both drinking and divination. It is impossible to tell exactly what kind of divination is meant here. In Babylon, it was customary to put drops of oil into a cup full of water, or drops of water into a container of oil, and to foretell the future from the shapes assumed by the drops. The biblical story of the cup makes a passing reference to the special feats of magic performed by high Egyptian dignitaries. Compare Joseph's words: "Such a man as I can indeed divine" (Gen. 44 : 15). The harsh punishment meted out for Benjamin's supposed theft — he "shall be my slave" (ibid., 17) — likewise indicates the special value attached to the Egyptian divining cup.

The figure shows a silver cone-shaped cup from the time of the Eighteenth Dynasty. The ten rings with their inscriptions form a scale for measuring the quantity of liquid. Some scholars hold that the cup was meant for medical use.

ᴀɴᴅ ʜᴇ has made me a father
to Pharaoh, and lord of all his
house and ruler over all the land
of Egypt.   (Gen. 45 : 8)

Joseph's functions in the court of Pharaoh correspond to the various duties of an Egyptian vizir, the king's vice-regent (cf. Gen. 41 : 40-45). The elevation of a Hebrew to such a high position in Pharaoh's court becomes entirely plausible in the light of our present knowledge of Semitic penetrations into Egypt in the patriarchal period. Groups of West Semitic tribes descended upon Egypt as part of the migration of peoples known as the Hyksos, i.e. 'rulers of foreign lands'. At the end of the 18th century B.C., the Hyksos seized control of Egypt and ruled it for several generations.

The dagger-handle reproduced here belonged to a high official of Semitic descent, as shown by the name — Nahman — written on the handle, in the inscription: "Nahman, who follows his lord". The dagger, which was discovered at Sakkarah in Egypt, is a masterpiece of craftsmanship, made, apparently, of electrum (an alloy of gold and silver). On the handle there is a hunting-scene: the hunter holds two staffs, one of which may have had a magical significance; and above him are a lion and a gazelle.

Egyptian nobles, and above all the kings, used seals in the form of a scarab with their names on them. The scarab seals shown here bear Semitic names, followed, in the case of two of them, by the title Hyksos. From left to right: a) Khyan (a Hyksos king, known also from Egyptian inscriptions); b) Samqan; c) Anat-her; d) Ja'qob-her. Some of these scarabs are made of steatite.

ΑND the sons of Israel carried Jacob their father, their little ones and their wives, in the wagons which Pharaoh had sent to carry him. They also took their cattle and their goods, which they had gained in the land of Canaan, and came into Egypt, Jacob and all his offspring with him.

(Gen. 46 : 5-6)

The descent of the Patriarchs into Egypt was a part of the migration of West Semitic tribes into Egypt at the beginning of the second millennium B.C. The reasons for these migrations were various: famine, trade and settlement in the Delta.

The upper figure (from a tomb at Thebes dating to the reign of Tutankhamon) shows one of the few examples known from Egyptian art of a wooden wagon with a protective covering. The wagon is drawn by oxen and in it is seated a Nubian princess on her way to visit Egypt. The wagon may well have been provided by Egyptians to convey the princess from her own country, as in the story of Jacob. The lower illustration is the famous wall-painting found in an Egyptian tomb at Beni Hasan (beginning of the 19th cent. B.C.). The painting portrays a group of Semites on their way to Egypt. The inscription accompanying the picture informs us that there are thirty-seven souls in the caravan, led by "Abisha (or, Abishar), ruler of a foreign land" (third from right). Both the men and the women are colourfully dressed. The men have pointed beards and are barefooted or wearing sandals (for the dress of the women, see p. 130). Most of the men are carrying defensive weapons (for the musical instruments, see p. 26 and for the water-skin, see p. 63). The first two men on the right are Egyptian officials who are presenting the members of the caravan to the ruler.

THEN Joseph made ready his chariot and went up to meet
Israel his father . . .   (Gen. 46 : 29)

In the Bible, the harnessing of a chariot is usually mentioned among the preliminaries to a military campaign
(e.g. Ex. 14 : 6). The procedure must have been elaborate, since the Egyptian chariot (like its Canaanite prototype) was a highly perfected instrument of war. There were three stages: first, the detachable parts of the chariot,
such as the yoke and the cross-piece, were assembled and attached to the body. Then the horses were harnessed
to the yoke and the reins. Finally, the quivers, shields and other weapons were placed in position on the chariot.
The painting reproduced here is from el-Amarna in Egypt, and belongs to the time of the Eighteenth Dynasty
(14th cent. B.C.). It gives a clear idea of the typical Egyptian chariot of the New Kingdom and the process of
harnessing it. The body of the chariot, made mainly of wood and leather, is tilted back on its axle and is thus
highly manoeuvreable. The wheels have six spokes. A bow-case is fastened to one side of the body and a quiver
to the other. A pair of horses is already in harness. Two slaves are engaged on the last stage of the preparations.

ꓮND from among his brothers he took five men and presented them to Pharaoh.   (Gen. 47 : 2)

Joseph presents five of his brothers to Pharaoh in order to obtain royal sanction for the settlement of the Hebrews in Goshen. Scenes of foreign envoys being received by Pharaoh are well-known in Egyptian art.
The picture reproduced here, from the tomb of an Egyptian noble in the vicinity of Thebes, shows inhabitants of Canaan doing obeisance to Tutankhamon (middle of the 14th cent. B.C.). The king is, as usual, portrayed on a scale larger than that of ordinary mortals. The leaders of the delegation are seen in the top row, also distinguished from the other members by their greater size. By their gestures they express their submission to Pharaoh. After them come slaves bearing the tribute, which consists of vessels, animals and skins. The figures at the head of the procession are prostrating themselves on the ground, in accordance with the etiquette repeatedly described in the el-Amarna letters (cf. also Gen. 42 : 6; 43 : 26). The envoys are dressed in the splendid blue and purple robes typical of the Canaanites (see p. 94). Before them, wearing the thin white garment of the Egyptians, stands an official, who, with a gesture, presents them to Pharaoh.

PUT them in charge of my cattle. (Gen. 47 : 6)

Jacob's family, who were known as shepherds in Canaan, carried on the family tradition in Egypt. Pharaoh requests Joseph to appoint his brothers as royal overseers of his herds, no doubt in recognition of their professional knowledge and experience. The cattle-overseers in Egypt used to inspect their herds and count them personally.

The illustration shows a miniature Egyptian model of a cattle-counting. The owner of the cattle is seated in a shady pavilion with a roof supported by columns, numbering his cows and bulls as they are driven past him by the cowherds. The model is taken from a tomb at Thebes, belonging to the Eleventh Dynasty (i.e. just before the patriarchal age).

THEN Joseph said to the people, "Behold, I have this day bought you and your land for Pharaoh. Now here is seed for you, and you shall sow the land. And at the harvests you shall give a fifth to Pharaoh, and four fifths shall be your own . . ."   (Gen. 47 : 23-24)

The acquisition of land carried out by Joseph on behalf of Pharaoh bears some resemblance to episodes known to us from the Egyptian records of a later period. In the time of the New Kingdom (second half of the second millennium B.C.), many estates were appropriated by the crown or the priesthood (cf. Gen. 47 : 22). Their division and sale, and the allocation of Pharaoh's share in them, were calculated on the basis of accurate measurements.

The picture — from the tomb of Menna at Thebes (Eighteenth Dynasty) — shows agricultural scenes, including the measuring of the crop on the royal estates. In the top row, officials dressed in white are measuring the crops, and, beside them, are servants stripped to the waist and holding a measuring line. In the middle row, scribes are recording the grain which is piled in heaps. In the bottom row, peasants are cutting the grain with sickles.

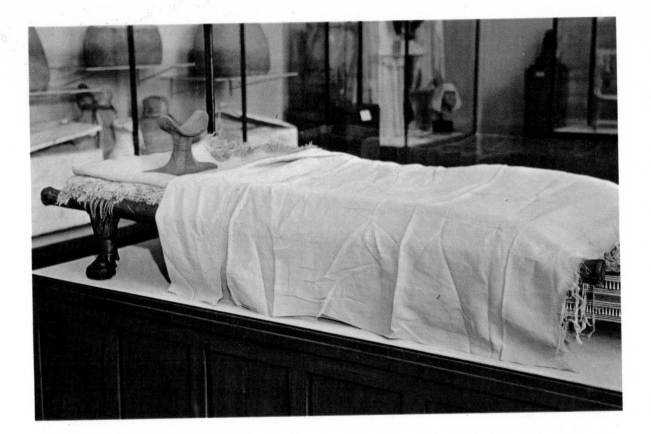

THEN Israel bowed himself
upon the head of the bed.
(Gen. 47 : 31)

The Egyptian habit of sleeping in a bed was foreign to the Semitic tribes of Palestine who used, no doubt, to sleep on skins spread on the ground. The Egyptians regarded sleeping in a bed as a sign of their superior civilization. Sinuhe the Egyptian (20th cent. B.C.), who dwelt for a long time among the Semites of Canaan, boasts of sleeping once more in a bed on his return to Egypt. The bed features among Egyptian domestic furniture from an early date. It consisted of a piece of cloth stretched on a wooden frame. The Egyptians liked to sleep with their heads lying much higher than their feet. To this end, they sometimes made use of a concave head-rest fixed on a stand. They also used so many pillows that they sometimes had to climb on to the bed by steps.
The picture shows a bed from the Eighteenth Dynasty, on which a head-rest has been placed.

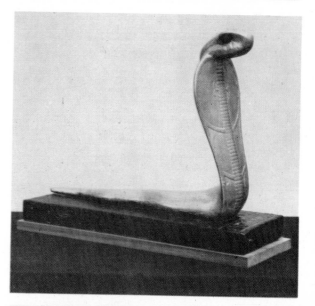

GATHER yourselves together, that I may tell you what shall befall you in days to come.

(Gen. 49 : 1)

The blessings given by Jacob to his sons reflect the fortunes of the tribes after their settlement in Palestine. The various metaphors from the animal and plant world are meant to give a vivid picture of each tribe's characteristic mode of life, the geographical peculiarities of its territory and its means of livelihood, all in the setting of the historical events that followed the conquest of Canaan.

The descriptions of the illustrations follow the order of the tribes in this chapter; the order of the pictures themselves is as follows: p. 120 from top left downwards: deer (text No. 6); wolf (No. 8); from top right downwards: boat (No. 2); ass (No. 3); serpent (No. 4); lion (No. 1). On p. 121 below, from left to right: archer (No. 7); repast (No. 5).

(1) "Judah is a lion's whelp: From the prey, my son, you have gone up; He stooped down, he crouched as a lion . . . The sceptre shall not depart from Judah" (Gen. 49 : 9-10). Judah, the largest and strongest of the tribes from which great kings sprang, is compared to a devouring lion, the king of the beasts.

In the picture, reproduced from the ivories of Megiddo, (14th-12th cents. B.C.), we see, on the right, a crouching lion and, on the left, a lion devouring its prey.

(2) "Zebulun shall dwell at the shore of the sea" (ibid., v. 13). In the time of the Judges, the tribe of Zebulun extended as far as the Mediterranean coast, and perhaps even controlled part of the Phoenician seaboard ("and his border shall be at Sidon"). It took an active part in the sea trade and shipping business.

The picture shows a model of a Phoenician ship from a tomb at Achzib, dating from the time of the Israelite monarchy.

(3) "Issachar is a strong ass, Crouching between the sheepfolds" (ibid., v. 14). Defeated in its efforts to master the strong Canaanite cities in the Valley of Jezreel and the Valley of Beth-shean, Issachar became "a slave at forced labor" to them instead. Hence the tribe is compared to the ass, the beast of burden.

The Egyptian painting reproduced here portrays a loaded ass driven on with a stick by a foreign slave.

(4) "Dan shall be a serpent in the way, A viper by the path" (ibid., v. 17). The tribe of Dan straddled some of the main routes of communication in Palestine. It was therefore well-placed to spring upon travellers suddenly from ambush, like the poisonous snake that lies in wait for the passing wayfarer.

The picture is of a snake wrought in gold from the tomb of Tutankhamon.

(5) "Asher's food shall be rich, And he shall yield royal dainties" (ibid., v. 20). Asher occupied Western Galilee: its wealth and prosperity may have resulted from its control of the passes through the hills. The Bible portrays Asher as entertaining his guests with a royal banquet, such as we find depicted on one of the Megiddo ivories. The king holds a bowl in his right hand and a flower in his left; in front of him there is a table with drinking vessels; on the other side of the table the guests are seated in pairs; two slaves are waiting on the king.

(6) "Naphtali is a hind let loose, That bears comely fawns" (ibid., v. 21). The territory of Naphtali stretched the length of Eastern Galilee, and it is compared to a swift hind that courses over hill and valley. The picture shows a deer drawn on the wall of a tomb of the Hasmonean period, excavated in Jerusalem.

(7) "Joseph . . . The archers fiercely attacked him, Shot at him and harassed him sorely; Yet his bow remained unmoved, His arms were made agile" (ibid., v. 22-24). The tribes of Joseph — Ephraim and Manasseh — which occupied the centre of Palestine and also part of Trans-Jordan, were famed for their warlike prowess in holding their ground against the Canaanites and Philistines in the wooded hills of Ephraim. The blessing therefore singles out the military alertness and the steadfast bow of the ancestor of the tribe.

The reproduction from the Megiddo ivories shows a bowman in the act of kneeling and stretching his bow.

(8) "Benjamin is a ravenous wolf" (ibid., v. 27). Benjamin, King Saul's tribe, though small, was renowned for courage in its valiant struggle with the Philistines.

Reproduced here is an amulet found at Arslan Tash in Syria (7th cent. B.C.), showing a she-wolf destroying an evil spirit.

So the physicians embalmed Israel . . . ; and they embalmed him (Joseph) and he was put in a coffin in Egypt.

(Gen. 50 : 2, 26)

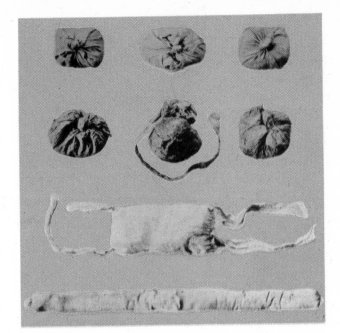

Although the Egyptian practice of embalming the dead was not, apparently, to the liking of the Hebrews, they nevertheless followed the local custom in the case of Jacob and Joseph, until their bodies could be returned to Canaan for burial (Gen. 50 : 25, 26). In embalming, the brain and the intestines were first removed from the body, which was then filled with preservative and wrapped in linen bandages. The picture below (from the tomb of Amenemopet, beginning of Nineteenth Dynasty), illustrates part of the process. It shows (on the right) artists fashioning the facial mask of the deceased, while others drill holes in beads of wood, stone and glass which are to adorn the neck of the mask. In the middle, we can see bowls containing the colours. On the left, is the embalmed and wrapped body.

The top figure on p. 123 shows bags of embalming materials. Those in the top rows contain natron, and the two below them chaff (from the tomb of the Pharaoh Tutankhamon).

The top figure on p. 122 shows a basalt sarcophagus. On the lid, the goddess Nephthys is seen lamenting the deceased whose name and titles are recorded on the sides. The deceased was the commander of mercenary forces in the Egyptian army (6th cent. B.C.). On the left are the words: "He was seventy days in the house of purification", i.e. in the embalming workshop. Presumably, the ritual mourning took place during these seventy days, which was the time that the Egyptians mourned for Jacob (Gen. 50 : 3).

Herodotus also states that the embalming took seventy days, whereas the Bible assigns only forty days to the embalming of Jacob: "for so many are required for embalming" (ibid.).

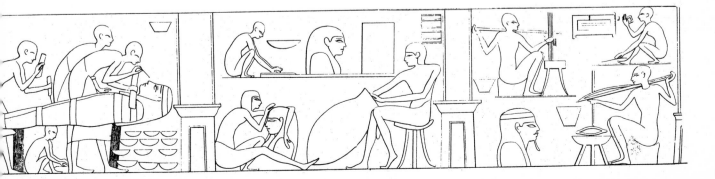

THIS is a grievous mourning
to the Egyptians . . .

(Gen. 50 : 11)

Jacob's burial is attended, as a mark of veneration, by the king's ministers ("the servants of Pharaoh"), the elders of Egypt, "chariots and horsemen . . . a very great company". The Egyptians, believing as they did that death was merely the transition to eternal life hereafter, used to accord magnificent funerals to their nobility.

The picture shows part of an Egyptian funeral procession crossing the Nile in small boats on its way to the city of the dead in Thebes. The figures below are professional mourners: note the expressive gesticulations. Those above are mourning-women loudly lamenting the dead: some of them are scattering ashes on their heads.

The pictures are reproduced from the tomb of Neferhotep, dating from the end of the Eighteenth Dynasty (14th cent. B C.).

EXODUS

N OW there arose a
new king over Egypt,
who did not know
Joseph.   (Ex. 1 : 8)

There have been numerous conjectures about the identity and date of the unnamed Pharaoh who enslaved the Israelites. One of the best known is based partly on the biblical statement that the Israelites built a store-city by the name of Raamses (Ex. 1 : 11). This is taken to be the city called in Egyptian "The House of Ramses", which was rebuilt in the reign of Ramses II (13th cent. B.C.). Hence, those who hold this view identify the "new king" with Ramses II, one of the greatest of the Pharaohs who, during a reign of sixty-six years, extended the borders of Egypt, suppressed revolts in Canaan, and erected some of the most magnificent buildings and cities in the Egyptian empire.

The picture is of the granite statue of Ramses II, probably from the temple at Karnak. The king is holding the royal sceptre and has a broad collar of gold and glass beads over his shoulders; on his head he is wearing the blue crown of Egypt, which is actually a helmet. On the front of it there is affixed the serpent uraeus, the symbol of Pharaoh's sovereignty.

A ND made their lives bitter with hard
service, in mortar and brick ... (Ex. 1:14)

The full meaning of the enslavement of the Israelites in Egypt is made clear by Egyptian pictures illustrating the
back-breaking tasks performed in the field and in constructional work by Egyptian and foreign forced labour.
Bricks in Egypt were made from the mud of the Nile, which is a mixture of clay and sand, with the addition of
straw or sometimes stalks and grass to bind and strengthen the clay. This we learn from Pharaoh's order: "Let
them go and gather straw for themselves" (Ex. 5 : 7).
The painting reproduced here (from the tomb of Rekhmire at Thebes, 15th cent. B.C.) shows how bricks were
made in Egypt. In the upper register on the left, there is a pool from which water is drawn for moistening the
clay. In the centre, workmen are kneading the clay with short-handled hoes, while labourers carry the clay to two
workmen who are making the bricks in moulds. Another workman is putting the bricks out to dry (top left).
The labourers include a bearded Semite and darker skinned Nubians. The inscription reads as follows: "The
making of bricks for the rebuilding of the workshops of the god Amon at Karnak." In the lower register the
building of the temple is shown.

WHEN you serve as midwife to the
Hebrew women, and see them upon the
birthstool, if it is a son, you shall kill him;
but if it is a daughter, she shall live.

(Ex. 1 : 16)

The Hebrew word *obnaim* (lit. "two stones", above translated "birthstool") means both the stool where the
woman in labour used to sit, and the round double table of stone on which the potter did his work. This same
term for two different objects used in making pottery and in labour may have been connected with the Egyptian
belief that God creates men and fashions them into various shapes on a potter's wheel, just as the potter fashions
pottery in his workshop.
The picture, showing an Egyptian scene of birth (the woman in labour attended by midwives) is from the temple
of Luxor, 14th cent. B.C. The woman giving birth, an Egyptian queen, is sitting on a chair with her hands held
by two midwives. The new-born child, a son to Pharaoh, is placed in the arms of the waiting handmaids.

THE midwives said to Pharaoh, "Because the Hebrew women are not like the Egyptian women; for they are vigorous and are delivered, before the midwife comes to them."

(Ex. 1 : 19)

The difference of the physical condition between the Egyptian and the Hebrew women is suggested by the contrast of their giving birth. According to the midwives' reports to the king — perhaps in order to exonerate themselves from failing to carry out the royal command — the Hebrew women gave birth so easily and quickly that, unlike the Egyptians, they had no need of the midwives. Perhaps there is here a note of contempt for the delicate, pampered Egyptian women who lacked the natural vitality of the Hebrews.

These differences are also reflected in Egyptian art, as shown in the paintings reproduced here. The picture on the left — from the tomb of Menna, 15th cent. B.C. — illustrates the slender figures and well-groomed bodies of the Egyptian ladies. They are wearing the thin, white dresses customary in Egypt and are adorned with brightly coloured collars on their necks, bangles on their arms, and rings in their ears. In their hands they hold gift-offerings of flowers and fruit. There is a striking difference between them and the Semitic women of the patriarchal period portrayed by the Egyptian artist in the picture on the right (detail from p. 114). These sturdy females are wearing coloured dresses of coarse material, without any personal adornment; three of them have one shoulder bare; they are all wearing low boots, no doubt for the hard journey on foot from Canaan to Egypt.

SHE took for him a basket made of bulrushes; . . . and she put the child in it and placed it among the reeds at the river's brink.

(Ex. 2 : 3)

Moses came into the world in the harsh days of Pharaoh's decree: "Every son that is born to the Hebrews you shall cast into the Nile" (Ex. 1 : 22). When Jochebed could no longer conceal her son, she put him in a basket — apparently made of reeds — and placed it in the reeds that fringed the Nile, in the hope that the child would somehow be saved. "And his sister stood at a distance, to know what would be done to him" (Ex. 2 : 4). In fact, the anxiously awaited deliverance came from an entirely unexpected quarter — from the royal house of Egypt.

The illustration on the left shows a tangle of papyrus reeds, reproduced from the tomb of Kenamon (15th cent. B.C.). The stalks, which look like inverted bells, are arranged in four rows. Some are bending under the weight of the birds that have sought shelter among them.

The figure on the right shows a coiled basket of a type common in ancient Egypt.

NOW the daughter of Pharaoh came down to bathe at the river, and her maidens walked beside the river ... (Ex. 2 : 5)

The grown-up princesses of the royal household of Egypt had special palaces, with gardens and baths attached. Sometimes the princesses were very numerous: Ramses II had 59 daughters, of whom 45 are known to us by name. In the biblical story of the finding of Moses, neither the king nor his daughter are named. In a later tradition, however, the daughter is called Thermuthis (Josephus, *Antiquities* II 9, 5 — § 224; *Book of Jubilees* 47, 5); or Batyah *(Babylonian Talmud, Megillah* 13a).

The relief — from the temple of Medinet-Habu built in the reign of Ramses III, 12th cent. B.C. — shows a daughter of Pharaoh, followed by her handmaids, going to offer a sacrifice, while a procession of female singers and musicians passes by. The princess is wearing a high head-dress, the emblem of the goddess Nekhbet which subsequently became the queen's emblem. Her head is covered by a wig, and in her hands she is carrying staves decorated with lotusflowers as an offering to the god. She is wearing a thin garment and sandals. The handmaids are dressed just like their royal mistress, but without the headdress.

AND he saw an Egyptian beating a Hebrew, one of his people.
(Ex. 2 : 11)

The painting is taken from the tomb of Puyemre at Thebes (15th cent. B.C.). It shows a bearded Semite leading a herd of cattle. The inscription in the middle of the picture is about wine made by the Apiru (= Hebrews?). The inscription at the bottom left mentions wine "from the ways of Hor", i.e. the district of Qantara which is close to the biblical Goshen.

If we could be sure that there is a geographical connection between the herdsman and the wine-makers, the picture would illustrate the way of life of Semitic tribes who were engaged in cattle-rearing and wine-making on the borderland of Egypt, i.e. in the area where the cattle-rearing Hebrews lived (Gen. 46 : 32, 34).

At the top left there is a reproduction of an overseer smiting a slave, a motif common in Egyptian art. In Egypt, as in all oriental countries, beating was a favourite means of exacting taxes from peasants and of compelling workers to work still harder. Obviously, such a method would have been applied with special rigour to foreign slaves; and the taskmasters and tax-gatherers were held responsible for its proper application (Ex. 1 : 11; 5 : 13).

NOW Moses was keeping the flock of his father-in-law, Jethro, the priest of Midian; and he led his flock to the west side of the wilderness, and came to Horeb, the mountain of God.

(Ex. 3 : 1)

The theophany in the burning bush took place at Horeb which is called here already "the mountain of God" in anticipation of the law-giving on Mount Sinai. Moses came to this spot in search of good pasturage; the Hebrew word *midbar* translated here "(the west side of) the wilderness" means actually pasturage. He had perhaps gone beyond the limits fixed — according to the custom of desert shepherds — for the pasturage of his father-in-law's flock and had entered the mountainous region of central Sinai, the only place where vegetation is found in summer-time. It is difficult to identify Horeb with any certainty (see p. 151).

The view here is of Jebel Serbal (6791 feet), seen looming on the horizon behind the oasis of Feiran and the lower hills surrounding it. Although this is not the highest peak in Sinai, it is the most imposing. Granite pinnacles rise above the surrounding valleys like gigantic towers, amid a landscape of majesty and infinite variety. The grandeur of this spectacle, which filled the ancient beholder with awe-struck wonderment, not unnaturally led the Christian monks of the 4th cent. A.D. to regard Jebel Serbal as "the mountain of God".

As had been promised to Abraham in the Covenant with God (Gen. 15 : 14), the Hebrews left Egypt "with great possessions". To the inhabitants of Canaan, the most striking manifestation of Egypt's wealth was its great abundance of precious metals accruing from the exploitation of the Nubian gold mines and the booty brought back from military campaigns in Asia.

Large quantities of gorgeous gold and silver vessels have been discovered in Egyptian tombs. On the left are some of the vessels from the treasure found in the tombs of the princesses at Lahun (time of the Middle Kingdom). It is hardly likely, of course, that objects of such magnificence were commonly possessed by the neighbours of the Israelite women.

The elegant dresses worn by Egyptian women were made of fine, white linen. Thanks to the dry climate of Egypt, various specimens of this fabric have been preserved to the present day. On the right, for example, we see a shawl, a kerchief and a dress, all made of linen.

TAKE your rod and
stretch out your hand
over the waters of
Egypt, over their rivers,
their canals, and their
ponds, and all their
pools of water, that they
may become blood . . .
(Ex. 7 : 19)

The early sages said: "These two plagues (blood and frogs) came from the Nile, because the sustenance of Egypt comes from the Nile, seeing that it is the Nile that rises and waters their soil" *(Lekah Tob, Ex. 7 : 28)*. The plague of blood affected not only the mainstream of the Nile, but also its confluents and canals, the pools and the ponds that the Egyptian nobles used to build for themselves on their estates. It is well known that the waters of the Nile are turned blood-red from time to time by pollution with fungi, plants and insects, and this phenomenon might provide an explanation of the plague. The many different words used by the Bible for the waters of the Nile conjure up a picture of the Egyptian landscape with its many artificial ponds and channels which were dug to make good the total lack of rain.

The lower picture shows such a pond on the estate of an Egyptian noble at Thebes in the 15th or 14th cent. B.C. In the water there are lotus flowers, while papyrus and other water plants surround the pond. Geese are swimming on the surface of the pond and the water is teeming with fish. Such pools were used for bathing, for the breeding of fish and fowl, and for ornamentation. The upper picture shows one of the net-work of irrigation channels running off the Nile, which covered Egypt then as now.

BEHOLD, I will plague all your country with frogs . . . behold, tomorrow I will bring locusts into your country and they shall cover the face of the land . . .
(Ex. 8 : 2; 10 : 4-5)

What is written about the frogs and locusts makes it clear that most of the plagues were only extreme aggravations of pests that normally afflict Egypt year by year. The frogs multiply every year after the inundation of the Nile; but on this occasion, hordes of them overran the country: "The Nile shall swarm with frogs, which shall come up into your house, and into your bedchamber, and on your bed, and into the houses of your servants, and of your people, and into your ovens and your kneading-bowls" (Ex. 8 : 3).

The locust is always one of the most dangerous natural pests in the East. But, this time, it descended upon the country with exceptional speed and in unprecedentedly large numbers: "Such a dense swarm of locusts as had never been before, nor ever shall be again . . . the land was darkened . . . and not a green thing remained, neither tree nor plant of the field" (Ex. 10 : 14-15).

The Egyptians attributed divine powers to the frog and regarded it as a symbol of fertility. Hence the goddess of fertility and childbirth, Heket, is sometimes represented with a frog's head. In the upper picture, we see the frog-shaped hieroglyphic sign for this goddess. Another hieroglyphic sign in the shape of a tadpole means 100,000 and is used to indicate a vast multitude.

The lower picture reproduces a painting of the desert locust as it appears in the tomb of Horemheb at Thebes (15th cent. B.C.). This locust, after multiplying rapidly in the favourable climate of the Sudan, invades the neighbouring countries and devours their crops.

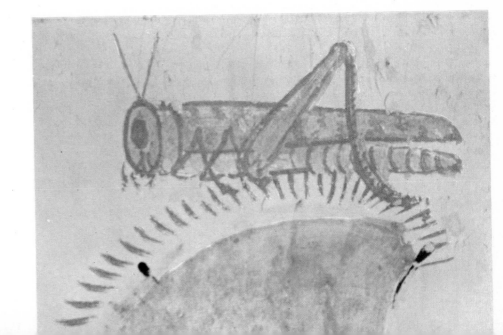

A̲ND all the first-born in the land of Egypt shall die, from the first-born of Pharaoh who sits upon his throne, even to the first-born of the maidservant who is behind the mill . . .   (Ex. 11 : 5)

The slaying of the firstborn was "more grievous than all the other plagues put together" (*Midrash Haggadol,* Ex. XI, 9). The two extremes of Egyptian society singled out by the biblical verse are meant to show that the plague afflicted all ranks of the people alike : from the crown prince — who sat on the royal throne even in his father's lifetime — down to "the maidservant who is behind the mill", an expression that, in Egyptian literature, signifies the poorest of the poor.

In the centre of the upper picture, Ramses III (beginning of the 12th cent. B.C.) is standing before the goddess Isis. The king is wearing ceremonial robes and holding the hand of the goddess who says to him: "Lo! I give thee many years of life." Behind him is his son, the crown prince, holding a fan at the side of which is written: "The crown prince who is over the two lands, the royal son, his beloved son."

The lower picture is of a coloured limestone statue from Gizeh (third millennium B.C.), showing a maidservant grinding corn in a hand-mill. There are piles of grain at the edge of the grinding-stone. The servant is wearing a short skirt and a wig covered by a cloth to keep out the dust.

THE time that the people of Israel dwelt in Egypt was four hundred and thirty years. (Ex. 12 : 40)

The length of the Israelite stay in Egypt is broadly in accordance with what was foretold in the Covenant of God with Abraham (Gen. 15 : 13). But, since the dates given in the Bible are only approximate, it is difficult to fit them into the framework of Egyptian chronology. It seems probable enough, however, that the sojourn in Egypt was connected with the Hyksos invasion at the end of the 18th cent. B.C. (see p. 113), while the Exodus took place at the beginning of the 13th cent. B.C. or a little earlier. The most powerful of the dynasties that ruled Egypt in this period was the Eighteenth Dynasty (1570-1305 B.C.), with which begins the New Kingdom.

The pictures show — from bottom to top and then from right to left — the five most famous rulers of this dynasty. In chronological order they are: Queen Hatshepsut (1486-1468 B.C.), the only woman to have wielded sovereign power in Egypt: her husband and successor, Thutmose III (1490-1436 B.C.), the great conqueror, in whose reign the Egyptian armies reached the banks of the Euphrates; Amenhotep III (1398-1361 B.C.), whose reign marks the cultural and artistic apogee of the New Kingdom; his son Amenhotep IV (1369-1353 B.C.), the great religious innovator, calling himself Akhenaton, whose political negligence brought about a disastrous decline in Egypt's power; and his son-in-law, Tutankhamon (1352-1344 B.C.), who chanced to be the only Pharaoh whose tomb almost entirely escaped depredation by robbers and retained most of its treasures intact to our own day. These were the Pharaohs under whose rule the Israelites dwelt in Goshen as resident foreigners (Heb. *gerim).*

WHEN Pharaoh let the people go, God did not lead them by way of the land of the Philistines, although that was near; for God said, "Lest the people repent when they see war, and return to Egypt."

(Ex. 13 : 17)

The "way of the land of the Philistines" was the short coastal route from Egypt to Canaan, which was part of an international highway running from Egypt to Aram-Naharaim. In Egyptian records from the time of the Exodus it is called "the ways of Hor", — the Egyptian god Horus — since it was the route traversed by the Egyptian kings at the head of their armies on their campaigns into Palestine and Syria. To protect their armies and safeguard their supply routes, the Egyptians established forts at frequent intervals along that part of the road that ran through the desert. In the reliefs of Seti I (c. 1300 B.C. — roughly the time of the Exodus) on the temple walls at Karnak, there is a row of scenes which form a kind of 'military map' showing the route from Sile (near the modern Qantara on the Suez Canal) to Raphia.

Sile, seen at the extreme right of the relief, is represented as a frontier fort on a branch of the Nile. The fort in the upper left hand corner may represent Raphia. A chain of forts and wells (about twenty in all) surrounds the chariots of Pharaoh who is on his way back to Egypt.

The Papyrus Anastasi I, a literary document from the reign of Ramses II (middle of 13th cent. B.C.), describes a section of these same desert halts. The Israelites would almost certainly have been trapped had they followed this fortified military route on their way out of Egypt. This is why from the outset they were made to avoid "the way of the land of the Philistines".

When the Israelites reached the edge of the desert, they were commanded to camp between the sea and the network of forts to the south of it. We are now able to reconstruct the first part of the Israelite march (see map) from non-biblical records, since the names of three places on the route mentioned in the Bible occur in other records. On a relief from the time of Seti I (see above), Migdol is represented as one of a chain of Egyptian fortresses on the military road from Egypt to Palestine; it is also mentioned in a document from the reign of Ramses II (13th cent. B.C.). Baal-zephon (after a Canaanite god of that name), was a sailors' shrine situated on the narrow strip of land which stretches along the north side of Lake Serbonis (see p. 144). In an Egyptian document of about 1100 B.C., the area of marshes and lakes to the north of Zoan (the Egyptian "House of Ramses"), is called *djouf* (with which the Hebrew *yam suf*, literally "sea of reeds", usually translated as the "Red Sea", is perhaps to be connected). The Israelites may have circumvented the network of Egyptian forts by following the route marked in red on the map. Since they did not take the usual road, Pharaoh might well suppose that "They are entangled in the land, the wilderness has shut them in" (Ex. 14 : 3).

Another widely held view, first suggested by the early Jewish commentators, places the Exodus much further south, identifying the "Sea of Suf" either with the tip of the Gulf of Suez, or with one of the Bitter Lakes to the north of it.

TELL the people of Israel to turn back and encamp in front of Pi-hahiroth, between Migdol and the sea, in front of Baal-zephon; you shall encamp over against it, by the sea.

(Ex. 14 : 2)

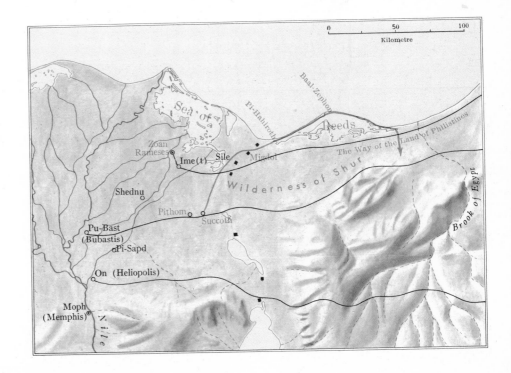

AND they said to Moses, "Is it because there are no graves in Egypt that you have taken us away to die in the wilderness?" ... (Ex. 14 : 11)

Even in the angry words of the Israelites we can hear a note of bitter irony about Egypt with its abundance of tombs. To ensure life after death it was essential, the Egyptians believed, to preserve the embalmed body of the deceased and to supply it in its tomb with its various needs (see pp. 122-123). Hence, in the course of time, Egypt became the land of sepulchres. During their long sojourn in Egypt, the Israelites could not have failed to notice the numerous tombs which were cut into the rocks or built laboriously and with great ostentation on the west bank of the Nile. In the third millennium B.C., the Egyptian kings erected huge pyramids to be their burial places. Later, in the New Kingdom, the kings had their tombs cut out of the rock in the Valley of the Kings (see illustration), to-day known as Biban el-Maluk ("the gates of the kings"). Situated at the foot of the hills to the west of Thebes, this valley can be approached only by a narrow path running between steep cliffs. Even so, the royal tombs had been broken into as early as the 12th cent. B.C. The ancient Greek geographer, Strabo, was greatly impressed by what he saw in the valley and described forty tombs worth visiting. So far, more than sixty royal tombs have been discovered there.

THE Egyptians pursued, and went in after them into the midst of the sea, all Pharaoh's horses, his chariots, and his horsemen.   (Ex. 14 : 23)

The Bible states that Pharaoh took with him a force of six hundred "picked chariots" (Ex. 14 : 7). The chariots were the pride of Egypt's army (see also p. 145); and it is no wonder that, at the sight of them, the Israelites were thrown into a panic and "cried out to the LORD" (ibid. 10). From the beginning of the New Kingdom, the chariot became the spearhead of Egypt's fighting force. With the great mobility of the horse, combined with the impact of the vehicle, and the "fire-power" of the archer riding it, the chariot was excellently suited for the pursuit of a retreating enemy and for long-distance campaigns beyond the borders of Egypt. The Egyptian chariot, which at the beginning of the Eighteenth Dynasty was still of the Canaanite type, was gradually perfected into a highly mobile and powerful instrument of war capable of covering large distances even in difficult terrain. Drawn by a pair of horses, it carried only two fighting-men — the charioteer and the archer. In ceremonial pictures, however, the king appears alone in his chariot at the head of his hosts. Thus, in the painting reproduced here from the tomb of Tutankhamon (14th cent. B.C.), we see the king alone in his chariot leading his forces in pursuit of Semitic tribes. Thus Pharaoh may have ridden at the head of his chariots in pursuit of the Israelites (Ex. 14 : 6-8).

THE LORD routed the Egyptians in the midst of the sea... But the people of Israel walked on dry ground through the sea, the waters being a wall to them on their right hand and on their left.

(Ex. 14 : 27-29)

According to the view set out on p. 141, the Israelites passed along Lake Sirbonis (Sabkhat Bardawil), the shallow lagoon on the north coast of Sinai, which can be identified with the biblical "Sea of Suf." Today, the waters of this lagoon are saline; but formerly it was a bay into which flowed one of the arms of the Nile; it must once have contained fresh water in which reeds could grow (the Egyptian word *djouf — suf* means water in which papyrus grows).

Lake Sirbonis is separated from the Mediterranean Sea by a spit bar, confined by the sea to the north and south. To this day it is usually safe to walk along this strip of land; but, occasionally, when a strong wind has been blowing, the waves break over it, flooding it temporarily and making it dangerous to travellers.

THE horse and his rider He has thrown into the sea.   (Ex. 15 : 1)

The Song of Moses gives the following detailed description of the drowning of the Egyptian chariot force —
horses, riders and all: "Pharaoh's chariots and his host He cast into the sea: And his picked officers are sunk in the
Red Sea" (Ex. 15 : 4). At the time of the Exodus, the Egyptians, like the other peoples of the ancient East, had
not yet begun to use cavalry in the modern sense, i.e. soldiers mounted on horseback. The horsemen and riders
mentioned in the song are simply the chariot-teams.
Several reliefs from the reign of Ramses II, found in the Ramesseum at Thebes, portray in great detail the battle
with the Hittites near Kadesh-on-the-Orontes. One of them (belonging roughly to the period of the Exodus and
reproduced above) shows the retreating Hittite chariots sinking in the waters. A confused mass of horses, chariots
and charioteers are seen struggling in the river; some of them are trying to swim to the bank.

Miriam, called here "the prophetess", sings a song of triumph, just as the
prophetess Deborah does on a later occasion (Judg. 5). In the great exaltation
after the parting of the sea, Miriam and her chorus of dancing and timbrel-
beating women provided the customary accompaniment for the male singers
and musicians (cf. Ps. 68 : 25). In Israel, as throughout the ancient East, women
took part in victory celebrations, dancing and singing well-known popular
songs (cf. 1 Sam. 18 : 6-7).
A scene of dance and song is represented on an Egyptian relief from the tomb
of Huy at Sakkarah, dating from the Nineteenth Dynasty (roughly contemporary with the Exodus). It shows a band of eight dancing women who
accompany their dance with rhythmic beating on timbrels. On the right, two
girls are dancing while keeping the beat with sticks held in their hands.

THEN Moses led Israel onward from the Red Sea, and they went into the wilderness of Shur; they went three days in the wilderness and found no water.   (Ex. 15 : 22)

After the Israelites had crossed the 'Sea of Suf' (in the English Bible translated 'the Red Sea'), they turned towards the desert wastes of the Sinai peninsula. That closest to the Egyptian border was the biblical wilderness of Shur which apparently stretched from "the way of the land of the Philistines" and Lake Serbonis southwards to the Tih plateau in Central Sinai. The word *shur* in Hebrew means "wall", and maybe it designated the line of forts erected by the Egyptians on their desert frontier, from Migdol near the Mediterranean coast in the north to the Gulf of Suez in the south (i.e. along the modern Suez Canal). The forts were intended to defend the soil of Egypt from Asiatic desert raiders and to control their movements into the land of the Nile.

By their daring march along the Sea the Israelites had outflanked the northern end of this fortified line and then continued south-east until they came to a waterless waste "in the way of Shur" (see map on p. 141).

The picture shows a sandy and rocky desert landscape in Northern Sinai.

THEN they came to Elim, where there were twelve springs of water and seventy palm trees; and they encamped there by the water.

(Ex. 15 : 27)

It is impossible to identify with complete certainty all the places listed in the route taken by the Israelites during the Exodus. The location of Elim, for one, cannot be fixed. But it was certainly one of the few fertile oases in the Sinai peninsula as is shown by the number of springs and palm-trees mentioned in this verse. In the Sinai desert there are places, especially in the wadis, where subterranean waters collect in sufficient quantities for palm-groves to thrive in the middle of the wilderness. Such oases are found along Wadi el-Arish at the northeastern corner of the peninsula (upper picture), on its eastern coast (Nuweibeh, Dhahab) and, the largest of them all, in southern Sinai in Wadi Feiran (lower picture). The economic importance of this last oasis is famous throughout the entire region. Throughout the ages, the nomads of the Sinai deserts were attracted by oases such as those shown here.

IN the evening quails came up and covered the camp . . . Now the house of Israel called its name manna; it was like coriander seed white, and the taste of it was like wafers made with honey.

(Ex. 16 : 13, 31)

The quail (upper picture) is a migratory bird which appears in Sinai occasionally in the spring on its way from the Sudan to southern and western Europe and regularly on its way back in the autumn. Huge flocks of these birds arrive, especially in the spring, so completely exhausted that it is easy to catch them with nets and even with bare hands. The Bible relates that the quails descended upon the Israelite camp in enormous numbers: the people gorged themselves so much that a plague broke out (Num. 11 : 31–34). From other countries, too, there are stories of epidemics resulting from the eating of quail-flesh; but the cause of the illness is still unknown.

Manna is a drop-like excretion from two kinds of scale-insects that live on the tamarisk tree. In the pictures below we see (from left to right): a) A female in the egg-sack *(Trabutina mannipara)*; b) the eggsack excreted by a female insect *(Najococus serpentinus)*; c) the female secretes large transparent drops of manna which dry and fall to the ground; d) dried grains of manna. The excretion by the manna insects occurs in June-July.

It may be noted that the Arabs call these grains *man* or *man min sama* — 'manna from heaven'. The Bible, however, lays stress on the miraculous nature of the occurrence: "Behold, I will rain bread from heaven for you" (Ex. 16 : 4).

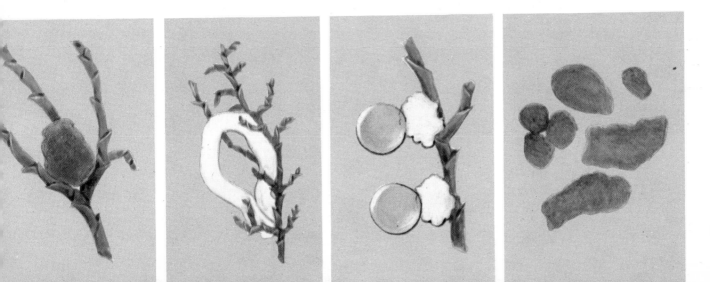

T HEN came Amalek and fought with Israel at Rephidim. (Ex. 17 : 8)

The Amalekites were a nomadic tribe of typical war-loving desert raiders roaming to the south of Canaan, in the Negeb and Sinai (Num. 13 : 29; 14 : 43, 45) and in the region of Kadesh ("the country of the Amalekites", Gen. 14 : 7). They suddenly fell upon the Israelites, attacking the stragglers at the rear of the column, as such raiders always do ("how he attacked you on the way, when you were faint and weary, and cut off at your rear all who lagged behind you", Deut. 25 : 18).

The picture reproduced here, which is painted on the famous chest from the tomb of Tutankhamon, graphically portrays the heat and fury of a battle between the Egyptian army and Asiatic tribes, prominent amongst whom are long-haired, bearded desert raiders. In contrast to the large shields with rounded tops of the Egyptians and the round shields carried by the Canaanite soldiers in the 13th cent. B.C., the shields of the desert raiders are rectangular and embellished with various designs. Their weapons consist principally of chariots, javelins, short swords and bows.

The battle depicted on this chest seems to have been fought in a desert region (like the battle described in the Bible) as indicated by the typical desert vegetation seen at the edges of the painting.

AND there Israel encamped before the mountain.   (Ex. 19 : 2)

The Bible does not give the exact location of the mountain of Sinai on which the Ten Commandments were given. Some maintain that this scriptural silence is deliberately intended to veil the material aspects of the awesome occasion.

A late Byzantine Christian tradition identifies the mountain of God with Jebel Musa ("the Mountain of Moses"), which rises to a height of 7500 ft. in the centre of a granite range in the south of the Sinai peninsula. At its foot, there is an extensive valley, called to-day er-Raha, wide enough for a large encampment. Here, according to Christian tradition, the Israelites were encamped while Moses "went up to God" (Ex. 19 : 3). It is true that there are not many springs of water in the immediate vicinity; these are found in abundance only at the oasis of Feiran, about 30 miles away. But the mountain itself, with its steep slopes rising sheer from narrow tortuous valleys is apt to arouse feelings of religious awe in the beholder.

[. . . I am the Lo]rd your God that [brought] you out of the land of E[gypt.]
[You shall not hav]e other gods be[fore] Me. You shall not make [for yourself an image]
[or any likeness] that is in the heavens above or that is in the earth [beneath]
[or that is in the water]s beneath the earth. You shall not bow down to them [nor]
[serve them, for] I am the Lord your [God, a jealous God visiting the iniquity]
[of fathers upon son]s to the third and to the fourth generation unto them that hate Me, [and doing]
[kindness unto thousands] unto them that love Me and keep My commandments. You shall [not]
[take up the name of the Lord] your God in vain for the Lord will not hold guiltless [him that]
[takes up His na]me in vain. Remember the day of the Shabbath [to hallow it :]
[six day]s you shall work and do all your business, and on the [seventh day]
a Shabbath for the Lord your God; you shall not do therein any business, [you,]
[and your son and your daughter], your slave and your handmaid, your ox and your ass and all your [cattle]
[and the stranger that is] in your gates. For six days did the Lo[rd make]
[the heaven]s and the earth, the sea and all th[at is therein],
and rested [on the] seventh day; therefore the Lord blessed the
seventh day and hallowed it. Honour your father and your moth[er, that]
it may be well with you and that you be long upon the ground [that]
the Lord your God gives you. You shall not do adultery. You shall not do murder. You shall [not]
[st]eal. You shall not [bear] against your neighbour vain witness. You shall not covet [the]
[wife of your neighbour. You shall] not desire the house of your neighbour, his fie[ld, or his slave]
[or his handmaid, or his o]x or his ass, or anything, that is your neighbour's.
[(?) And these are the statute]s and the judgements that Moses commanded the [sons of]
[Israel] in the wilderness, when they went forth from the land of Egypt. Hear
[O Isra]el, the Lord our God, the Lord is one; and you shall l[ove]
[the Lord your G]o[d with al]l y[our heart . . .]

A‌ND God spoke all these words, saying, "I am the Lord your God, who brought you out of the land of Egypt out of the house of bondage."
(Ex. 20 : 1-2)

Two versions of the Ten Commandments are found in the Bible, the first in Ex. 20 : 2-17, and the second in Deut. 5 : 6-21. The oldest manuscript containing the Commandments is a papyrus discovered in Egypt and known as the Nash Papyrus (after its purchaser); it was probably written in the 2nd or 1st century B.C. Unfortunately, the writing on it is careless and the ink has flaked off in some places, so that scholars differ about the reading of some of the words. Apart from the Ten Commandments, the papyrus also contains that portion of Deuteronomy known as the *Shema* (Deut. 6 : 4-9).

This collocation on a single papyrus of two such widely separated biblical passages finds its explanation in the Mishnah: "(The priests in the Temple at dawn) recited a Benediction and recited the Ten Commandments, the *Shema,* and the 'And it shall come to pass if ye shall hearken', and 'the Lord said to Moses'" (*Mishnah Tamid,* 5 : 1). The text of the Commandments in the Nash Papyrus is essentially based on that in the Book of Exodus. Both are distinguished by the cosmological reason given for the Sabbath ordinances — God's resting on the seventh day — in contrast to the social motivation of Deuteronomy: "That your manservant and your maidservant may rest as well as you. You shall remember that you were a servant in the land of Egypt" (Deut. 5 : 14-15). In certain details, however, e.g. *ed shav* (false witness, Deut. 5 : 20) instead of *ed sheqer* (lying witness, Ex. 20 : 16) — the papyrus shows the influence of Deuteronomy. Finally, there are a few instances in which the papyrus differs from both Massoretic versions, as in putting "Neither shall you commit adultery" before "You shall not kill".

YOU shall not make your-
self a graven image, or any
likeness of anything that is in
heaven above, or that is in the
earth beneath, or that is in the
water under the earth.

(Ex. 20 : 4)

The prohibition of making graven images
is one of the basic tenets of the religion of
Israel. By force of this prohibition the God
of Israel was comprehended without any
effigy, as a deity far beyond all human visua-
ization, "Who has no body, nor can He be
conceived in bodily terms". This is what
made the Law of Israel fundamentally different from all the embryonic forms of mono-
theism that appeared in various parts of the
Ancient East. The biblical wording of the
prohibition reflects the primeval oriental
conception of the universe as divided into
different parts: the firmament above the
earth, the earth beneath the heaven (cf. Gen.
1 : 6-8) and the abyss under the earth (Deut.
33 : 13; Ps. 24 : 2 etc.). This conception is
illustrated, for instance, by several reliefs on
Babylonian boundary stones *(kudurru)* (see
p. 274). One of them—of King Meli-Shipak
who lived in the 12th cent. B.C. — is reproduced here. On the rounded top register of
the stone we see the symbols of the chief
gods of the heavens (from left to right): a
crescent (the moon-god, Sin); an eight-
pointed star (Ishtar, the queen of heaven);
the sun-disc (the god Shamash). The symbols in the second register are: horned caps
mounted on facades of temples (Anu, the
god of the sky and the supreme deity of the
Sumerian and Akkadian pantheon, and Enlil,
the storm-god); a ram's head on a pole
above a goat with a fish's body (Ea, the god
of sweet water, wisdom and sorcery). The
last symbol in this register is not clear (it
may be that of Ninhursag, the lady of the
mountains and goddess of fertility). Below
all these come three registers of symbols of
the various gods whose main sphere of influence is the earth. In the bottom register,
the serpent and the scorpion symbolize the
denizens of the water under the earth.

Now these are the
ordinances which you
shall set before them.
(Ex. 21 : 1)

Ever since advanced civilizations developed in the Ancient East at the end of the fourth millennium B.C., society required legal systems. From time to time, collections of laws are discovered that were promulgated hundreds of years before the biblical code. The Sumerians were the first legal codifiers; and the most ancient collection of laws yet brought to light is that of Urnammu, King of Ur, who lived at the end of the third millennium B.C.

The stele erected by the king shows (second row from the top) the moon-god, who was also the god of Ur, empowering Urnammu to make laws. In the two scenes on the right and left the king is seen offering a libation, while the god hands to him the symbols of sovereignty and justice — the rod, the ring and the line. However, nothing like the moral argumentation of the biblical code has been found in any other ancient oriental collection of laws, not even in those of a later date.

WHEN an ox gores a man or a woman to death, the ox shall be stoned, and its flesh shall not be eaten; but the owner of the ox shall be clear. But if the ox has been accustomed to gore in the past, and its owner has been warned but has not kept it in, and it kills a man or a woman, the ox shall be stoned, and its owner also shall be put to death. (Ex. 21 : 28-29)

The oldest known law code in a Semitic tongue was discovered near the city of Eshnunna, east of the Tigris. It is from the beginning of the second millennium B.C. and is earlier than the famous laws of Hammurabi. The code, which is made up of 60 sections, contains occasional similarities to the laws of the Bible, such as that relating to the goring ox (for a picture and translation of this section see next page).

Both sets of laws stress two principles. First, the responsibility of the owner is conditional upon his having received a previous warning (Ex. 21 : 29). Secondly, if an unsuspected ox (i.e. one that has not yet gored three times) kills another ox, then the owner of the ox which did the goring and the owner of the one that was gored share the damage equally. However, the Bible adds the responsibility of the ox, which is to be stoned as a murderer, whether its owner has been warned previously or not. This is in accordance with God's words to the sons of Noah: "For your lifeblood I will surely require a reckoning; of every beast I will require it" (Gen. 9 : 5). If the ox was a known gorer, its owner bears the full responsibility. Thus if it has killed a freeborn man, the owner's punishment is legally death; but he is permitted to buy off his life by a money payment. Such a ransom is the only penalty imposed by the Eshnunna code. If the ox has killed a slave, the punishment in both the Bible and the Eshnunna code is a ransom.

The picture above — an Egyptian palette from the beginning of the third millennium B.C. — shows a bull (symbolizing the king) goring a man. The lower picture — an Egyptian wall-painting from the period of the New Kingdom — shows two bulls locked together in a fight.

IF a thief is found breaking in and is struck so that he dies, there shall be no bloodguilt for him; but if the sun has risen upon him, there shall be bloodguilt for him. (Ex. 22 : 2-3)

The Eshnunna code also resembles the biblical laws in the case of housebreaking. If a householder catches a thief in the act of breaking in during the night, he may kill him on the spot. But if the thief is caught during the hours of daylight, he can ransom himself by payment; if he cannot pay, he is sold as a slave. In contrast to this, the Law of Hammurabi punishes housebreaking by death, regardless of whether the crime was committed by day or by night. The distinction between day and night is common to the biblical laws, the ancient code of Eshnunna and later legal codes. In all these, a thief in the night may be killed on the spot, while the daylight robber is only liable to a fine. The remarkable parallels between the laws of the Bible and those of Eshnunna, which in some cases are similar even in their wording, are perhaps due to the fact that both codes were in use by the West-Semitic tribes who expanded south-east to the realm of Eshnunna and north-west to Canaan.

Trespass and Unlawful Entry—Eshnunna Code, §12-13

A man who is caught in the field of a mushkenum (a farmer dependent on the king) inside the fence at high noon shall pay 10 shekels of silver. He who is caught inside the fence at night shall die, he shall not get away alive. A man who is caught in the house (on the premises) of a mushkenum inside the building at high noon shall pay 10 shekels of silver. He who is caught at night shall die, he shall not get away alive.

The Goring Ox (v. previous page)—Eshnunna Code, §53-55

If an ox gores a(nother) ox and causes its death, both ox owners shall divide (between them) the price (realised from the sale) of the live ox and the value of the dead ox (cf. Ex. 21 : 35).

If an ox known to gore habitually and the ward authorities have had (the fact) made known to its owner, but he does not have his ox dehorned (?) it gores a man and causes his death, then the owner of the ox shall pay 2/3 of a mina of silver (cf. ibid. 29).

If it gores a slave and causes (his) death, he shall pay 15 shekels of silver (cf. ibid. 32).

Y OU shall utterly overthrow them and break their pillars in pieces. (Ex. 23 : 24)

The injunction on the Israelites to destroy the shrines of the peoples conquered by them was one of the most stringent of all the commandments. The stone "pillars" (Heb. *mazzeboth*) mentioned in this verse were set up everywhere in the ancient East. The example shown here is a Canaanite stele from Beth-shean, of characteristically Egyptian style. On the left side of the relief, the god Mekal is portrayed sitting on his throne and holding a sceptre in his left hand and the symbol of life in his right hand. Before him stand the architect Amenemopet and his son, holding staves decorated with lotus flowers in their left hands and making a sign of reverence with their upraised right hands. The lower part of the relief contains a dedicatory inscription. The stele had been broken, apparently on purpose. Archaeological evidence from the time of Joshua's conquest of Canaan and the Bible itself (e.g. the action of Gideon) indicate that the Israelites at times did carry out the above injunction literally and destroyed the idols and holy stones of the Canaanites (see also p. 258).

AND I will send hornets before you which shall drive
out Hivite, Canaanite and Hittite from before you.

(Ex. 23 : 28)

The Bible promises that the *tsirah* (usually translated "hornet") will put the Canaanites and Hittites to flight before the Israelites (cf. Deut. 7 : 20; Josh. 24 : 12). This is evidently to be understood metaphorically as the panic and terror that will seize upon these peoples, as it is written: "The LORD, your God will lay the fear of you and the dread of you upon all the land that you shall tread" (Deut. 11 : 25). There was, indeed, an ancient Greek tradition that the inhabitants of Phaselis in Lycia were actually forced by a plague of hornets to abandon their country. The picture is a reproduction of the gold covering to the bed-canopy of Queen Hetep-heres in the middle of the third millennium B.C. The figures embossed on the gold plate are hieroglyphic signs. The insect represented in the illustration symbolizes Lower Egypt and the reed on the right — Upper Egypt. These were the two emblems of the Pharaohs.

AND Moses wrote all the words of the Lord . . . (Ex. 24 : 4)

The art of writing was already known to the Western Semites at the time of the Exodus and the Law-giving. Interestingly enough, it is in the Sinai peninsula that early Semitic inscriptions have been preserved. They are written in what modern scholars call the proto-Sinaitic script and were discovered at Serabit el-Khadem, close by the copper and turquoise mines in the southwest of the peninsula. This script can be dated to the 15th cent. B.C. It was apparently used by Semites who had been brought to Sinai by the Egyptians to work in the mines. Though basically a pictorial script, it already has the character of an alphabet and thus marks a revolution in the history of writing. Inscriptions in a script resembling the proto-Sinaitic have been found in Palestine at Shechem, Gezer, Lachish and Beth-shemesh, all of them dating from the 18th to the 13th cent. B.C. Indeed, some scholars hold that proto-Sinaitic is actually derived from the proto-Canaanite script found in Palestine and was brought to Sinai from there. Attempts to decipher proto-Sinaitic have therefore started from the assumption that the Sinai miners spoke a Canaanite dialect and worshipped Canaanite gods. The suggested decipherment and translation of the lower inscription (by W. F. Albright), reproduced below runs as follows:

Right-hand row from top to bottom:

ḏt bʿtn mṯ nqb = 'O serpent lady, O lord of mine(s)'

Left-hand row:

mʿ hb ʿlt = 'Pray, receive a burnt offering'

The reference here is apparently to sacrifices offered to the god of the mines whose figure is seen on the right.

ᴀɴᴅ let them make me a sanctuary, that I may dwell in their midst. According to all that I show you concerning the pattern of the tabernacle, and of all its furniture, so you shall make it.

(Ex. 25 : 8-9)

The tabernacle, the portable sanctuary of the people who went forth from Egypt, was constructed after the solemn making of the Covenant between God and Israel at Mount Sinai. It accompanied the Israelites throughout the period of their wanderings, and after the conquest of Canaan it was set up at Shiloh (Josh. 18 : 1). As described in the Bible and shown in the proposed restoration here, it consisted of three walls made of boards of gold-covered acacia wood (Ex. 26 : 15-29). Over these boards were stretched curtains, "of fine twined linen and blue and purple and scarlet stuff", made "in skilled work" and embroidered with the figures of cherubim (ibid. 1-6). These fine curtains were covered by undyed curtains of goats' hair (ibid. 7) and over them skins of rams and goats (ibid. 14). At the entrance to the tabernacle there were five gold-covered acacia-wood pillars with a screen hanging from them (ibid. 36-37). The Holy of Holies was separated from the rest of the sanctuary by a veil (Heb. *parokhet*) hung from four pillars (ibid. 31-33). All the boards and pillars were wedged into sockets and bases to ensure stability. Those inside the tabernacle, like all the vessels there, were overlaid with gold, and the inner curtains were of the most splendid kind. This magnificence was meant to emphasize the holiness of the tabernacle.

For the court of the tabernacle, the various ritual appurtenances which it contained and the special place set aside for them, see the following pictures.

THEY shall make an ark of
acacia wood . . .   (Ex. 25 : 10)

Many of the fittings of the tabernacle — the ark, the table, the boards, the
four pillars of the veil, and the copper-covered altar — were made of
acacia-wood. This contrasts with the variety of woods — cypress, cedar and
olive — used by Solomon in the construction of the Temple at Jerusalem.
Two kinds of trees are found in the wide valleys and ravines of the Sinai
desert and the Negeb: *Acacia spyrocarpa* and *Acacia Raddiana.* We can be
sure that the tabernacle and its fittings were made of the wood of these trees,
since there are no others in Sinai. The trunk of the acacia is very hard and
durable. Both species are conspicuous in the otherwise barren landscape of
Sinai, especially the second *(Acacia Raddiana)* with its umbrella-like top
(shown in the picture).

AND you shall make two cherubim of
gold . . . The cherubim shall spread out
their wings above, over-shadowing the
mercy seat with their wings, their faces
one to another . . .   (Ex. 25 : 18, 20)

The fittings of the tabernacle included cherubim of two kinds: a) figures of hammered gold at either end of the mercy seat (Ex. 25 : 18-22); b) figures woven into the curtains of the tabernacle: "with cherubim skilfully worked shall you make them" (Ex. 26 : 1). There were similar cherubim also on the veil (ibid. 31).

The ancient Jewish sages conceived the cherubim as being "in the likeness of a man, with wings like those of a bird" *(Midrash Haggadol, Terumah)*. Figures like the biblical cherubim, having human faces, bird's wings and an animal's body and legs (see p. 22) feature in the religious beliefs of the ancient East. In one of the wall-paintings at Mari from the beginning of the second millennium B.C., there are representations in various colours which may give us an idea of the many-coloured cherubim woven into the curtains of the tabernacle (the picture on the right). The cherubim on the mercy seat of the ark symbolize the divine throne. A similar function was performed by the cherubim at the side of the thrones depicted on the sarcophagus of Ahiram, king of Byblos, and on an ivory plaque from Megiddo belonging approximately to the 13th cent. B.C. (picture on the left). So, in the Bible, God is sometimes explicitly called "the LORD of hosts who sits enthroned on the cherubim" (2 Sam. 6 : 2; cf. 1 Sam. 4 : 4; 2 Kings 19 : 15; Ps. 80 : 1; 99 : 1). Elsewhere God is described on solemn occasions as riding on a cherub (2 Sam. 22 : 11; Ps. 18 : 10).

Aɴᴅ you shall make a table of acacia wood ... And you shall make a lampstand of pure gold ... And there shall be six branches going out of its sides ...

(Ex. 25 : 23, 31-32)

The table and the lampstand *(menorah)* stood opposite each other in the Holy Place outside the veil, the table at the north side of the tabernacle and the lampstand at the south side (Ex. 40 : 22, 24). The table and the ark both had the same "moulding of gold round about" (Ex. 25 : 11, 24). The lampstand had seven branches in all, two sets of three springing from either side of a central stem. Each of the branches was decorated with an almond-shaped cup, a capital and a flower, and was topped by a lamp. Archaeological finds from the Bronze and Iron Ages include lamps with seven wicks; but they do not branch out from the shaft. The candelabrum of the Second Temple was apparently made to resemble that in the tabernacle, as shown by the relief on the Arch of Titus at Rome (lower picture). The candelabrum there is carried on poles on the shoulders of Roman soldiers in the triumphal procession. An earlier representation of these holy vessels (candelabrum and table) is found on a coin of Mattathias Antigonos, the last of the Hasmonaean kings (40-37 B.C.). The obverse shows the table and the reverse the seven-branched candlestick (upper pictures).

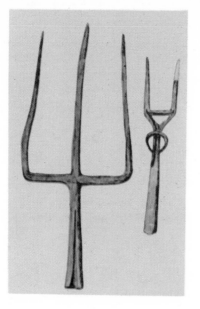

You shall make pots for it to receive its ashes, and shovels and basins and forks and fire pans; all its utensils you shall make of bronze. (Ex. 27 : 3)

Amongst the ritual implements found in excavations in the ancient Near East are several which somewhat resemble the implements of the tabernacle as described in the Bible.

Pots and containers which were used in the offering of sacrifices (see figure on right) were discovered in the Middle Bronze Age temple at Gebal (Byblos). In the excavations of Gezer — in a layer of the Late Bronze Age — forks have been disclosed (see figure above), some of which are three-pronged, like the fork in the sanctuary of Shiloh ("with a three-pronged fork in his hand", 1 Sam. 2 : 13). With these forks the priests used to turn over the sacrificial flesh or move it from place to place.

For this reason, the forks are mentioned only in connection with the altar for burnt offering (Ex. 38 : 3; Nu. 4 : 14) and not in connection with the inner altar or the table of showbread, neither of which served for the offering of sacrifices.

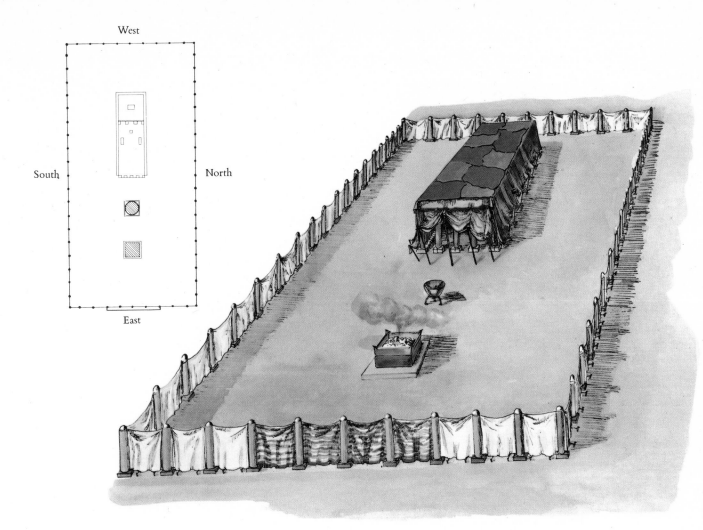

West

South

North

East

YOU shall make the court of the tabernacle . . . a hundred cubits long for one side . . . And likewise for its length on the north side there shall be hangings a hundred cubits long . . . And for the breadth of the court on the west side there shall be hangings for fifty cubits . . . The breadth of the court on the front to the east shall be fifty cubits.

(Ex. 27 : 9-13)

The court of the tabernacle, a plan and reconstruction of which are shown here, was in the form of a rectangle: one hundred cubits long by fifty cubits wide (i.e. roughly 150 × 75 ft.). This rectangle can be divided into two equal squares. In the western of these two squares stood the tabernacle, while the eastern contained the ritual appurtenances of the court, the most important of which was the altar for burnt offering (Ex. 27 : 1-8). The court was fenced off by draperies of fine twisted linen hung from pillars set in bronze bases. At the entrance to it, on the eastern side, there hung a curtain of "blue and purple and scarlet stuff and fine twisted linen embroidered with needlework" (ibid. 16), like that at the entrance to the tabernacle (Ex. 26 : 36).
Between the altar of burnt offering and the entrance to the tabernacle stood the bronze laver on its bronze base (Ex. 30 : 17-21), placed there so that the priests could wash their hands and feet before officiating. The materials used in the making of all these appurtenances were simpler and cheaper than those used in the making of the tabernacle and its implements: bronze instead of gold, linen hangings (apart from the curtain at the entrance to the court) instead of costly many-coloured curtains. This was because the sanctity of an object diminished the further it was removed from the Holy of Holies.

AND you shall make holy garments for Aaron your brother, for glory and for beauty.

(Ex. 28 : 2)

Eight articles for the priestly vestments are described in the Bible, four of which were worn by all the priests alike: 1) linen breeches "from the loins to the thighs" (Ex. 28 : 42); 2) a coat; 3) a girdle round the coat; 4) a mitre or turban (ibid. 39-40). In addition to these, there were four more worn by the High Priest alone: 5) a robe of wool dyed blue, worn over the coat, its hem fringed with golden bells and pomegranates (ibid. 31-35 and see p. 168); 6) over this an ephod made of gold, coloured wool and linen "skilfully worked". The ephod was suspended from two shoulder-pieces on each of which there was an onyx stone (ibid. 6-12), each onyx being engraved with the names of six of the tribes of Israel; 7) the breastplate which was hung over the ephod on the priest's chest and tied to the ephod by gold chains above and by a blue lace below. In its component materials it was similar to the ephod. It was inlaid with twelve stones, one for each of the tribes of Israel (see next page); 8) hung upon the forehead of the High Priest, over the turban, there was a plate of pure gold, engraved with the words: "Holy to the LORD" (ibid. 31-38).

The most striking of these eight vestments was the ephod, which is mentioned also in the prophetic books of the Bible and presumably even in Ugaritic literature and in the Assyrian letters from Cappadocia. Unfortunately, no pictorial representation either of the ephod or of any other of the priestly vestments has yet been discovered. The reconstruction given here is thus necessarily based on the biblical text and on garments known to have been worn in that period.

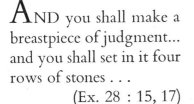

A ND you shall make a breastpiece of judgment... and you shall set in it four rows of stones . . .

(Ex. 28 : 15, 17)

The stones set in the ephod fall into two groups; first, the two onyx stones on the straps by which the ephod was suspended from the shoulders of the High Priest (Ex. 28 : 9-12); and secondly the twelve stones on the Priest's breastplate (ibid. 17-21). The latter were of twelve different kinds and twelve different colours and each stone was engraved with the name of one of the tribes. The stones on the breastplate were smaller than those on the shoulder-pieces. They were set into the surface of the plate with only their upper part showing. Hence they were also called "stones for setting" (Ex. 25 : 7; cf. 28 : 17). They were arranged in four rows of three stones each and every stone had a gold setting ("they shall be set in gold filigree", ibid. 20). All the stones together, both those on the shoulder-pieces and those on the breastplate, were "a remembrance for the sons of Israel . . . before the LORD" (ibid. 12, 29).

In the illustration are shown the stones of the breastplate in the order in which they are listed in the Bible (from left to right, and from top to bottom). The conjectured identification of each stone is given below in English and in Latin (according to N. Shalem): 1) Sard–Carnelian *(Lapis Sardius)*; 2) Plasma *(Plasma)*; 3) Jasper–Agate *(Jaspis; Jasp-Achatis)*; 4) Turquoise; 5) Lazurite *(Lapis Lazuli)*; 6) Chalcedony *(Chalcedonium)*; 7) Amber *(Succinum)*; 8) Agate *(Achatis)*; 9) Amethyst *(Amethystus)*; 10) Mother of Pearl; 11) Black Onyx *(Onyx)*; 12) Jasper-Onyx *(Jaspis)*.

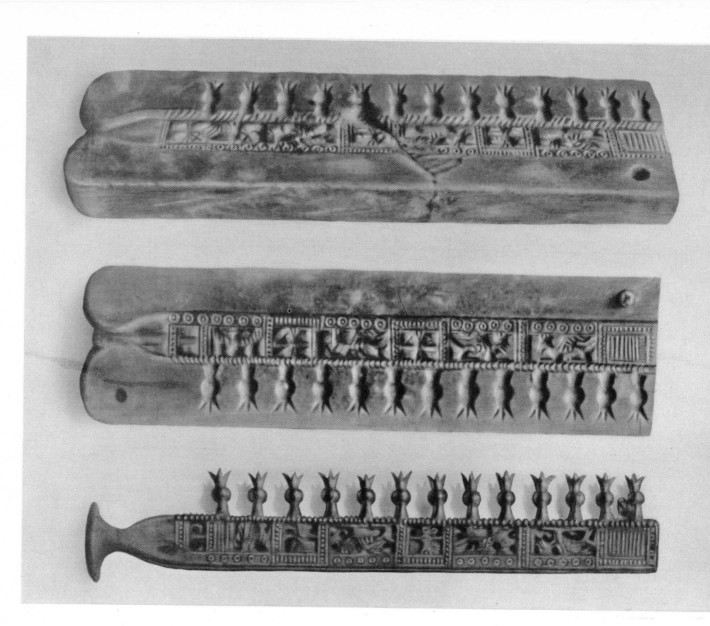

A golden bell and a pomegranate, a golden bell and a pomegranate, round about on the skirts of the robe.   (Ex. 28 : 34)

The robe of Aaron's ephod was adorned with blue and purple pomegranates and fringed with gold bells (see
picture on p. 166). When Aaron entered the tabernacle to officiate there, "its sound shall be heard" (Ex. 28 : 35).
While the ring of bells may have had a magical significance for other peoples, in ancient Israel it served merely
to enhance a solemn occasion.
An example of this kind of decoration is seen in the picture shown here of a mould for pomegranate-shaped
ornaments which was discovered in the excavations at Ugarit (Ras Shamra) and belongs to the 14th or 13th cent.
B.C. Near the mould, the excavators found bars of gold, silver, and electrum, and vases and jewellery intended
for recasting. Below — a modern cast made from this mould.

YOU shall make an altar to burn incense upon; of acacia wood shall you make it. A cubit shall be its length, and a cubit its breadth; it shall be square and two cubits shall be its height; its horns shall be of one piece with it. And you shall overlay it with pure gold...

(Ex. 30 : 1-3)

The altar for incense (the inner altar) stood opposite the *parokhet* veil, before the entrance to the Holy of Holies (Ex. 30 : 6; 40 : 26). In its general structure it resembled the outer bronze altar in the court. Both were square; both were carried on the shoulders with poles and both had four horns, one at each corner. Apart from the different metals with which they were overlaid, the gold-covered altar of incense was much smaller and was in the form of a square pillar with a block on top. It was intended only for the burning of incense, and not for burnt-offerings, sacrifices or libations (Ex. 30 : 7-8). Archaeologists have unearthed many small altars which were apparently intended for the burning of incense. In form they are similar to the gold altar described in the Bible; but they are made of stone or pottery and did not necessarily belong to sanctuaries. About a dozen such incense altars from the Iron Age have been found in Palestine and in neighbouring countries, eight of them at Megiddo. The photograph shows a stone altar of this type from the period of the Israelite Monarchy which came to light recently at Megiddo.

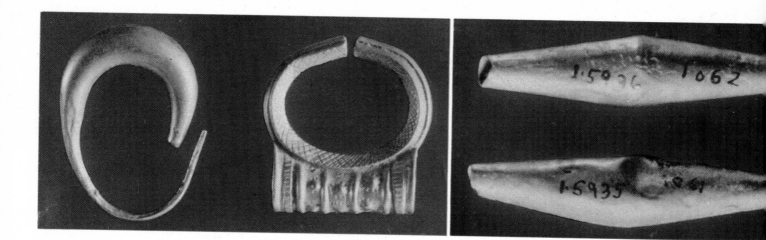

AND Aaron said to them, "Take off the rings of gold which are in the ears of your wives, your sons, and your daughters, and bring them to me." (Ex. 32 : 2)

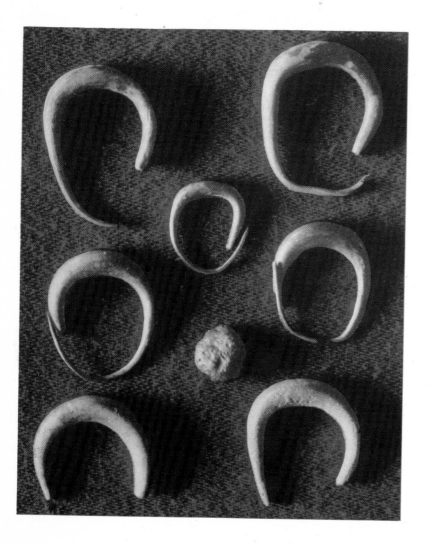

The raw material for the molten image (Heb. *masekhah*) made by Aaron to satisfy the Israelites' demand was provided by the earrings worn by the men and women alike (on nose- and ear-rings see p. 72). Perhaps there is a hint here of the religious significance attributed to such rings and pendants in antiquity. In the ancient East they sometimes took the form of tiny figurines which were used as amulets. Hence perhaps their Aramaic name, *qedasha* ('holiness'). The gold rings of the Israelites were melted down into liquid metal from which the calf was cast.

On this view, the Hebrew *masekhah* (Ex. 32 : 4; from the root *nasokh* = to pour out) is taken to mean a cast image. According to another interpretation, however, the word refers to overlaying and the calf was made of wood with only a covering of gold (cf. ibid. 20).

Many earrings, dating from the second millennium B.C. like those shown here, have been found in excavations in Palestine. They are circular in shape, open at one side and tapering off towards the opening. Sometimes they are enhanced by the addition of a ring of wrought gold. The jewellery shown here of the Patriarchal age comes from the excavations of Tell el-Ajjul (Beth Eglayim).

AND he received the gold at their hand, and fashioned
it with a graving tool, and made a golden calf...

(Ex. 32 : 4)

The making of the golden calf, with its attempted representation of God in visible form and its imitation of the doings of the land of Egypt (cf. Lev. 18 : 3), which they had just left, was the Israelites' worst falling from grace in the wilderness.

The words accompanying the making of the calf — "these are your gods, O Israel, who brought you up out of the land of Egypt" (Ex. 32 : 4) are repeated during the later calf-worship in the reign of Jeroboam, son of Nebat (1 Kings 12 : 28).

It is sometimes assumed that the calf was patterned after Apis, the sacred bull of Egypt. A similar view was held by the early Rabbis: "Moses said, 'Lord of the Universe, Thou didst enslave Thy children only in Egypt out of the whole world . . . and Thy children learnt from them and they too have made a calf'" (Shemot Rabbah, 43). Aaron followed the usual method of making idols in the ancient East and cast the calf in gold which he obtained by melting down the earrings (see preceding picture). Then he shaped the lines of the image with a fine engravers' tool until he had created "a molten calf". The Egyptians sometimes cast statuettes of their sacred bull in bronze, like the one reproduced here. Between the horns appear a sun-disc and the uraeus (the sacred snake). Though this particular figurine is from the 7th or 6th cent. B.C., it is representative of much earlier types.

AND all the women who had ability spun with their hands...

(Ex. 35 : 25)

Spinning and weaving were done in the home (Prov. 31 : 19), or in special workshops, mainly by women but occasionally also by men. The usual raw material was wool or flax, but sometimes goat-hair was used too (Ex. 35 : 26). Egyptian art provides us with illustrations of every stage of the work, from the preparation of the raw material right up to the finished cloth. One such example is a wall-painting from the tomb of Khnumhotep at Beni Hasan (beginning of the second millennium B.C.). On the right, a girl is shown spinning simultaneously on two spindles (no mean feat). The material to be spun is passed to her by the girl kneeling before her who prepares it for spinning by rolling it along her thigh. The thread to be spun passes from the ball before the kneeling woman to the (white) stone dish; the spun threads are collected in the red pottery dish. Two other women are busy weaving on a horizontal loom such as was commonly used in Egypt in the Middle Kingdom. The woman in the centre of the painting is supervising the work.

E has filled them with ability to do every sort
of work done by a craftsman or by a designer or by
an embroiderer in blue and purple and scarlet stuff
and fine twisted linen, or by a weaver—by any sort
of workman or skilled designer.   (Ex. 35 : 35)

The biblical differentiation of the various terms applied to the
manufacture of cloth and woven material is evidence of the
high standard of craftsmanship attained by the skilled designers
of antiquity. The work of the weaver (Heb. *oreg*), i.e. the
weaving of plain cloth, was relatively straight-forward, since
the construction of the looms was very simple (see the illustration on the preceding page). One set of threads was passed
over and under another set, thus producing the warp and woof
of Lev. 13 : 48 ff. The work of the 'skilled designer' (Heb.
hosheb), by contrast, was much more complicated, consisting
as it did of weaving pictures and designs into the cloth. The
production of a colourful pattern required the use of different
coloured threads and complicated combinations of the warp
and woof. The "embroiderer" (Heb. *roqem*) picked out various
scenes and designs on the cloth in precious stones and silver and
gold knots (see illustration). In the words of the rabbis: "The
embroiderer works with a needle . . . the cunning workman
on a loom" (*Babylonian Talmud, Yoma* 72b).
The illustration shows a fine example of woven material made
by a 'skilled designer', which has been preserved in the tomb of
Pharaoh Thutmose IV (late fifteenth cent. B.C.). This is part
of a tapestry of Pharaoh Amenhotep II, whose name is woven
into the left-hand corner. On the right is a design of lotus
flowers woven of blue and red threads: some yellow, brown
and black threads are also used.

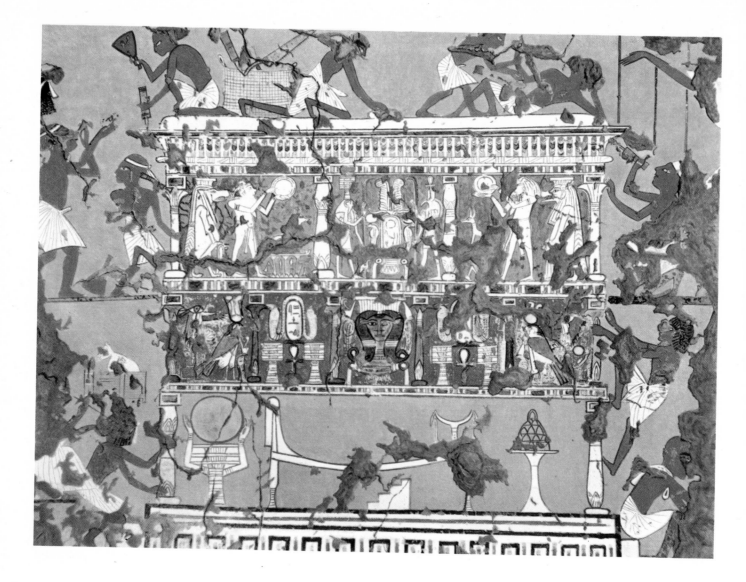

THEN he made the upright frames for the tabernacle of acacia wood . . . (Ex. 36 : 20)

The carpenters' work was especially important in the construction of the tabernacle. The boards supporting the curtains of the tabernacle, the ark, the table of showbread, the incense altar, the altar for burnt offering, and the four pillars of the veil were all made of wood and called for accurate, skilled workmanship. The boards were placed side by side to form continuous walls. The builders of the tabernacle evidently drew on the accumulated technical experience of the lands of the ancient Orient, where master craftsmen also fashioned ritual accessories of wood. The carpenters of Egypt, which had no plentiful local supply of wood like Canaan, attained a high level of proficiency and developed a multiplicity of tools to meet their various technical requirements. The picture — a reproduction from the tomb of Apy (13th cent. B.C.) — shows a catafalque with its furnishings designed for a royal tomb. The workmen are putting the finishing touches to the work with the usual carpentry tools — saw, chisel, drill and hammer. Above, the overseer is standing beside a laggard workman and warning him to mend his ways before the master comes and sees him. The other workmen are absorbed in their tasks. The catafalque, with its appurtenances and colourful emblems, was constructed for ritual purposes.

174

HE made it and all its utensils of a talent of pure gold.   (Ex. 37 : 24)

Of the appurtenances of the tabernacle, some — e.g. the mercy-seat, the cherubim, the table implements, the dishes, spoons, bowls and flagons, and the lampstand with its snuffers, and its trays — were made of pure gold: others — e.g. the ark, the poles, the table and the altar for incense (Ex. 26 and 37) — were of wood overlaid with gold. The mercy-seat, the cherubim and the candlestick were hammered and fashioned from a single bar of "pure" gold. This was presumably not refined gold, but the type of natural gold used in Egypt which was from 72.1% to 99.8% pure. Overlaying wooden implements with gold was also an Egyptian practice. The products of the Egyptian royal goldsmiths and their various practical uses were known throughout the ancient East and no doubt served as a pattern for the gold-work in the tabernacle.

The relief from Sakkarah reproduced here belongs to the Sixth Dynasty (second half of the third millennium B.C.). It illustrates the smelting and casting of gold. At the top right six men are blowing through tubes to fan the flame in a crucible. Opposite them on the left two others are weighing the gold and recording its weight. At the bottom, the metalworkers are placing the moulded objects of gold on tables for the final shaping. In the middle there is an assortment of gold objects arranged on a shelf.

HE made the holy anointing oil also, and the pure fragrant incense, blended as by the perfumer.
(Ex. 37 : 29)

The art of the perfumer consisted in preparing the anointing oil and the fragrant incense. The process was as follows: choice spices — myrrh, aromatic cinnamon and cassia (Ex. 30 : 22-24) — were soaked in water, boiled for a long time and then kept in olive oil until the oil became impregnated with their perfume. This concoction, called in the Bible "holy anointing oil", was used for anointing the priests and the implements of the tabernacle. The incense burnt every day in the tabernacle was a compound of several herbs, ground very fine.
The Egyptian perfumers, too, prepared various cosmetics by mixing scented herbs with oil. The picture (from a Theban tomb, c. 1500 B.C.) shows an apothecary's workshop. Three workmen are pounding the dried herbs with a pestle and mortar. The man on the right is stirring the blend of scented herbs into the oil in the bowl. The stooping figure on the right is shaping the cooled ointment into balls. The jars to the right and left apparently contain a mixture of spices and wine. The man standing beside them, to the left of the picture, is straining the wine from one of the jars into a cup.

THEY were twelve stones with their names according to the names of the sons of Israel: they were like signets, each engraved with its name, for the twelve tribes.   (Ex. 39 : 14)

The special stones set in the ephod and the breast-plate were engraved with the names of the twelve tribes whom the High Priest represented before the Lord (see p. 166). The gold plate, which was a kind of fillet on the priest's turban, also bore an inscription: "And they made the plate of the holy crown of pure gold, and wrote upon it an inscription, like the engraving of a signet, Holy to the LORD" (Ex. 39 : 30).
The craftsmen responsible for the fittings of the tabernacle engraved the names on the stones by the method employed in the ancient world in engraving a signet-ring with its owner's name.
The picture, from the tomb of Ti (Fifth Dynasty) at Sakkarah, illustrates the art of engraving. The man seated is holding in his left hand a cylinder seal through the length of which he is piercing a hole with a tool held in his right hand. The inscription above him reads as follows: "Drilling a cylinder seal by a seal-maker".

176

LEVITICUS

WHEN any man of you brings an offering to the LORD . . .　　　　(Lev. 1 : 2)

Sacrifices were the distinguishing feature of all ancient worship. In the Mosaic law, too, they occupied a central position in the ritual. The Israelite ritual lays stress on sacrifice as a means of bringing the worshipper closer to God. His offering only has a meaning if it gives outward expression to inner spiritual longing and the soul's devotion to God, as described by the prophets and psalmists: "The sacrifice acceptable to God is a broken spirit: A broken and contrite heart, O God, Thou wilt not despise" (Ps. 51 : 17).

The picture reproduces a section of a fresco from the palace of Zimrilim, King of Mari (18th cent. B.C.) portraying a sacrificial procession. The sacrificer's round cap and beard are characteristic of the West Semitic tribes akin to the Israelites; whereas his fringed robe is in the style of the Mesopotamian Akkadians. The bull to be sacrificed is being led by the ring in its nose. It is adorned with a crescent and the ends of its horns (of which only one is visible) appear to have been gilded.

W HEN you bring a cereal offering baked in the oven as an offering, it shall be unleavened caked of fine flour mixed with oil, or unleavened wafers spread with oil.

(Lev. 2 : 4)

The meal offerings (Heb. *minhah*) were sacrifices consisting of agricultural produce — wheat or barley. They were offered in various forms: as meal, unleavened cakes (leaven being forbidden to be placed on the altar), or parched grains (Heb. *qali*).

Various ovens, which were used for different purposes, including baking, have been brought to light by excavation in Palestine. The picture above is of a pottery oven from Hazor belonging to the Late Bronze Age.

The meal offerings were prepared in special utensils such as the griddle (Lev. 2 : 5), which may have been similar to the flat pottery platter found at Lachish in a temple belonging to the middle of the second millennium B.C. (lower picture, showing both sides). It is perforated on one side; but the perforations are not pierced right through.

Meal offerings were part of the ritual of all ancient peoples. The Egyptians used to put beside their meal offerings "offering tables" of stone on which were reproduced loaves of bread, cups and bowls containing fruit, spices, etc. These "offering tables" took the place of a sacrifice similar to the regular meal offering of the Bible. The middle picture shows an offering table of the Fifth Dynasty (middle of the third millennium B.C.). It is made of alabaster and inscribed with the hieroglyph meaning "offering".

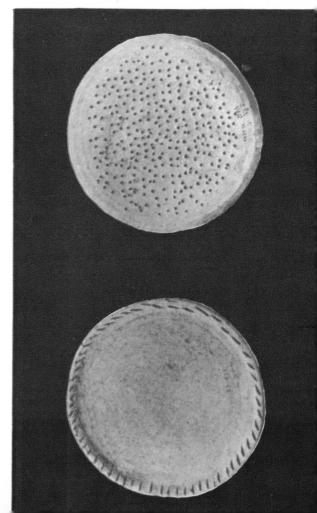

IF a man's offering is a sacrifice of peace offering if he offers an animal from the herd, male or female, he shall offer it without blemish before the LORD. (Lev. 3 : 1)

Only ritually clean and domesticated animals — i.e. cattle, sheep and goats — were used for sacrifices. The early Rabbis gave the following explanation: "The bull flees from the lion, the sheep from the wolf, the goat from the tiger. Said the Holy One Blessed be He: 'You shall not bring before Me such as pursue, but only such as are pursued'" *(Vayyiqra Rabba, 27).*

Oxen were used for various types of sacrifice, including the "peace offering" which was eaten at a joint repast. The skeletal remains of oxen found in excavations in Palestine belong to the short-horned breed common in the country in biblical times. From the art of antiquity it is clear that oxen were also the usual sacrificial animals throughout most of the ancient East.

The upper picture shows a wall-painting from the tomb of Amenemhet from Thebes (Eighteenth Dynasty), representing a bull being led to sacrifice.

The lower picture shows the breed of oxen common in the Bible-lands to-day.

If his offering for a sacrifice of peace offering to the LORD is an animal from the flock, male or female, he shall offer it without blemish. If he offers a lamb for his offering, then he shall offer it before the LORD.

(Lev. 3 : 6-7)

The term "flock" in the Bible (Heb. *tson*) includes both sheep (see lower picture) and goats. Sheep and goats, as the commonest domesticated animals kept by the Israelite tribes, were the earliest and most usual sacrificial animals in the Israelite ritual. They might be used for most of the different kinds of sacrifice; and for the Paschal offering a "lamb . . . from the sheep or from the goats" was obligatory (Ex. 12 : 5). Sometimes the Law specifies that the animal sacrificed must be a sheep and not a goat, as in the case of the guilt offering (Heb. *asham*) which consisted of a male sheep, usually a ram, i.e. a fully grown sheep with horns (see picture in bottom centre). The priests' ordination offering likewise consisted of a ram (Ex. 29 : 19-22; Lev. 8 : 20-29). In the Ugaritic myths, too, there are references to the sacrifice of rams. In Egypt, Syria and Mesopotamia it was customary to sacrifice non-domesticated sheep and goats as well, as illustrated on the 9th-8th cent. relief from Carchemish reproduced above. It shows the worshippers carrying the sacrificial animals — apparently mountain-goats — on their shoulders.

IF his offering is a goat, then he shall offer it before the LORD.

(Lev. 3 : 12)

The goat is hardier than the sheep and more used to meagre mountain pasture (see illustration below). The type of goat called *saïr* (literally 'the hairy one') in the Bible was used, both male and female, for the sin offering. Of the other two kinds of he-goat named in the Bible, the one called in Hebrew *tayish* is of little importance and does not receive much mention in the sacrificial laws; but the second (Heb. *atud*) features prominently in the sacrifices offered by the tribal leaders at the inauguration of the tabernacle (Num. 7 : 17 et al.) and is referred to as a sacrificial animal in the biblical poetry (Is. 1 : 11; Ps. 66 : 15 et al.).

The unfinished Egyptian relief reproduced above depicts the sacrifice of an ibex to the dead. It is from a stele of a Theban king from the end of the third millennium B.C.

BUT if he cannot afford a lamb, then he shall bring, as his guilt-offering to the LORD for the sin which he has committed, two turtle-doves or two young pigeons, one for a sin offering and the other for a burnt offering.

(Lev. 5 : 7)

Birds as well as animals were used for sacrifice. Indeed, birds are included in the first sacrifices mentioned in the Bible — those offered up by Noah after the flood (Gen. 8 : 20). The only birds that were at all domesticated in Israel were the dove and the closely related turtle-dove. These are the only two birds which the Bible permits for sacrificial use, both males and females (see picture). Moreover, they could not be used for any sacrifice except the burnt offering and the sin offering. They were generally offered up by the poor instead of the more expensive animals. Other ancient peoples used other kinds of birds as well in their sacrifices.

The picture above shows an Egyptian wooden model of men and women bringing sacrifices; they are led by two men followed by two women holding ducks in their right hands; the first woman carries on her head a basket with jugs. The model is from the tomb of Meketre (end of the third millennium B.C.).

FOR the breast that is waved and the thigh that is offered I have taken from the people of Israel, out of the sacrifices of their peace offerings, and have given them to Aaron the priest and to his sons, as a perpetual due from the people of Israel.　　　　　　　(Lev. 7 : 34)

What was left of the ordinary peace offering, after all the fat parts had been burnt on the altar, was eaten by the sacrificer and his family, with the exception of the special portions — namely, the breast and the right thigh — set aside for the priests. The sacrificer used to wave the breast together with the fat of the sacrifice "before the LORD" (Lev. 7 : 30); hence the expression "wave breast". Then the fat was burnt on the altar, while the breast was given to the priest. The right thigh was apparently also waved; but evidently the waving was not such an essential part of the ritual in this case and therefore it was called simply "the thigh that is offered". The custom of putting aside the breast and the right thigh for the priest to eat was widespread in the ancient East. The accompanying picture shows the separation of the thighs from the body of an ox that has just been sacrificed; it is taken from a painting found at Gizeh and dates to the Old Kingdom of Egypt.

NEVERTHELESS among those that chew the cud or part the hoof, you shall not eat these: the camel ... and the rock badger ... and the hare .. and the swine ... (Lev. 11 : 4-7)

Different categories of ritually pure and impure creatures are distinguished here: a) land animals; b) water animals; c) fowl; d) "creeping things" (for instance reptiles). The Mosaic Law gives no explanation for the impurity of certain creatures, but merely points to the physical features which "make a distinction between the unclean and the clean" (Lev. 11 : 47). The two main indications of a pure land animal are that it both chews the cud *and* is two-hoofed.

Thus the camel, though a ruminant, is considered impure, since it has fleshy soles to its feet and not hooves. The picture above shows camels on an Assyrian relief at Nimrud from the 8th cent. B.C.

The hare, several species of which are found in Palestine, likewise does not cleave the hoof, though it is included by the Bible amongst the cud-chewing animals on account of the ruminant-like movements of its jaws. The picture on p. 187 below shows a hare on a relief from the tomb of Meten, dating from the Old Kingdom of Egypt.

The biblical pig (Heb. *hazir*) includes both the domesticated and the wild species ("the boar from the forest", Ps. 80 : 13). This animal was also considered impure by the Egyptians, so much so that, according to Herodotus, swineherds in Egypt were subject to religious and social discrimination. Although pigs were reared in Egypt from time immemorial, they are first portrayed in Egyptian art only in the New Kingdom (see lower figure).

THESE you may eat, of all that are in the waters. Everything in the waters that has fins and scales, whether in the seas or in the rivers, you may eat. But anything in the seas or the rivers that has not fins and scales, of the creeping creatures in the waters and of the living creatures that are in the waters, is an abomination to you.   (Lev. 11 : 9-10)

In place of a detailed list of the names of ritually pure and impure fish, the Mosaic code simply specifies the external signs by which a fish may be recognized as pure. We must also bear in mind that only part of the Israelite tribes dwelt near the sea and that, in the biblical period, Israel was essentially a nation of tillers of the soil, not of fishermen. It is true that one of the gates of Jerusalem was called "the Fish Gate" (Zeph. 1 : 10; Neh. 3 : 3; 12 : 39), apparently after the near-by fish-market. But we have it on the authority of Nehemiah that "fish and all kinds of wares" were brought to the Jews of Jerusalem by Tyrians (Neh. 13 : 16). Amongst the fish permitted for eating we find the mouth-breeding fish (Tilapia), common in the Sea of Galilee (Tilapia zillii), shown on the right; while the forbidden fish included, for instance, the catfish (Clarias lazera), left figure.

AND these you shall have in abomination among the birds, they shall not be eaten, they are an abomination: the eagle . . .

(Lev. 11 : 13)

Instead of specifying the distinguishing signs of purity or impurity in birds, the Mosaic Law gives a list of the various impure species. We may say that the common feature of most of the birds forbidden for eating is that they are birds of prey or carrion. These can be divided into various classes: 1) keen-sighted birds that hunt their prey by day, such as the hawk *(Milvus,* lower row, second from left) and the falcon *(Accipiter nisus,* lower row, first from left)* ; 2) night-birds of prey, such as the owl *(Athene noctua,* on right above) with its extremely keen hearing and its silent flight; 3) fish-eating water-fowl, like the long-legged and long-necked heron *(Ardea cinerea,* lower row, third from left); 4) carrion-birds, such as the large, broad-winged vulture with its bald head and neck *(Gyps fulvus,* above on left). A scavenger of a different kind was the common Palestinian raven *(Corvus corax —* lower row, extreme right).

AND these are un-
clean to you among the
creeping things that
creep upon the earth...
(Lev. 11 : 29)

"The creeping things that swarm upon the earth" being naturally repulsive to man, are not usually considered to be edible. Nevertheless, in the Mosaic Law it is not touching them while alive that makes a person unclean, but only touching their dead bodies (Lev. 11 : 31). The "creeping things" in contrast to "the living creatures that are in the waters" (ibid. 10) are small creatures of various kinds, reptiles, many small mammals and invertebrates. All alike have short legs and move with their bodies close to the ground. Of the eight animals listed in these verses not all can be identified with certainty. Most of them belong to the lizards.
The lower picture shows the green lizard *(Lacerta viridis)*; the upper picture the chameleon *(Chamaeleon Chamaeleon)*, both of them mentioned in v. 30 of the same chapter.

THE priest shall command them to take for him who is to be cleansed two living clean birds and cedarwood and crimson stuff and hyssop.

(Lev. 14 : 4)

A man who had recovered from leprosy was obliged to purify himself through sacrifice and ritual acts of atonement performed by the priest. On the first day, the priest sprinkled him seven times with hyssop, cedar-wood and scarlet cloth that had been dipped in the blood of a bird. These are the same three ingredients that were added to the charred flesh of the red heifer (Nu. 19 : 6). The hyssop was also used for the sprinkling of impurity-removing water on persons made unclean by contact with a corpse (ibid. 18). One the eve of the Exodus from Egypt, "a bunch of hyssop" was used in making the sign of blood on the houses of the Israelites to save them from the slaying of the firstborn (Ex. 12 : 22-23). Thus the hyssop became a symbol of physical cleanliness and moral regeneration, as in the words of the Psalmist: "Purge me with hyssop, and I shall be clean" (Ps. 51 : 7).
The picture at the top left is of a cedar of Lebanon *(Cedrus libani),* the tallest and most majestic of all the trees of the Middle East. Its wood is very durable and has a pleasant scent. Although it was not grown in ancient Israel, it was well known to the Hebrews.
The right-hand picture is of the hyssop *(Majorana syriaca)* which grows in rock-crannies and abounds in hilly regions. This highly aromatic plant is to this day used by the peoples of the East as a seasoning for their food.
At the bottom there is a picture of the kermes (the crimson-worm of the ancients). The epithet "crimson" refers to the red dye extracted from the eggs of kermes insects which live on oak-trees. The species that was common in ancient Phoenicia and in northern Israel is known as *Kermes biblicus* and other related species. After the eggs had been removed from under the outer shard of the female insect, they were carefully rolled into a large ball from which the dye was then extracted.

HE shall take a censer full of coals of fire ... and two handfuls of sweet incense beaten small, and he shall bring it within the veil.

(Lev. 16 : 12)

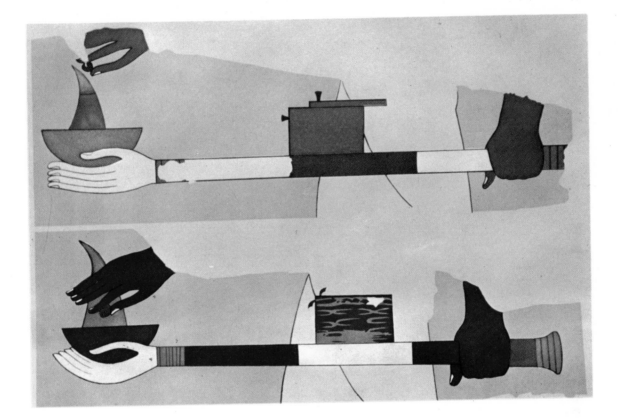

The incense was an offering of spices in the form of fine powder which, when burnt, gave off aromatic smoke. It was usually offered up on the gold altar. Only once a year did the High Priest offer up the incense not on the gold altar, but in a censer — in the solemn service for the Day of Atonement, at the moment when, in his vestment of white linen, he entered the Holy of Holies. The intention was that the smoke of the incense rising from the censer at that moment should cover the mercy-seat over the Ark and conceal the cloud of the glory of the Lord that rested upon it from the priest's eyes, lest he die (Lev. 16 : 13).

The picture here, reproduced from the tomb of Amenemhet at Beni Hasan (Twelfth Dynasty), shows how incense was offered in a censer. The long white handle is apparently of ivory inlaid with some other material, possibly bronze and gold. The censer, in which the incense is burning, is laid on the hand-shaped bowl. The dark-coloured balls of incense are stored in a small container in the middle of the handle. One of these balls, which has been taken out of the half-open container, is about to fall from the hand of the sacrificer into the flame. Smoke is seen rising from the censer.

YOU shall not do as they do
in the land of Egypt, where you
dwelt, and you shall not do as
they do in the land of Canaan,
to which I am bringing you . . .
(Lev. 18 : 3)

The aim of the Mosaic Law was to raise the Israelites — 'a holy nation' — to a high moral standard and to separate them from other nations in their secular conduct and religious practice. To this end, it sought to hedge about the life of the individual with legal restrictions and to sanctify the whole people by laws conducive to moral conduct and self-control. The Law warns the Israelites against the excesses of the Egyptians and Canaanites, which were part of the ritual of idolatry.

The picture below represents a cult-scene from the city of Mendes in the Nile Delta. The ram was sacred to the god Min whom the Egyptians regarded as the source of fertility. Greek authors describe this cult as highly immoral; yet the Ptolemies worshipped this god and brought it offerings, as portrayed in the picture.

The upper picture is a reproduction of an ivory relief of the Canaanite fertility goddess (the goddess Qadesh?) from Ugarit (14th cent. B.C.). The goddess is seated on a throne between two goats. Her breasts are bare, and in her uplifted hands she is holding branches or grain-stalks which the goats are rearing up on their hind legs to reach. The relief is a masterpiece influenced by Aegean art; it illustrates the Canaanite fertility cult which was accompanied by licentious rites in honour of the fertility goddess.

YOU shall not steal,
nor deal falsely, nor lie
to one another.

(Lev. 19 : 11)

The portion of Leviticus beginning with the words "You shall be holy"
(chap. 19) contains the moral commandments which are the indis-
pensable basis of "a kingdom of priests and a holy nation" (Ex. 19 : 6).
Some parallels to these ethical precepts can be found in other ancient
codes of conduct; they differ, however, from the biblical law in that
they contain no commandments for the creation of a moral society
as a whole; still less do they show any awareness of holiness in the
biblical sense. These codes were known only in certain limited circles
and were in general applicable only to crises in human lives, such as
sickness or death.
A good example is provided by an Assyrian ritual text, known as the
shurpu tablets, which contain the loftiest expression of morality
found in ancient Mesopotamian literature. The subject of the text is
the exorcising of a sick man's malady by the common Mesopotamian
magic practice of burning an effigy of the evil spirit held to be responsible; hence the name *shurpu* = burning (Heb. *serepha*). In the *shurpu*
tablet reproduced above, the magicians question the sick man about
his sins. In its present form, the text belongs to the 7th cent. B.C.;
but the main part of it was composed much earlier, between the 15th
and the 12th centuries B.C.
The picture below shows a section (chap. 125) of the Egyptian *Book
of the Dead* of which several papyrus copies exist. Some of the provisions of this book, the so-called "negative confessions", are similar
to the moral prohibitions of the Mosaic Law. The soul of the deceased
stands before the gods of righteousness and, as proof of its purity,
enumerates the crimes which it has *not* committed.

Shurpu Tablet II

(1) [Incantation. I call on you] great gods,
(2) . . . [god] and goddess, lords of salvation,
(3) (Namely), [so-and-so the son of] so-and-
so, whose (guardian) god is so-and-so,
whose (guardian) goddess is so-and-so,
(4) . . . who is sick, full of anxieties, sad, (and)
sleepless.
(5) Has he eaten that which is taboo to his
god? Has he eaten that which is taboo
to his goddess?
(6) Has he said for yes "no," has he said for
no "yes"?
(7) . . . Has he pointed a finger (against . . .)?
(8) . . . Has he said that which is incongruous?
(11) Has he forgotten his goddess?
(12) Has he spoken evil?
(13) Has he said that which is coarse?
(14) Has he caused wickedness to be spoken?
(15) Has he (bribed) a judge?
(18) Has he oppressed a weak woman?
(19) And driven (her) out of her city?
(20) Has he alienated son from father?
(21) Has he alienated father from son?
(22) Has he alienated daughter from mother?
(23) Has he alienated mother from daughter?
(24) Has he alienated daughter-in-law from
mother-in-law?
(25) Has he alienated mother-in-law from
daughter-in-law?
(26) Has he alienated brother from brother?
(27) Has he alienated friend from friend?
(28) Has he alienated companion from companion?
(29) Has he failed to set free one in confine-
ment, release one in fetters?
(30) Has he refused to allow a prisoner to see
the light of the day?
(31) Has he said concerning a captive "Seize
him!", concerning a bound one "Bind
him"?
(36) Has he despised father or mother, treated
with contempt the elder sister?
(41) Has he uttered a slander?
(42) Has he used false scales?
(47) Has he entered his neighbour's house?
(48) Has he approached his neighbour's wife?

The Book of the Dead (from chapter 125)
(reconstructed from different manuscripts)

What is said on reaching the Broad Hall of the
Two Justices, absolving X of every sin which
he has committed, and seeing the faces of the
gods:
I have not committed evil against men.
I have not mistreated cattle.
I have not committed sin in the place of truth.
I have not blasphemed a god.
I have not done violence to a poor man.
I have not done that which the gods abominate
I have not defamed a slave to his superior.
I have not killed.
I have not caused suffering to anyone.
I have not had sexual relations with the wife of
(another) man.
I have not had sexual relations with a boy.
I have neither increased nor diminished the
grain-measure.
I have not taken milk from the mouths of
children.

YOU shall have just balances, just weights, a just ephah, and a just hin . . .   (Lev. 19 : 36)

To prevent dishonesty in business dealings, the Mosaic Law gives the use of just weights and measures the force of a divine moral imperative. The verse quoted above makes obligatory reliable scales ("just weight") and correct dry *(ephah)* and liquid *(hin)* measures. *Hin* is a word of Egyptian origin meaning a "pot", which was the Egyptian liquid measure since the Middle Kingdom. The biblical *hin* was equivalent to about eleven pints. It is used in the Bible as a measure of oil for offerings (Heb. *minhah*) (Ex. 29 : 40 *et al.),* of wine for libation (Lev. 23 : 13 *et al.),* and of water (Ezek. 4 : 11).

The picture below shows a fragment of an Egyptian vessel excavated at Samaria. Written on it in hieroglyphic characters are the words "81 hin", certifying to the capacity of the vessel.

In the upper picture we see Egyptian "just balances" for weighing the hearts of the deceased when they are brought to trial before the judge of the dead in the underworld. The picture is taken from the Egyptian "Book of the Dead" (see previous page) which contains prayers and descriptions of the after-life.

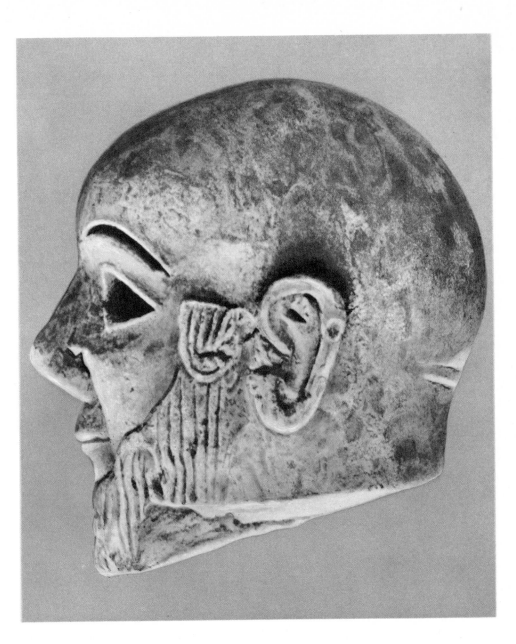

THEY shall not make tonsures upon their heads, nor shave off the edges of their beards . . .
(Lev. 21 : 5)

The shaving of the head and the edges of the beard had already been forbidden the whole people in Lev. 19 : 27. This prohibition is now repeated, to emphasize that priests too are included in it, apparently because such practices were common among priests of other nations (i.e. in Egypt). Other verses in the Bible (Is. 15 : 2; Jer. 16 : 6; 41 : 5; 47 : 5) imply that these practices were popular mourning rites, adopted by the Israelites, apparently from foreign people. The Mosaic Law insists on the complete and unequivocal renunciation of foreign practices.

Shaving the head and cutting the beard or the 'edge of the beard' was a regular practice in the ancient world and not only a special sign of mourning (see p. 105). Cutting the side-locks was also customary among the Ishmaelite-Arab tribes, as is evident from Jeremiah's description of them as having the corners of their hair cut (Jer. 9 : 26; 25 : 23).

The custom of preserving the fringe of the beard is sometimes found amongst the peoples of Mesopotamia, as shown by the head from Mari belonging to the third millennium B.C. which is reproduced here.

AND you shall take on the first day the fruit of goodly trees, branches of palm trees, and boughs of leafy trees, and willows of the brook ... (Lev. 23:40)

The Feast of Tabernacles, which is pre-eminently agricultural in character (see next page), was distinguished by two commandments: that of sitting in the booth (Heb. *succah*) and that of taking the 'four species'. Some scholars have regarded these two commandments as complementary; but in Jewish tradition and practice the booth and the four species are quite separate. Proofs of this abound in the sayings of the early Rabbis and other records from the time of the Second Temple, such as the well-known story of how the people pelted King Alexander Jannaeus with their citrons at the celebration of the Feast of Tabernacles. "The goodly tree" (on right above) is traditionally the *Citrus medica var. Lageriformis,* the earliest species of citrus fruit introduced into Palestine from eastern Asia. The "branches of palm trees" (above, left) are the abundant leaves of the date-palm *(Phoenix dactylifera L.)* which provides man with food, clothing (from the fibre) and shelter. Tradition identifies the "boughs of leafy trees" (below, left) with the stems of the myrtle *(Myrtus communis L.).* The "willows of the brook" *(Salix acmophylla)* grow on the banks of streams (below, right) in the Jordan valley, beside Lake Huleh, in Galilee, and in the coastal plain. The traditional *lulab* is made up of the three types of branches tied together. The citron (Heb. *ethrog)* is held separately.

THAT your generations may
know that I made the people of
Israel dwell in booths when I
brought them out of the land
of Egypt .   (Lev. 23 : 43)

Dwelling in booths is in keeping with the agricultural character of the
"Feast of Ingathering". During the fruit-harvest, the country-folk lived out
in the fields in booths (Is. 1 : 8), just as they do to this day during the
grape-gathering in the hills of Hebron. The biblical word for booth (succah)
signifies protection and shelter from sun, wind and rain (Is. 4 : 6; Jonah
4 : 5; 2 Sam. 22 : 12). The Bible explains the commandment as a reminder
of the Exodus. It has also preserved for us a detailed description of how
booths were made at the Feast of Ingathering in Nehemiah's day: "For
from the days of Joshua the son of Nun to that day the people of Israel had
not done so. And there was very great rejoicing" (Neh. 8 : 17).
To this day, the inhabitants of the Sinai desert are in the habit of making
"houses" of palm-fronds fastened to the trunks of trees with branches for
roof. The raw-material for such booths — which are easily put up or taken
down, according to the requirements of nomad life — is provided by the
palm-trees of the desert oases. It was in booths like these that the Israelites
presumably lived during their wanderings in the desert. In this photograph
we see such a temporary abode at Dhahab on the eastern coast of the Sinai
peninsula.

A ND your threshing shall last to the time of vintage, and the vintage shall last to the time for sowing ... (Lev. 26 : 5)

The Law describes God's bounty to Israel in terms of the agricultural seasons, as befits an agricultural people. The Law promises such abundance that the threshing will continue up to the grape-harvest and the grape-harvest last into the sowing season. The biblical words for "threshing", "vintage" and "sowing" denote clearly defined seasons of the farmer's year.

Similar terms also occur on an agricultural calendar engraved in the old Hebrew script on a stone tablet found in the excavation of Gezer (dating probably to the 10th cent. B.C.). The inscription gives a consecutive list of the seasons of the year: "(1) His two months are (olive?) harvest; His two months are (2) planting (grain); His two months are late planting; (3) His month is hoeing up [of] flax; (4) His month is harvest of barley; (5) His month is harvest and feasting; (6) His two months are vine-tending; (7) His month is summer fruit". The sequence of agricultural activities is therefore as follows: gathering (of olives?), sowing, late sowing, flax-hoeing, barley-harvest, wheat-harvest, grape-harvest, gathering of summer fruits. The word *yrhw* in the Gezer inscription is apparently a dual form meaning "two months". Some seasons (gathering, sowing, late sowing, grape-harvest) lasted for two months, others (flax-hoeing, barley-harvest, general harvest, summer fruits) only one. If this interpretation is correct, the Gezer inscription records the complete annual calendar of the ancient Israelite farmer.

NUMBERS

THE LORD spoke to Moses in the
wilderness of Sinai . . .   (Nu. 1 : 1)

Geographically, the Sinai peninsula comprises three main regions (see map): a) the coastal plain to the north;
b) the central plateau; c) the mountainous region to the south. The coastal plain is an area of shifting sand, confined
within narrow limits on the east, but expanding on the west. The central plateau is not of uniform structure, being
broken up and intersected by vales and ridges. Cliffs of whitish limestone rise in sheer precipices from the gravel-
strewn surface of the ground. The Arabs call the plateau "the desert of the nomads" *(Badiyet et-Tih)*. The southern
part of the peninsula is a region of high mountains intersected by deep, ephemeral water-courses and their tributary
channels, of pinnacles, rocky massifs and deep gorges. The valleys reach a depth of several hundred feet. The loftiest
peaks in this southern region are: Jebel Katerina (8652 ft.), Jebel Musa = Mount Moses (7486 ft., see p. 151) and
Jebel Serbal (6791 ft., see p. 134). The whole region is a desert with very little rainfall. Water rushes down the
many dry valley beds only after the rare torrential downpours, and then only for a few hours. In this primordial
waste, barren yet swept by violent storms, man ekes out a bare existence in the oases that afford shelter from the
savage elements.

THE people of Israel shall encamp each by his own standard,
with the ensigns of their fathers'
houses . . .   (Nu. 2 : 2)

The Israelite host in the desert was disposed in military
order by fighting units (Heb. *degel;* see next page). The
word *ot* (= ensign) is used only here in the military
sense of the emblem or device of a sub-division of the
fighting unit. This emblem was attached to a wooden
staff and carried by a special standard-bearer.

The use of standards in the ancient East for military and
ceremonial purposes goes back to the third millennium
B.C. and it is still customary to this day. According to
Jewish tradition, the standards of the Israelites bore
special symbols and inscriptions. In the Dead Sea Scroll
of 'The War of the Sons of Light against the Sons of
Darkness' we read that inscriptions on the standards were
changed with each new phase in the conflict. For example,
when the army marched out to battle the inscription
borne aloft read: "The Community of God"; when
battle was joined it became: "The War of God"; when
the army returned to camp it was: "The Salvation of
God".

The lower figure shows a Sumerian standard-bearer
marching at the head of a military procession. The
emblem borne aloft at the top of the staff is the figure of
a bull. The picture is made of shell inlaid in bitumen.
It comes from Mari and belongs to the middle of the
third millennium B.C.

The upper picture, from the tomb of Thanuny at Sheikh
Abd el-Gurnah in Egypt (15th cent. B.C.) shows a line
of five Nubian mercenaries. They are armed with
staves; the last man is carrying a standard on which are
depicted two wrestlers.

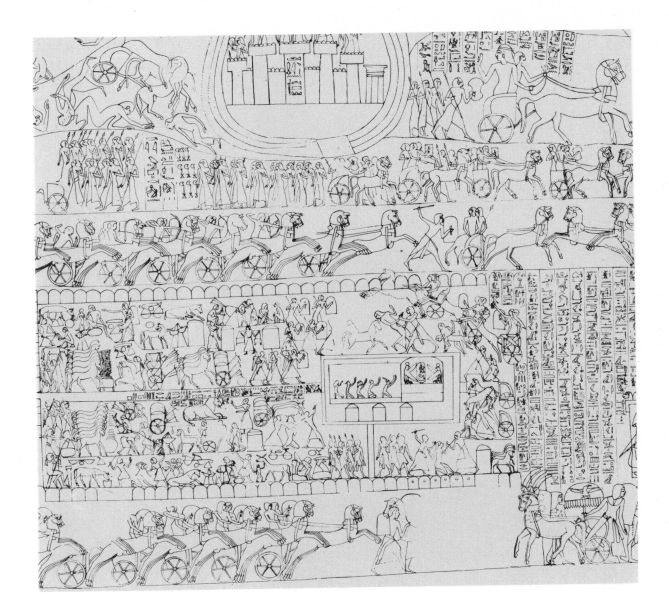

So they encamped by their standards, and so they set out,
every one in his family, according to his fathers' house.

(Nu. 2 : 34)

Various commentators have been puzzled by the biblical description of the Israelite encampment in the wilderness. The four fighting units encamped in military order, the camp itself within its gates (Ex. 32 : 26-27), the drill followed in pitching camp and the order of the march did not seem to conform with the customs of that period. However, reliefs from the time of the Exodus prove that the great armies of that period already had a camping drill and marching order similar to those described in the Bible.

The picture shows the camp of Ramses II (from the reliefs at Abu Simbel in Egypt) in his famous battle with the Hittites near Kadesh-on-the-Orontes in northern Syria in the early 13th cent. B.C. On this campaign Ramses set out with four armies, but only part of them arrived in time to take part in the decisive phase of the battle. The Egyptian camp is drawn up in the form of a rectangle which is fenced in by the warriors' shields, and there are openings for gates. All the services of the army are concentrated inside the camp. It includes the royal tent, in which representatives of various subject peoples are saluting the emblem of the Pharaoh. In this connection it will be recalled that the Israelites pitched their camp round the "tent of meeting" (Nu. 2 : 2).

Aₙᴅ thus you shall do to them, to cleanse them: sprinkle the water of expiation upon them . . .   (Nu. 8 : 7)

The Levites' office as bearers and guardians of the tabernacle was one of great sanctity; hence particular care had to be taken to ensure their absolute ritual cleanliness. This was the purpose of the special ceremony described here which included sprinkling them with water of expiation and shaving off all their hair (Nu. 8 : 7). The "water of expiation" is presumably the same as the "water for impurity" in Nu. 19 : 9: the sprinkling of it was apparently intended to cleanse a man of any possible impurity contracted by contact with the dead. We find the sprinkling of water (though not "water of expiation") both in the rites for cleansing a leper (cf. Lev. 14 : 7) and in some biblical passages dealing with ritual purity (Ezek. 36 : 25; cf. Zech. 13 : 1).
Such purification by sprinkling was also practised by other peoples of the ancient East including Egypt, where it concerned mainly funerary rites. Here, for example, is a picture from the tomb of Neferrompet (Nineteenth Dynasty) showing a priest sprinkling purificatory water on the deceased and his wife. The priest is clothed in a leopard-skin, which was one of the special garments worn by Egyptian priests.

A<small>ND</small> wash their clothes and
cleanse themselves. (Nu. 8 : 7)

The washing of clothes was customary for the cleansing of either a slight or a grave defilement. Hence, the Levites were commanded to wash their clothes before they started to officiate in their special functions in the sanctuary. This practice was widespread in the ancient East, being observed with special rigour by priests. The fine linen vestments of the Egyptian priests, for example, had to be washed nearly every day to preserve their whiteness and purity. Hence, the important ministers at the Egyptian court included "Pharaoh's Launderer" and the "Chief Launderer of the Palace". In the tombs of Egyptian nobles there are pictures of washermen working under the supervision of the chief launderer.

The picture reproduced here illustrates the various tasks performed by the washermen. It comes from the tomb of Ipui, a Theban craftsman who lived in the reign of Ramses II (13th cent. B.C.). The different stages of laundering are portrayed in sequence from bottom to top: two washermen are working beside large jars, while two others are wringing out the laundered linen. Above them others are stretching out the laundry and hanging it up to dry. In the top register a man is sitting and folding the dry laundry; above his head there is a line on which hang the clothes that have already been washed.

וואנשי הסרך יהיו מבן ארבעים שנה ועד בן חמשים ועד בן חמשים שנה ויהיו פקודי שנה מבן חמים שנה ויריבך אשֿ וה שטרים
ויהיוגבאורך חם מבן ארבעים שנה ועד בן חמשים ועל מנעוטי החללים ושול לכ השלל ומטהרי הארץ ושומרי הכלים
ויערך הצורה נול יהיו מבן חמש ועשרים שנה ועד בן שלשים ובני נער ויבואו ואשר לואיבאו לצאותם בצאתם
מירשלים ללכת למלחמה עד שובן ונגל נסה או עוד או אור אר הגר או איש אשר פיק עולק בבשרי מואיש מנוגע בבשרו
בשרו בל אלה לוא ילכו אתך למלחמה נולך יהיו אנשי נריבת מלחמה תמימי רוח ובשר ועתידים ליום נקם וכל צדק וכל
איש אשר לוא יהיה טהור ממקורו ביום המלחמה לוא ירד אתך כיא מלאכי קודש עם צבאותם יחד ורוח יחדה
בין כל מחנותמה לבין חרי נאמת ולענ שלאצנ חרי ערית ובל עירית כאמה ובל ערית דבר רע לא יראה סביבות כל מחנותם

In another passage (Nu. 4 : 23) it is stated that the Levites were on active service in the sanctuary from the ages of thirty to fifty. There is a similar regulation in the Dead Sea Scroll of the "Manual of Discipline for the Future Congregation of Israel": "At twenty-five, he is to take his place in the formal structure of the holy community and be eligible for communal office. At thirty he may take part in litigation and in rendering judgments and may occupy a position on the staff of the militia". The sect of the Scrolls was thus also of the opinion that the service of the Levites began at the age of twenty-five, but that they did not commence their fully responsible active service in the Sanctuary and on the battle-field until the age of thirty.

The picture is a reproduction of col. 7 of "The War of the Sons of Light against the Sons of Darkness". The first three lines deal with the allocation of duties in the fighting force according to the age of the warriors: (line 1) "The men of the militia shall be from forty to fifty years old; the camp prefects shall be from fifty to sixty years old; the officers (line 2) also shall be from forty to fifty years old. And all those who spoil the slain and those who collect the booty and those who cleanse the earth and those who guard the arms (line 3) and he who prepares the provisions — all of them shall be from twenty-five to thirty years old . . ."

AND when you go to war in your land against the adversary who oppresses you, then you shall sound an alarm with the trumpets . . . (Nu. 10 : 9)

The trumpets, which were made of hammered silver, served for various purposes: to summon the whole community, to give the sign for the hosts to move, as battle-signals, and as an accompaniment of the sacrifices on joyous occasions, festivals and new moons — "for remembrance before your God" (Nu. 10 : 10). Trumpets were used for signals in war, because their sharp and penetrating metallic note could be clearly heard even above the din and turmoil of battle. The ceremonial and military use of trumpets was common in the ancient East, especially in Egypt of the New Kingdom, as the paintings of the period show. In the one reproduced here, from a tomb of the reign of Amenhotep IV (14th cent. B.C.), we see a unit of the king's bodyguard, composed of Nubians, Libyans, Canaanites and Egyptians, exercising for battle. The trumpeter is facing the ranks of the soldiers, so that he can transmit to them by trumpet-blast the battle-orders which he receives.

A detailed description of the trumpets and their various notes has been preserved in the Dead Sea Scroll of "The War of the Sons of Light against the Sons of Darkness".

So they set out from the mount of the LORD three days' journey; and the ark of the covenant of the LORD went before them ... to seek out a resting place for them. (Nu. 10 : 33)

The oases of Sinai were few and far between, and only experienced nomads knew their location and size. For this reason Moses requested his Midianite father-in-law, Hobab, who was well acquainted with the desert tracks, to accompany the Israelites: "For you know we are to encamp in the wilderness, and you will serve as eyes for us" (Nu. 10 : 31). It is not clearly stated here whether Hobab actually agreed to remain with the host, but we are told that it was the Ark of the Covenant of the Lord that showed the tribes the way in the desert.

The picture shows a typical oasis in southern Sinai near the foot of Jebel Katerina, the highest mountain massif in the peninsula. Such oases provide water for man and beast, a supply of vegetables and fruit, and shelter from the sun's rays. Sometimes the water stored beneath the gravels of the wadi beds rises so close to the surface that it can easily be reached by digging shallow wells. Where the water is plentiful, vegetables and fruit (especially dates) can be grown without much effort.

NOW the rabble that was among them had a strong craving; and the people of Israel also wept again, and said, "O that we had meat to eat." We remember the fish we ate in Egypt for nothing, the cucumbers, the melons, the leeks, the onions and the garlic.

(Nu. 11 : 4-5)

Wandering in the desert, the Israelites long for the abundance of Egypt. Their remembrance dwells especially on the fleshpots (Ex. 16 : 3) and the various spiced vegetable dishes in which Egyptian cooking excelled. The picture reproduced here is from the wall-paintings in the tomb of Nakht, an Egyptian dignitary of the 15th cent. B.C. It demonstrates the abundant variety of Egyptian food. Apart from meat and fish, their ordinary fare contained fruit, vegetables and various seasonings. The food was adorned with flowers and served with the elegance and good taste characteristic of the ancient Egyptians.

THE people went about and gathered it, and ground it in mills
or beat it in mortars, and boiled it in pots . . .   (Nu. 11 : 8)

In antiquity, flour was made from grain in two ways: a) by milling, i.e. grinding the grain between a lower and
an upper millstone until it was reduced to a kneadable powder; and b) by pounding the grain in a mortar with a
pestle. The mortar and pestle were already known in the Mesolithic period, whereas the millstone was not
invented until the Neolithic Age. Even before the development of agriculture, prehistoric man used to pound and
grind the seeds of wild plants which he collected in the fields. Most of the pounding and grinding implements
found in excavations in Palestine are made of hard basalt. In the plate we see mill-stones on the lower left — on
the lower right a pestle and mortar from Gezer belonging to the second millennium B.C.
The illustration on the upper left shows a three-legged mortar from Hazor, of the period of the Israelite kings.
The picture on the upper right shows a deep and large cooking bowl from Hazor, of the same period. Its wide
mouth and ring-base made it convenient for placing on a hearth. That the pot (Heb. *parur*) of our verse was a
vessel of this kind is indicated by the fact that it was used for cooking pounded grain as well as broth (Judg. 6 : 19)
and meat (1 Sam. 2 : 14).

AND whether the land that they dwell in is good or bad, and whether the cities that they dwell in are camps or strongholds.

(Nu. 13 : 19)

The spies were sent to reconnoitre the land of Canaan and collect information about the character of the people and the nature of the country, especially the strength of its fortresses. This was the kind of military intelligence which has always been sought by army leaders. Later, during the conquest of Canaan, Joshua cautiously avoided a frontal attack on the fortified cities of Canaan, no doubt as a result of the exact information about them which he possessed.

The reproduction here from a series of Egyptian reliefs from the reign of Seti I (c. 1300 B.C., see p. 140) shows a fortified city, called on the relief "the town of the Canaan". It stands on a mound with steep, smooth sides surrounded by a deep moat. The city wall is topped by turrets and parapets and the gate in it is fortified and protected by two towers. The upper wall may belong to the inner fortress in the centre of the city which contained the king's palace and other public buildings. This structure is typical of all the fortified Canaanite cities of this period, as witnessed by excavations in Palestine. The spies hardly exaggerated in their report that "the cities are fortified and very large" (Nu. 13 : 28).

The "camps" of this verse refer to open encampments outside the walls, or to quarters in cities such as Hazor, Carchemish, and Qatna (in central Syria), where a large lower city, surrounded by an earthen wall, sprawled at the foot of the fortified mount.

AND whether the land is rich or poor, and whether there is wood in it or not . . . (Nu. 13 : 20)

Apart from military intelligence (see preceding page), the spies were instructed to collect information about the nature and economic resources of Canaan. The various parts of the country differ in economic importance (see also p. 267). The coastal plain has abundant water resources and fertile soils; the hills of the lowlands are well suited for vineyards and olive groves. The central mountains were covered by forests in antiquity, and some of the wide valleys intersecting them from east to west are among the most fertile parts of the country. As against this "rich land" there is the "poor": the Negeb, the Judaean desert and parts of the Jordan valley. The spies, who travelled along the mountains, saw before their eyes the typical landscape of Canaan: on the one hand, fields of corn, orchards and woods; and on the other — east of the water-shed — barren grey hills, dry and desolate, the few green spots between them only serving to emphasize their desert character.

In the picture on the right is the typical "rich" country of the Sharon; on the left — the "poor" and semi-desert Northern Negeb.

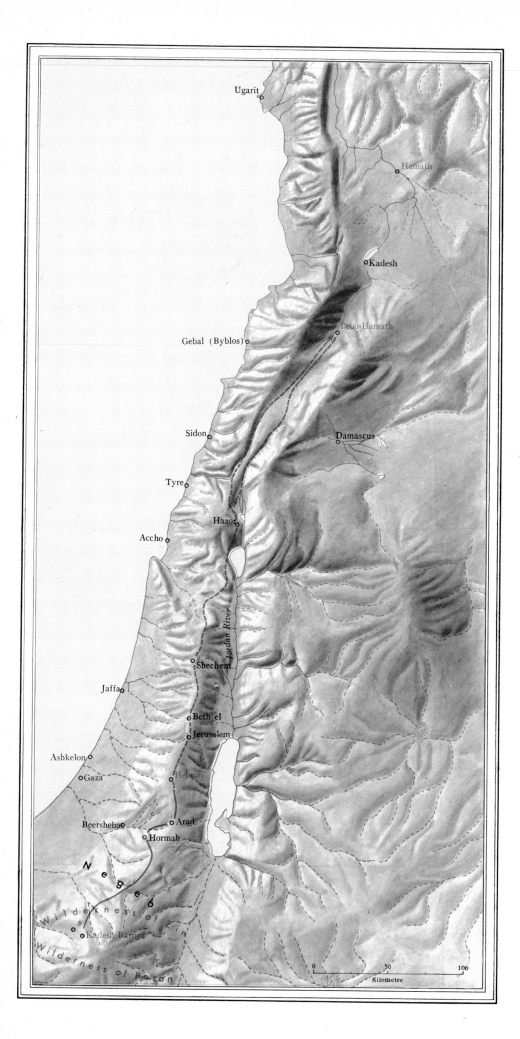

So they went up and spied the land from the wilderness of Zin to Rehob, near the entrance of Hamath.

(Nu. 13:21)

The spies went forth from Kadesh Barnea, crossed the wilderness of Zin at the southern end of Canaan, and reached Lebo Hamath situated on its northern border (cf. p. 243). Here the Bible also mentions Rehob, which was apparently situated, "in the valley which belongs to Beth-rehob" in the neighbourhood of Dan (Judg. 18:28). The spies traversed the Negeb and the central mountain range (Nu. 13:17), that is to say, they proceeded along the high-road which follows the watershed. It appears that they did not intend to scout the rich and closely settled lands of the Shephela, the coastal plain and the valleys, but only the sparsely settled mountain-country. The Israelites hoped, so it seems, to penetrate at first into these areas only; but, even there, the cities they saw filled the spies with awe: "Yet the people who dwell in the land are strong, and the cities are fortified and very large; and besides, we saw the descendants of Anak there" (ibid. 28). The spies paid particular attention to the Hebron region, which is the main theme of the passage.

AND Hebron was built seven years before Zoan in Egypt.

(Nu. 13 : 22)

In this verse the Bible provides us with a unique piece of chronological information about the founding of Hebron by describing it as nearly contemporary with the founding of Zoan (called in Greek Tanis), the Hyksos capital in the eastern part of the Nile delta. The founding of Zoan may have served as the starting-point of an era, witness the "Stele of year 400" discovered in the excavations of San el-Hagar, the site of ancient Zoan.

When Ramses II built his capital at Zoan and re-named it "The House of Ramses" (see p. 127), he set up a monument to commemorate the four-hundredth anniversary of the rule of the Egyptian god Seth in that place. This was apparently the number of years from the founding of the city to the anniversary celebrations which were held in the reign of Ramses's father at the end of the 14th cent. B.C. It follows that Zoan, and with it Hebron, were founded at the end of the 18th cent. B.C.

The figure at the top left of the stele is the god Seth who was a favourite deity of the peoples of Asia, including the Hyksos. Some details of his dress are typically Canaanite.

TURN tomorrow and set out for the wilderness by the way to the Red Sea.

(Nu. 14 : 25)

The Israelites were punished for their backsliding over the report of the spies by their defeat at Hormah (see next page) and were not allowed to enter Canaan the short way. They thus had no choice but to make a wide, wearisome detour through the wilderness to the Gulf of Elath, here called Red Sea. After many hardships, they reached the Red Sea near Ezion-geber where narrow, barren valleys run down between high rocks to the blue waters. The grandeur of the landscape with its changing colours, as shown in this modern photograph, must have made a profound impression on the weary host of Israelites moving slowly through dangerous country towards the distant Promised Land.

BUT they presumed
to go up to the heights
of the hill country...
(Nu. 14 : 44)

The Israelites presumed to try to enter Canaan the short way through the Negeb by the highroad leading to Arad and from there to the hills of Judah. However, they failed to conquer the country from the south, since the Canaanites and Amalekites were guarding the approaches to the mountains and the northern Negeb and blocked their advance (see p. 220). The "heights of the hill country" controlled by the Canaanites are in the region east of Beersheba in the southern foothills of the Judaean range.

The illustration shows the tops of the mountains of the northern Negeb near the Arabah; such mountains bar the entrance to Canaan from the south.

AND for the drink offering you shall offer a third of a hin of wine, a pleasing odour to the LORD.   (Nu. 15 : 7)

The 'drink-offering' (Heb. *nesekh*) completed the animal sacrifices and the offerings of vegetable produce (see pp. 179-185). The sacrifices listed in this portion of the Bible were in three forms: an animal sacrifice (Heb. *olah* or *zebah*), a meal-offering (Heb. *minhah*), and a libation *(nesekh)*. The libation was naturally made with the choicest and most festive of drinks — wine "which cheers gods and men" (Judg. 9 : 13):

Libations were customary among other ancient peoples. The Egyptian practice is illustrated by the picture reproduced here from the Tomb of the Two Sculptors, near Thebes, of the Nineteenth Dynasty. The worshipper is standing in front of a double brazier on which are piled birds and fruits as an offering to the god Min, and four jars. He is pouring the libation on to the brazier from a large vessel in his hands. Behind him stands his wife, with her right arm raised towards the offerings in a gesture of adoration. At the worshipper's feet, a youth is bringing lotus-flowers and a bird in one hand, and a dish of spices in the other. The plant growing between two braziers has a symbolic significance.

AND behold, the rod of Aaron for the house of Levi had sprouted and put forth buds, and produced blossoms, and it bore ripe almonds.

(Nu. 17 : 23)

After the murmuring of the people against Moses and Aaron (Nu. 16 : 41-42) God sent a portent to indicate the pre-eminence of the house of Aaron and the tribe of Levi. When the twelve chiefs of the Israelite tribes placed their staffs — the symbols of their high rank (Gen. 38 : 18, 25) — in the tent of meeting, only the staff of Levi burst into flower and bore fruit. The rapid flowering of the staff and the ripening of the fruit in a single night reflect the characteristics of the almond-tree (see illustration). While winter is still at its height, the white or pink almond blossom stands out against the landscape as the harbinger of nature's revival in the spring. In the dedication of Jeremiah to his prophetic mission, the almond branch (Heb. *shaked*) symbolizes the speedy coming to pass of the words that God will put into his mouth: "for I am watching over (Heb. *shoked*) my word to perform it" (Jer. 1 : 12). According to a later Jewish tradition, the staff of the Messiah too will be an almond branch.

AND every open vessel, which has no cover fastened upon it, is unclean.   (Nu. 19 : 15)

The Mosaic laws of ritual cleanliness differentiate between the various kinds of implements that may become unclean. An earthenware vessel can be defiled on its inside, and is therefore unclean if open at the top (see lower illustration); but if it is well closed by "a cover fastened upon it", it retains its ritual cleanliness, even in the tent of the dead. The binding (Heb. *tsamid*) which closes the vessel is interpreted by some scholars, on the analogy of the Arabic *samad,* to be a kind of cover. The meaning of the Hebrew *tsamid petil* in this verse would then be "a cover fastened by cords". Archaeological evidence also suggests that what is meant here may be a lid attached to the vessel by cords passing through holes made in the lid and through the handles of the vessel. Such a lid would keep the vessel tightly closed and preserve it from defilement.

The illustration shows a vessel of this kind from the period of the Israelite kingdom, found at Hazor.

AND the people of Israel, the whole congregation, came into the wilderness of Zin . . .
(Nu. 20 : 1)

According to the Books of Numbers and Joshua, "the wilderness of Zin" extended to the border of Edom and constituted the southern border of Canaan and of the territory of Judah (Nu. 34 : 3; Josh. 15 : 1; cf. map on p. 239). Apparently it included "the wilderness of Kadesh" (Ps. 29 : 8). It thus stretched right across the Negeb and even included the lower slopes of the Negeb mountains towards the Arabah. A region of extensive plains on the west, becoming gradually steeper towards its eastern end, it is intersected by wadis that run into the Brook of Egypt, in the beds of which there is arable soil. An archaeological survey of the region has revealed that in the beginning of the second millennium B.C. it contained highly developed settlements. After a long interval, they were resettled in the time of the Israelite and Judaean Monarchy. The settled population lived by grazing and agriculture, and also by their control of the caravan-routes into Egypt.

The photograph shows a typical scene in the wilderness of Zin on the modern road from Quseima to Nitsana.

WHEN the Canaanite, the king of Arad, who
dwelt in the Negeb, heard that Israel was coming by
the way of Atharim, he fought against Israel, and
took some of them captive.   (Nu. 21 : 1)

The Canaanite king of Arad barred the advance of the Israelite tribes from the Negeb to Canaan (see p. 215) and,
according to the Book of Deuteronomy, inflicted a severe defeat: "and (they) chased you as bees do" (Deut. 1 : 44).
The name Arad is preserved in a large mound (see picture) to the east of Beersheba. It stands at the south-eastern
end of the Judaean foothills, rising above the wide expanses of the Negeb to the south. The potsherds found on
the site show that it was first occupied in the Chalcolithic Age (fourth millennium B.C.). The city flourished in
the Canaanite period and was still in existence in Israelite times. It controlled the eastern part of the Negeb, and
its king was apparently the head of a league of several Canaanite cities of the region. Such, at least, is the natural
inference from the fact that he routed the Israelites at a neighbouring city, Hormah, which may be the modern
Tell Malhata (el-Milh) between Arad and Beersheba.
When, years later, the Israelites made their second and successful attempt to conquer Canaan, the king of Arad
was one of the thirty-one kings defeated by them (Josh. 12 : 14). It would seem that the city was subsequently
included in the Negeb district of Judah (cf. Josh. 15 : 21, where 'Eder' is presumably a scribal error for 'Arad').

S○ Moses made a
bronze serpent, and set
it on a pole...
        (Nu. 21 : 9)

The bronze serpent of Moses was made at God's express command to deliver the people from the plague of snakes that afflicted them in the desert: "and if a serpent bit any man, he would look at the bronze serpent and live" (Nu. 21 : 9). It is noteworthy that, according to the Israelite itinerary, this incident occurred in the region of Punon which in ancient times was the main source of copper in the Arabah (see Nu. 21 : 4, 10; 33 : 41-43).

The ancients had ambivalent feelings about the snake. On the one hand, it was a dreaded reptile; but, at the same time, they attributed to it miraculous powers of deliverance from destructive forces. In Egyptian art, the sacred snake is depicted as guardian and protector. The snake-cult was also widespread in Canaan, as is testified by archaeological finds.

The figure on the left shows a bronze snake from Lachish dating to the Late Bronze Age, i.e. roughly contemporary with the Exodus.

On the right is shown a standard of the same period from Hazor; it is also of bronze but overlaid with silver. It bears a relief of the head of a goddess with two snakes on either side.

The bronze snake made by Moses was a symbol designed only for a particular emergency and not as a permanent feature of the Israelite cult. It was therefore broken up and its worship banned by Hezekiah, King of Judah, "for until those days the people of Israel had burnt incense to it; it was called Nehushtan" (2 Kings 18 : 4).

THEN Israel sang this song: "Spring up, O well! — Sing to it! — The well which the princes dug, which the nobles of the people delved, with the scepter and with their staves." (Nu. 21 : 17-18)

Water is very rare and precious in the desert. It was therefore wholly appropriate that the Israelites should burst into a joyous song of thanksgiving at the finding of a well. The song describes the digging of the well and its legal acquisition by the leaders of the people. Water songs of this kind are to this day still sung by the Beduin tribes; they demonstrate the vital importance of wells in the desert regions of the Negeb and Trans-Jordan. In the Middle Ages, nomadic Arabs used to celebrate the finding of a well with songs and dances. Several places in the Holy Land were called Beer (well) or Beeroth (wells). The Moabite Beer-elim (Well of God) mentioned in Isaiah (15 : 8) is sometimes identified with Beer, where the Israelites dug a well (Nu. 21 : 16), which may be situated in the well-watered Wadi eth-Themed.

The illustration shows a deep well of the type found in the desert regions of the Negeb. The mouth of the well is ringed by stones which bear grooved marks made by the ropes used for drawing up buckets of water.

BUT Sihon . . . he gathered all his men together and went out against Israel . . . and fought against Israel. And Israel slew him . . . and took possession of his land from the Arnon to the Jabbok, as far as to the Ammonites . . . for the boundary of the Ammonites was strong.

(Nu. 21 : 23-24)

On the last stage of their long journey, the Israelites marched along the eastern edge of Moab up to the "plains of Moab" opposite Jericho (Nu. 21 : 12-20; see p. 236). From the Brook Zared — the dividing-line between Edom and Moab — they proceeded to the River Arnon (ibid. 12-13) which had formerly belonged to the kingdom of Moab, but at the time of the Exodus formed the frontier between Moab and the kingdom of Sihon the Amorite. When the Amorite ruler sought to check the advance of the Israelite tribes by engaging them in battle at Yahaz, he was utterly defeated. In spite of this success, the Israelites made a detour round the fortress-girt country of the Ammonites and did not attempt to attack it (Deut. 2 : 19). The map shows (top right) the chain of Ammonite border forts based on the archaeological survey carried out in Trans-Jordan.

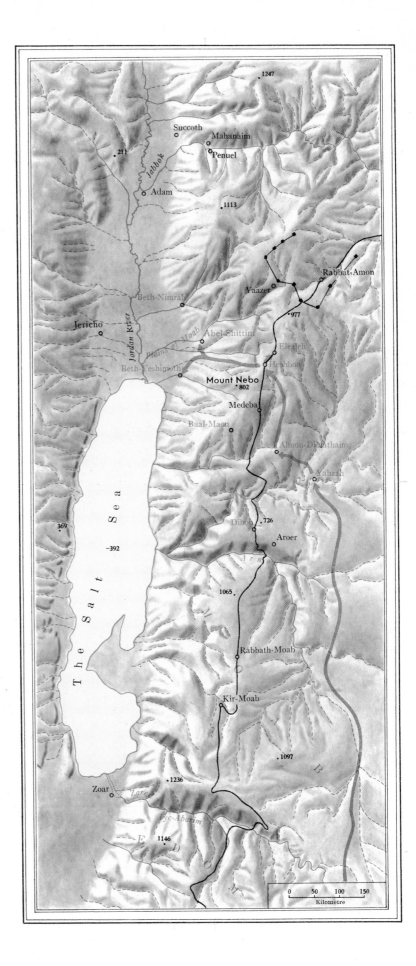

ND Israel took all these cities, and Israel settled in all the cities of the
Amorites, in Heshbon, and in all its villages.   (Nu. 21 : 25)

The country of the Amorite king Sihon was the first region east of the Jordan to be conquered by the Israelites on
their march towards Canaan. It is probable that the Amorite kingdom was founded only a short time before the
war with the Israelites. We know that Sihon conquered the southern part of his territory, up to the Arnon, from
the king of Moab (Nu. 21 : 26). An ancient ballad preserved in the Bible (ibid. 27-28) describes the Amorite war
with Moab and the part played by the city of Heshbon in this struggle:

> "Come to Heshbon, let it be built, let the city of Sihon be established.
> For fire went forth from Heshbon, flame from the city of Sihon.
> It devoured Ar of Moab, the lords of the heights of the Arnon".

Thus, whole districts of Trans-Jordan changed hands more than once in a short space of time: first from Moab to
Sihon, then from Sihon to Israel.

The name of Heshbon, the capital city of Sihon, is still preserved in the Arab village Hisban which is situated on
the ancient King's Highway on the Trans-Jordan plateau, about twenty miles east of Jericho. None of the archaeological finds made so far on the site are earlier than the Nabataean period. In the division of Canaan amongst the
tribes, the city fell to Reuben. It was also included in the cities of Gad, being on the border between the two
tribes (Josh. 13 : 17, 26).

The illustration shows a hill ridge near Heshbon, and the Wadi Hisban, which passes below the site of the city.

So Balak the son of
Zippor, who was king
of Moab at that time...
(Nu. 22 : 4)

Balak the son of Zippor, one of the ancient kings of Moab, is mentioned in several other passages of the Bible
(Josh. 24 : 9; Judg. 11 : 25; Micah 6 : 5). About 1300 B.C., the period of decline in Trans-Jordan — which had
lasted for hundreds of years — came to an end when the Semitic tribes in the region organized themselves into
kingdoms. The main concern of these newly formed states was to consolidate themselves against inroads from
the desert. It was their fear of bold, land-hungry migrating tribes that presumably moved the kings of Edom and
Moab to refuse the Israelites passage through their land: "Behold a people has come out of Egypt; they cover the
face of the earth, and they are dwelling opposite me" (Nu. 22 : 5).
The illustration above, reproduced from a stele found at Balua in Moab, represents one of the ancient Moabite
rulers. He is standing between two deities — a god on the left and a goddess on the right — and raising his hands in
a gesture of submission to the god. The hat, profile and beard resemble those of the Shasu Beduin portrayed on
Egyptian reliefs. The stele is dated by some scholars to the 12th or 11th cent. B.C. The inscription above the
figures has not yet been deciphered.

AND sent messengers to Balaam the son of Beor at Pethor, which is near the River...
(Nu. 22 : 5)

Balaam came from the city of Pethor which lay on the west bank of the Euphrates at the point where the river Sajur flows into it from the west, about twelve miles south of Carchemish. This district (according to Deut. 23 : 4) was part of the territory called "Aram-Naharaim" which stretched along both banks of the Euphrates. Pethor appears in Assyrian records first as Pitru. Later, however, after its conquest by the Assyrian king Shalmaneser in the ninth cent. B.C., its name was changed to Ana-ashur-utir-asbat, i.e. "to the god Ashur I gave back I have taken (the city)."

Of the magicians and seers found in Mesopotamia, the best known were the priests called in Akkadian *baru* (seers), who fulfilled functions similar to those of Balaam. They pronounced the will of the god to his worshippers and they were also called upon to invoke blessings and curses by means of charms and incantations. Therefore, we need not be surprised at the king of Moab's sending for such a man as far as a twenty days' journey (the distance from Moab to the Euphrates).

The photograph shows the Euphrates between Pethor and Carchemish.

THEN the angel of the LORD stood in a narrow path between the vineyards, with a wall on either side.

(Nu. 22 : 24)

The angel of the Lord who stations himself as an adversary in Balaam's way, chooses the right place for stopping the ass: a narrow passage between the walls of a vineyard. The incident probably occurred in the territory of Moab where vineyards were plentiful (Isa. 16 : 6-11), after Balaam had crossed the desert which separates Aram-Naharaim from Trans-Jordan. We know that the King's Highway, the ancient international road which passed through Edom and Moab, occasionally cut across cultivated fields and vineyards (Nu. 20 : 17; 21 : 22).
Boundary walls of stones or wayside hedges were an integral part of ancient vineyards (Isa. 5 : 5; Prov. 24 : 31). To this day such walls are a characteristic feature of the landscape in Israel.

GOD brings them out of Egypt; they have as it were the horns of a wild ox.   (Nu. 23 : 22)

Balaam the magician, seeing the Israelite hosts encamped before him, eulogizes in poetical parables their present might and future greatness. He compares them to the most powerful creatures known in the East: to the lion and to the aurochs (translated above "wild ox"). The aurochs, with its majestic horns (Heb. *toafot),* was a symbol of heroic power. Thus, Hammurabi, the king of Babylon, proclaims himself to be "the fiery wild ox who gores the foe".

In the Ugaritic epic we read that, when Baal and Moth fought together, they gored each other like wild oxen. On a relief from Ugarit (on the right) Baal is represented with the horns of an aurochs on his head. In the poetic imagery of the Bible, too, the aurochs symbolizes invincible strength as in the verse above. In the Blessing of Moses, the might of the tribe of Joseph is glorified in similar terms: "His horns are the horns of the wild ox; with them he shall push the peoples" (Deut. 33 : 17).

The aurochs *(Bos primigenius)* was once common in Mesopotamia, both in its wild and domesticated forms; some beasts still exist in the region. It also featured prominently in Mesopotamian art, as, for example, in the reliefs (left figure) found at Gozan (Tell Halaf) on the river Khabur. These reliefs are on the upright basalt slabs (orthostats) ornamenting the facade of the royal palace and probably belong to the 9th cent. B.C.

B<small>EHOLD</small> a people!
As a lioness it rises up
and as a lion it lifts
itself ... (Nu. 23 : 24)

In Balaam's discourse, as in the Blessings of Jacob and Moses (Gen. 49 : 9; Deut. 33 : 20, 22), the lion — the king of animals and the most dangerous of the beasts of prey — is used to symbolize the military prowess of Israel. The awesome spectacle of the lion rearing up to devour its prey sank deep into the imagination of the ancients. This moment, in which the fate of man and beast is decided, makes even the stoutest-hearted hunter quake. Such scenes naturally stirred the artistic imagination of the poets, painters and sculptors of antiquity and left their mark on many poems and other works of art in the ancient East.

The example reproduced here, like the one on the previous page, is a relief of a lion rampant from a stone slab from the palace at Gozan (Tell Halaf; probably from the 9th cent. B.C.).

LIKE valleys that stretch afar, like
gardens beside a river. (Nu. 24 : 6)

Balaam has a prophetic vision of the dwellings and settlements of Israel spread out like broad valleys and flourishing like gardens by the river-side or like leafy aloes that turn the whole landscape green and "like cedars beside the
waters" (Nu. 24 : 6). In the Book of Isaiah, Israel is again compared to a garden: "like a watered garden" in the
time of God's grace (Isa. 58 : 11), and "like a garden without water" (Isa. 1 : 30) in the time of God's wrath.
In the view we see river willows and vegetation bordering the banks of one of the streams which combine to form
the Jordan. To-day, as in biblical times, the fertile soil of the Jordan valley makes it like "gardens beside a river".

A<small>ND</small> took a spear in his hand . . . and pierced both of them, the man of Israel and the woman, through her body.

(Nu. 25 : 7-8)

In a frenzy of religious zeal, which served as an inspiration to later generations (1 Macc. 2 : 26; 4 Macc. 18 : 12) Phinehas the priest leapt to his feet and, with a single thrust of a spear, transfixed Zimri the son of Salu and the Midianite woman who together had put Israel to shame and brought down God's anger upon the people by inciting them to worship Baal of Peor in Moab.

In antiquity, the spear was used for thrusting at close quarters, in contrast to the javelin which was thrown. The blade and wooden shaft of the spear were longer than those of the javelin. At the moment of thrusting — especially when the victims were on their knees or flat on the ground, as here — the spear was held in both hands and thrust downwards with full force. The size of the weapon and the impetus of the thrust enabled Phinehas to pierce both the recumbent bodies at one blow.

The stele reproduced here was discovered in the territory of ancient Moab near the modern Sihan and belongs probably to the second half of the second millennium B.C. It shows a warrior about to deliver a spear thrust; he is holding the weapon in both hands, with the point downwards.

THEN drew near the daughters of Zelophehad the son of Hepher, son of Gilead, son of Machir, son of Manasseh, from the families of Manasseh the son of Joseph. The names of his daughters were Mahlah, Noah, Hoglah, Milcah and Tirzah.

(Nu. 27 : 1)

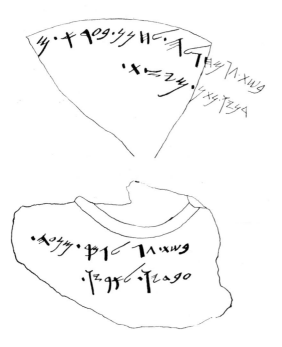

The right granted to the daughters of Zelophehad of inheriting property within their own family served as a precedent for the laws governing inheritance by degree of kinship (Nu. 27 : 6-11). This section also reflects the territorial situation which occurred in the area of the tribe of Manasseh. The names mentioned here — both those of the daughters and those of their ancestors — were also the names of districts and villages within the borders of this tribe. In the narrative of the Book of Joshua (ch. 17), the heritage of the daughters of Zelophehad was in the territory of Manasseh, on the western bank of the Jordan, while Gilead went to the remaining children of Manasseh (ibid. 5-6). The district of Hepher, so called after the daughters' grandfather, was situated apparently in the central Sharon; together with Arubboth and Socoh it later formed one of Solomon's administrative districts (1 Kings 4 : 10).

In the Samaria ostraca, which are reproduced here, the names of several settlements in Manasseh occur, amongst them Noah and Hoglah. The ostraca, which are from c. 800 B.C., were found in the store-house of the palace of the Israelite kings in Samaria. They were certificates of the dispatch of taxes in kind — especially wine and oil — to the king of Israel from the places mentioned. Each certificate bears the date of dispatch at the top and the name of the official responsible at the bottom. The ostracon above is inscribed as follows:

"[In the fifteenth year. From] *Hoglah* to Hanan (son of) Baara. Ma[ranyau (son of) Natan] from Yatsit."

The ostracon below bears the inscription:

"In the fifteenth year. To Gomer from *Noah*. Obadyau to Abiyau."

AND took all the spoil and
all the booty, both of man and
of beast.   (Nu. 31 : 11)

The Israelite treatment of their conquered foes depended on
whether the war was by divine commandment or an optional
war waged with divine consent (Deut. 20 : 10-15; cf. p. 276).
In a holy war, such as that against Midian, the men and women
were ruthlessly exterminated and only the virgins were taken
prisoner (Nu. 31 : 18). The booty were divided equally
"between the warriors who went out to battle, and all the
congregation" (ibid. 27). Special portions of the booty were
set aside as tribute for the Lord. the priests and the Levites
(ibid. 28, 41, 47).

The picture shows an Assyrian relief from Nimrud of the 8th
cent. B.C. which depicts spoils and captives similar to those
taken by the Israelites from the Midianites. The procession is
headed by a female captive leading four camels. She is followed
by an Assyrian soldier at the head of a herd of cattle and sheep
taken as booty.

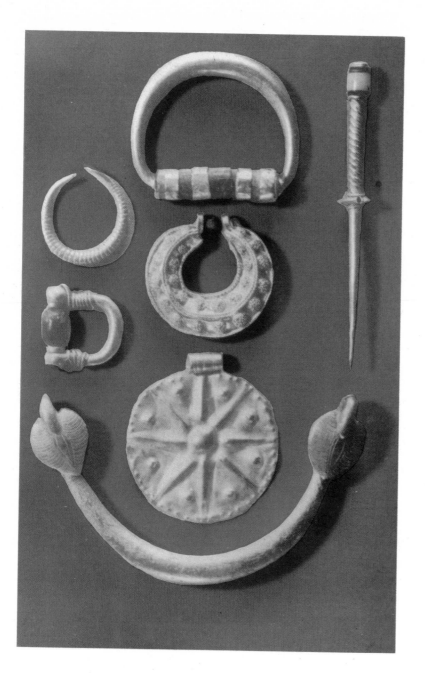

ARTICLES of gold,
armlets, and bracelets,
signet rings, earrings,
and beads . . .

(Nu. 31 : 50)

The metal objects taken as spoils by the Israelites from the conquered Midianites (Nu. 31 : 22; see also the previous page) included gold jewellery which was taken by the captains of the army and brought to the Tent of Meeting "as a memorial for the people of Israel before the LORD." Before the invention of coinage, such objects served in the ancient East as a reserve of valuables for use in an emergency. Jewellery had an additional value to far-roaming nomad peoples such as the Midianites, in that they were an easily portable form of personal possessions. Not all the items of jewellery mentioned in this verse have been identified. The first (Heb. *etsadah*) may have been an arm ornament (see 2 Sam. 1 : 10). The second (Heb. *tsamid*) was certainly worn on the arm (see Gen. 24 : 22; Ezek. 16 : 11). The use of signet-rings and earrings is well known from biblical literature; but the identity of the last item in the list (Heb. *kumaz*), mentioned also in Ex. 35 : 22, is unknown. The examples shown here of the gold ornaments mentioned above were found in the excavation of Beth Eglayim (modern Tell Ajjul) south of Gaza. They belong to the Middle Bronze Age (the patriarchal period).

WE will build sheepfolds here for our flocks, and cities for our little ones.   (Nu. 32 : 16)

Those experienced cattle-rearers, the tribes of Gad and Reuben, chose for themselves the territories of Yaazer and Gilead beyond the Jordan, because "the place was a place for cattle" (Nu. 32 : 1). They then proceeded to build folds for their sheep, as was customary in cattle-rearing districts. Fortified sheepfolds of a unique type (the so-called "kites"), which were evidently intended to serve as fortified posts for the protection of the shepherds and their flocks from the depredations of desert raiders, have been discovered in Trans-Jordan. Their date is uncertain, but they may go back as far as the biblical period. A good example of these structures and the way in which they were used is provided by the scene reproduced here from one of the rock-drawings of the Safaites (an Arab tribe of the first millennium A.D.) found in the desert to the east of Amman. It shows an enclosure with a narrow entrance protected by extended walls. These may be the *mishpetayim* (a Hebrew word of uncertain meaning) mentioned in the Song of Deborah as a feature of the territory of Reuben in Trans-Jordan: "Why did you tarry among the sheepfolds (Heb. *mishpetayim*), to hear the piping for the flocks?" (Judg. 5 : 16). Animals are shown inside and outside the entrance, with men apparently driving them inside, either for the night, or to protect them from threatening danger.

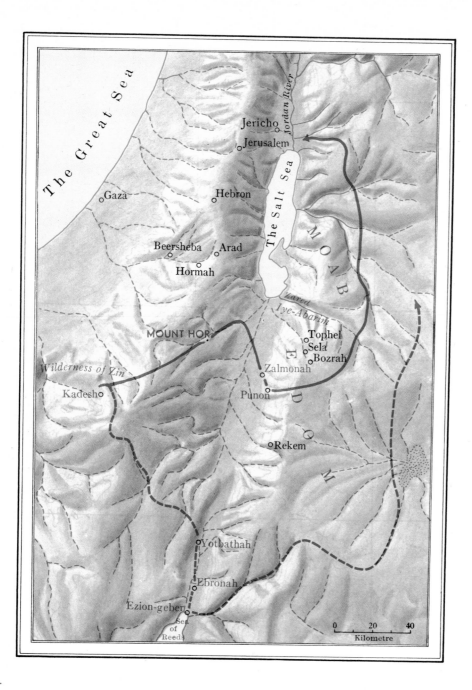

Chap. 33 of the Book of Numbers contains a detailed list of the camping stations of the Israelites on their long, circuitous march from the borders of Egypt to the plains of Moab. Today, it is no longer possible to identify most of these places, since they were only temporary halts the names of which have not been preserved. However, as the number of possible ways through the desert is limited by topographical factors, and the positions of the few watering places are fixed, our modern map gives a good general idea of the route followed by the Israelites, even though the names of the oases are no longer the same.

The central oasis on the route was Kadesh Barnea (see p. 250). From there they proceeded to Mount Hor and thence to the Arabah. The two lines drawn on our map indicate the view held by many scholars, that the Israelites reached Canaan by two different routes. The dotted line follows the route given in Nu. 20 : 14-21 ; 21 : 4, while the continuous line is a reconstruction from Nu. 33 : 41-50.

AND encamped at Yotbathah.　　(Nu. 33 : 33)

One of the desert halts to which the wandering Israelites were attracted was the oasis of Yotbathah, described in the Bible as "a land with brooks of water" (Deut. 10 : 7). In the Israelite itinerary, Yotbathah is placed before Ebronah and Ezion-geber on the Gulf of Elath. Assuming, therefore, that the Israelites proceeded southwards from Yotbathah along the Arabah, the oasis is presumably to be identified with the modern Ain Ghadyan (22 miles north of Elath). This is the most plentiful source of water in the southern Arabah and therefore fits the biblical description: "brooks of water". Nearby, there is a salt-marsh called today Sabkhat et-Tabah which may be a corruption of the ancient name. On the mound close to Ain Ghadyan, potsherds and a fort have been found, dating to the time of the Kings of Judah. In the Roman-Byzantine period the site was occupied by a Roman military station called ad Dianam. Not far away, the road from the Dead Sea meets the road from the Mediterranean to the Gulf of Elath.
As seen in the photograph here, Ain Ghadyan is a typical example of a well-watered, palm-girt oasis.

AND they set out from Yotbathah and encamped at Ebronah. (Nu. 33 : 34)

In the itinerary of the Israelites, Ebronah comes between Yotbathah and Ezion-geber (see previous page). If we are right in supposing that the Israelite line of march was from north to south along the Arabah, Ebronah must lie somewhere between Ain Ghadyan and Elath (see map on p. 236). A suitable spot is the oasis which the Arabs call Ain ed-Dafiyeh, six miles north of modern Elath (see picture). Here there is a spring flowing into a pool. In the rainy season, the spring-water is supplemented by rain-water which runs down from the wadis in the hills. In years of heavy rainfall, the whole valley is turned into a salt-marsh which drains into the Red Sea. In winter, this oasis is a suitable camping site for any large host of nomads. Tests recently made show that the waters of Ebronah are not very saline. The exact site of the ancient station has not yet been identified.

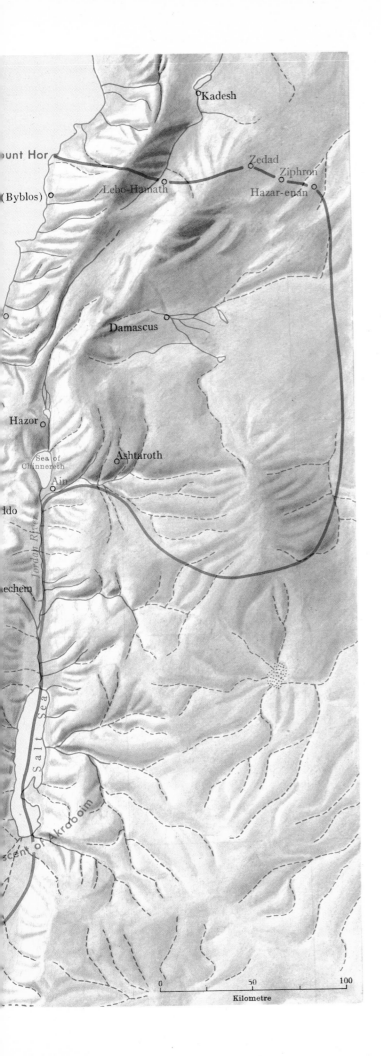

W<small>HEN</small> you enter the land of Canaan (this is the land that shall fall to you for an inheritance, the land of Canaan in its full extent). (Nu. 34 : 2)

"The land of Canaan in its full extent" as described in ch. 34 of the Book of Numbers is the Promised Land, the goal of the long Israelite wandering in the desert. The frontiers of the land drawn here include the region of the Lebanon and the Phoenician coast up to and beyond Gebal (Byblos), the Valley of the Lebanon up to Lebo Hamath (which was south of Kadesh-on-the-Orontes), Mount Hermon and the territory of Damascus. They do not include Gilead and all the southern districts of Trans-Jordan, since these did not belong to Canaan. Chapter 34 traces only the boundaries of the territory of the nine and a half tribes (cf. ibid. 13-15). The eastern border from the Sea of Galilee southwards is the Jordan. For the border-lines, see below, pp. 240-244.

Although the land of Canaan, as delineated in this chapter, was not conquered by Israel in its entirety until the reigns of David and Solomon, it was a concrete geographical reality well-known as such at the time of the Exodus. Its boundaries are, in fact, those of the Egyptian province of Canaan which had been conquered by Egypt as far back as the 16th and 15th centuries B.C. Its northern border was re-affirmed at the beginning of the 13th cent. B.C. by the Hittite king and Ramses II after the battle of Kadesh. Gilead and southern Trans-Jordan had no settled population in the centuries preceding the Exodus and are not mentioned at all in non-biblical sources. That is why they were not included in the geographical and political concept 'Canaan' (cf. Nu. 32 : 29-30; Josh. 22 : 9), a concept which continued to exist even after the destruction of the Egyptian empire.

YOUR south side shall be from the wilderness of Zin along the side of Edom, and your southern boundary shall be from the end of the Salt Sea on the east; and your boundary shall turn south of the ascent of Akrabbim and cross to Zin and its end shall be south of Kadesh-Barnea; then it shall go on to Hazar-addar, and pass along to Azmon; and the boundary shall turn from Azmon to the Brook of Egypt, and its termination shall be at the Sea.
(Nu. 34 : 3-5)

The southern border of Canaan ran across the Negeb from south of the Dead Sea to the River of Egypt and thence to the western border, the Mediterranean Sea. The demarcation of the southern border given in Josh. 15 : 3-4 and Ezek. 47 : 19 is broadly the same as that given here. In periods of expansion, such as the reigns of David, Solomon, Jehoshaphat, Amaziah and Uzziah, the Israelites pushed their southern border down to Elath and the Red Sea, which is the natural limit of the country on the south-east.

The Brook of Egypt is the modern Wadi el-Arish (see view on p. 241). Its lower reaches still formed the actual frontier at the time of the Kingdom of Israel. Altogether, with its tributaries and side-channels, it constitutes a natural barrier between the Negeb and the Sinai peninsula.

A prominent natural feature on the southern frontier is Tell Qudeirat (Kadesh; see picture on lower left), which controls the most copious springs in the northern Negeb. Although the steep acclivity known to-day as "The Ascent of Akrabbim (Scorpions)" lies between the tip of the Dead Sea and Kadesh, as described in the Bible, its identification with the biblical ascent of the same name is by no means certain (air-view on upper left).

FOR the western boundary, you shall have the Great Sea and its coast; this shall be your western boundary. (Nu. 34 : 6)

Whenever the Bible mentions "the sea" without any further designation, the reference is to the Mediterranean, the western boundary of Canaan. The term thus came also to be used as a synonym for "west", just as the word for "front" (Heb. *qedem*) was used in the sense of "east". The words occur together in the expression "frontwards and seawards", i.e. "east and west" (Heb. *qedmah weyammah*). In Akkadian inscriptions, the Mediterranean is called the "Upper Sea", in contrast to the "Lower Sea" which is the Persian Gulf (see p. 20). In the Bible it is given various names: the Great Sea, the Sea of the Philistines (Ex. 23 : 31), the Western Sea (Deut. 11 : 24). The Mediterranean is mentioned here and elsewhere in the Bible as the natural border of the Promised Land on the west, as the Euphrates is mentioned sometimes as the border to the north-east (ibid. 24; Josh. 1 : 4). Many a time, however, the country is defined as the land area enclosed by two seas: "I will set your bounds from the Red Sea to the Sea of the Philistines" (Ex. 23 : 31).

The Israel coast of the Mediterranean, having virtually no bays and indentations, was unsuitable for shipping and could not provide the harbourage required for international sea-trade in ancient times. It therefore acted as a natural barrier to foreign invasion.

The view shows the sea-coast at Ashkelon, the part of the Mediterranean that in the Bible is called "the Sea of the Philistines".

THIS shall be your northern boundary: from the Great Sea you shall mark out your line. to Mount Hor; from Mount Hor you shall mark it out to the entrance *(Lebo)* of Hamath, and the end of the boundary shall be at Zedad; then the boundary shall extend to Ziphron, and its end shall be at Hazar-enan; this shall be your northern boundary. You shall mark out your eastern boundary from Hazar-enan to Shepham; and the boundary shall go down from Shepham to Riblah on the east side of Ain; and the boundary shall go down, and reach to the shoulder of the sea of Chinnereth on the east;

(Nu. 34 : 7-11)

Although not all the points listed on the northern border have been identified, its general outline is clear enough. It stretched from the Phoenician coast to the edge of the desert beyond Damascus. The most important points along this line were Mount Hor, Lebo Hamath and Zedad. Mount Hor, like the identical expression in Nu. 20 : 23 referring to the Negeb, simply means high mountain peak. Lebo Hamath seems to be a place name; perhaps it is the city of *Labu* in the south of the district of Hamath which is mentioned in Egyptian and Assyrian sources and is identified with the modern village of Lebwe about 45 miles north of Damascus. It was a fixed point of the northern frontier of Canaan (Josh. 13 : 5; Ezek. 47 : 20; 48 : 1) between the Hermon (Anti-Lebanon) and the Lebanon ranges. According to another view, Lebo Hamath is the "entrance to Hamath" (Heb. *lebo* means "approaches of"), meaning the road at the northern end of the Lebanon range which runs northwards from there to Hamath. Zedad is the modern village of Sedad which is 36 miles east of Lebwe, to the north-east of the Hermon on the edge of the Syrian desert (see upper picture).

The northern boundary of Canaan ended on "the shoulder of the Sea of Chinnereth on the east", i.e. the slopes of the mountain range on the east shore of the Sea of Galilee (see lower picture).

AND the boundary shall go down to
the Jordan and its end shall be at the Salt
Sea . . .   (Nu. 34 : 12)

Rising at a height of 210 ft. above sea level, the Jordan proper twists and turns for the 152 miles of its tortuous course (84 miles as the crow flies) to lose itself in the Dead Sea 1280 ft. below sea level. After leaving the Sea of Galilee, it flows through a broad plain and is joined on both sides by many ephemeral streams and a few perennial rivers. The region where the three tributaries join to form the river is called the Land of Jordan (Ps. 42 : 6), and the tangled thickets on its banks the Jungle of Jordan (Jer. 12 : 5; 49 : 19). The depth of the river varies during most of the year from three to ten feet; in the spring it is somewhat deeper. When the river is at its lowest, it can easily be forded by camel and it presents little difficulty even to crossing on foot; there are about thirty known fords between the Sea of Galilee and the Dead Sea. Although the Jordan separates the territory through which it flows into two distinct regions, it is far from being an impassable geographical barrier and offers no obstacle to military incursions. As a matter of fact, the Jordan was never a fixed political frontier in ancient times: both the biblical Kingdom of Israel and the Hasmonaean state spread across it eastwards as far as the desert. The picture shows the Jordan in its lower course with its meanderings.

DEUTERONOMY

THESE are the words that Moses spoke to all Israel beyond the Jordan in the wilderness, in the Arabah . . . (Deut. 1 : 1)

It may well be that this verse does not refer to any one particular place, but to various parts of Sinai and Trans-Jordan where Moses addressed the Israelites in the course of their wanderings. This is the first occurrence in the Bible of the geographical term Arabah. Usually it is applied to the region along the lower course of the Jordan (Deut. 1 : 7; 11 : 30; Josh. 12 : 3); but here it refers to the long rift valley, extending from the Dead Sea to the Gulf of Elath and separating the mountains of Edom on the east from the Negeb plateau on the west, still called the Arabah today. This is the most desolate part of Palestine; the watering-places are very few and far between and the soil is, for the most part, saline.

At no time in history have there been more than a few permanent settlements in the whole region, and those mainly on its eastern, better-watered side.

The photograph shows a typical view of the Arabah.

O VER against Suf, between Paran and Tofel, Laban, Hazeroth, and Di-zahab. (Deut. 1 : 1)

We do not possess sufficient evidence to identify these Israelite camping stations with certainty. Everything turns on the location of Mount Sinai. If we accept the theory that the mountain is in the southern part of the peninsula, it follows that we must look for Hazeroth and Di-zahab in the same area, which extends to the Sea of Suf (Red Sea) mentioned in this verse. There are two modern places in this region, the names of which may be derived from the biblical names: Ain Hadhrah = Hazeroth, and Dhahab = Di-zahab.

Dhahab, seen in the accompanying photograph, is the chief oasis on the eastern shore of southern Sinai, two to three days' journey from Jebel Musa (Mount Moses). It is on the north-south road from Elath to the south of the peninsula and is also the terminus of the west-east road that runs from coast to coast across southern Sinai. The remains of a port and an important Nabataean settlement have been found there, together with copper slags which suggest that in the Nabataean period metal was worked at Dhahab. But, so far, no evidence bearing on the earlier biblical period has come to light.

AFTER he had defeated ... Og the king of Bashan, who lived in Ashtaroth and in Edrei. (Deut. 1 : 4)

From various passages in the Bible we know that Og, King of Bashan "reigned in Ashtaroth (and) in Edrei" (Josh. 13 : 12; cf. 12 : 4). Our verse is presumably to be construed as follows: "after smiting at Edrei Og, King of Bashan, whose capital was at Ashtaroth"; for we know from Nu. 21 : 33 that the battle in which Og was defeated by the Israelites took place at Edrei. The name Edrei is preserved in the modern Deraa, a small town on a hill in the Yarmuk valley and an important road junction, 30 miles east of the Jordàn. Potsherds found on the mound on which the village is situated (see picture) testify to the continuous occupation of the site from the early Canaanite period (third millennium B.C.) right down to the present day. Edrei reached the height of its prosperity and importance in the period of the Israelite Kingdom.

SO you remained at Kadesh many days . . .   (Deut. 1 : 46)

Kadesh Barnea lay on the borders of the Wilderness of Paran and the Wilderness of Zin, close to the territory of Edom (Nu. 20 : 14). It had been a sacred place from the earliest times. The other names given it in the Bible — En-mishpat (the "Well of Judgment", Gen. 14 : 7) and the Waters of Meribath-kadesh (the "Waters of Strife") seem to indicate that the cult places and tribal courts of the nomads were located in this oasis (see p. 296). Because of its natural advantages, Kadesh became the main Israelite base in the desert, and there the tribes were welded into a nation during their long years of wandering. The name Kadesh is preserved in the small oasis of Ain Qedeis, but the important centre of population in this region was situated near the copious spring at Ain Qudeirat.

In the middle of the oasis of Ain Qudeirat there is a mound on which stood a strong fortress erected by the kings of Israel. Many remains from the age of the patriarchs, the period of the Israelite Monarchy and the Nabataean, Roman and Byzantine periods have been found on the site of Kadesh Barnea and in its environs. There is no doubt that this was the most important oasis on the northern fringe of the Sinai desert and fully capable of supporting a large encamped host for "many days".

The picture shows the tell of Kadesh Barnea with ruined walls in the foreground and the valley of Kadesh in the background.

THEN we turned, and journeyed into the wilderness in the direction of the Red Sea . . . and for many days we went about Mount Seir . . . So we went on, away from our brethren the sons of Esau, who live in Seir, away from the Arabah road from Elath and Ezion-geber. (Deut. 2 : 1-8)

After the affair of the spies and the rout at Hormah (Nu. 14 : 45; Deut. 1 : 44) the Israelites turned southwards to the Red Sea. From there they continued their march northwards and skirted Mount Seir (cf. Nu. 21 : 4). By this detour around the territory of the sons of Esau they avoided any provocation that might lead to war. The photograph shows the barren shores of the Gulf of Elath, called here the Red Sea. The landscape is virtually unchanged since biblical times. The towering ridges of Mount Seir can be seen on the horizon.

THE Caphtorim, who came from Caphtor . . .
(Deut. 2 : 23)

The commonly accepted identification of Caphtor with the island of Crete, although not quite certain, is well attested. Some passages in the Bible state explicitly that the Philistines came from the island of Caphtor (Jer. 47 : 4; Am. 9 : 7); while, in others, the Philistines appear in poetic parallelism with the Cherethites (Cretans) (Ezek. 25 : 16; Zeph. 2 : 5). That Caphtor is the ancient name of Crete seems to be proved by its occurrence in documents from Mari and Ugarit (and perhaps also in Egyptian sources) dating to the second millennium B.C. Certain it is that the Caphtorites (whether identical with the Philistines or not) were one of the "Sea Peoples" who established themselves on the coast of Palestine after the great wave of migrations that swept across the Mediterranean to Asia and Egypt. The island of Crete was the centre of the Minoan culture, which reached a high level of development in the 19th–15th cent. B.C., and which greatly influenced the countries of the eastern Mediterranean.

The reproduction here is from the royal palace at Knossos, the capital of Crete (16th cent. B.C.). The figure of the Minoan prince painted on the wall of the palace is a good example of the sophisticated and stylized character of Minoan art.

RISE up, take your journey, and go over the valley of the Arnon... (Deut. 2 : 24)

The Arnon (Wadi el-Mojib), which rises in the mountains of Moab and flows into the Dead Sea, is the second largest of the rivers of biblical Palestine. Together with its tributaries it constitutes one of the most abundant sources of water in Trans-Jordan. In the last part of its course it has cut a deep canyon and flows between sheer, dark red walls of Nubian sandstone. The Arnon was thus destined to become a political boundary and served as such, first between the kingdom of Sihon and Moab ("for the Arnon is the boundary of Moab, between Moab and the Amorites", Nu. 21 : 13); then between Moab and the territories of Reuben and Gad (see next page). From time to time, the kingdom of Moab expanded to the north of the Arnon, as happened in the period before the invasion of the Amorites under Sihon; again in the reign of Eglon, King of Moab in the time of the Judges, and once more in the 9th cent. B.C., in the reign of King Mesha.
The illustration shows the Arnon flowing into the Dead Sea.

FROM Aroer, which is on the edge of the valley of the Arnon, and from the city that is in the valley . . . (Deut. 2 : 36)

Aroer stood on an isolated height (see illustration), almost two miles north of the Arnon, near the place where the King's Highway crossed the river canyon. Its position made it a place of strategic importance and the key to the control of the frontier which, at various periods, ran past it (see previous page). Aroer was one of the points which marked the boundary of the territory of Reuben and Gad (Josh. 13 : 9, 16). Here Joab, the commander of David's army, began his census of the tribes of Israel (2 Sam. 24 : 5).
The boundary line apparently ran south of Aroer, down in the canyon of the Arnon where there was a lower town, a kind of suburb of the upper city — "the city that is in the valley" (ibid.).
The potsherds found in the mound of Aroer indicate that the site was occupied, with interruptions, from the third millennium B.C. down to the coming of the Arabs, including the period of the Israelite Monarchy. It is mentioned as a Moabite city on the Mesha Stone and also in the Book of Jeremiah (48 : 19).

THE Sidonians call Hermon Sirion, while the Amorites call it Senir.   (Deut. 3 : 9)

In the biblical description of the extent of the Israelite conquest in Trans-Jordan, the words "from the valley of the Arnon to Mount Hermon" (Deut. 3 : 8) lead to a short digression on the different names given to the Hermon — Sirion, Senir, and, in one place, "Sion" (Hebrew text of Deut. 4 : 48). But the question still remains whether all these names refer to the whole of the Anti-Lebanon range, or indicate particular peaks in it. Possibly the name Sirion, the only one that occurs in non-biblical sources from the early second millennium B.C. onwards, is used for the whole range, while Senir is reserved for its northern and Hermon for its southern part. Certainly, Senir and Hermon are twice described in the Bible as adjacent peaks (Song of Sol. 4 : 8; 1 Ch. 5 : 23). Tradition has identified the Hermon with the modern Jebel esh-Sheikh. This mountain, which rises to a height of 9363 ft. and is snow-capped for most of the year (it was called in Aramaic *Tur Thalga,* "the mountain of snow"), filled the ancients with veneration and awe. Hence, it was from the earliest times regarded as holy by various peoples (Heb. *herem* = "sanctified object") and thought to be the abode of the god Baal Hermon (1 Ch. 5 : 23). At the foot of the Hermon rise the springs which form the head-waters of the Jordan. The majesty of the mountain proclaims the might of the Creator: "Tabor and Hermon joyously praise Thy name" (Ps. 89 : 12).
The illustration shows a view of Mount Hermon taken from Upper Galilee.

 And there you will serve gods of wood and stone . . . (Deut. 4 : 28)

In the ancient East, life was bound up to a great extent with religion and ritual. If, therefore, Israel was exiled to a foreign land and lived in the midst of a foreign people, it would take part, in consequence, in idolatrous worship (cf. 1 Sam. 26 : 19). The Law, the Prophets and the Psalms are full of sarcastic references to the idols of other nations "that neither see, nor hear, nor eat, nor smell" (Deut. 4 : 28; cf. 2 Ki. 19 : 18; Ps. 115 : 4-7; Isa. 37 : 19; Jer. 10 : 3-5). This realization that the idols worshipped as gods in the temples of the nations were nothing more than so many inanimate objects underlies the whole religious conception of the Bible, and finds its most characteristic expression in the jibes of the prophets and psalmists at the impotence of the idols.

The stone statue in the upper picture, which was found on the site of Samal (Zenjirli) and dates from the 9th cent. B.C., is of a Syro-Hittite god (apparently the storm god). On the pedestal of the statue there is a relief of a dwarf squatting between two lions.

The lower picture is a reproduction of a painted wooden statue of the Egyptian goddess Nebethet (Nephthys), sister of Isis. It probably dates to the 6th cent. B.C.

AND cisterns hewn out, which you did not hew . . .   (Deut. 6 : 11)

The earliest permanent settlements in the hill regions of Palestine clustered in areas where springs were plentiful, such as the Vale of Shechem and the vicinity of Hebron. Only when it became common practice to collect rainwater in cisterns, cut out of the rock and plastered to prevent the water from seeping away, did the hill regions become densely populated. The earliest of such rock-cut cisterns go back to very ancient times; by the time of the Israelite conquest (at the end of the Bronze Age) they were found everywhere. Because they were so important, the Bible includes them amongst the attractions of the Promised Land (Deut. 6 : 11). The ancient cistern was usually bottle-shaped, with a narrow mouth and a wide base.
The cistern-mouth reproduced here is one of several excavated at Hazor; it dates to the Late Bronze Age (approximately the period of the Israelite conquest). It is quite possible that some of these cisterns — in which traces of plaster have been found — were used for storing water as early as the Middle Bronze Age.

B<small>UT</small> thus shall you deal with them: you shall break down their altars, and dash in pieces their pillars . . .   (Deut. 7 : 5)

"For you are a people holy to the L<small>ORD</small> your God" (Deut. 7 : 6) — such is the reason given the Israelites for the commandment to destroy all the emblems of idolatry that, in the course of centuries, had become an integral feature of Canaanite life (see p. 157). The ruins of Canaanite temples excavated at Lachish, Hazor and elsewhere in Palestine indicate the thoroughness with which the Israelite conquerors of Canaan razed the idolatrous sanctuaries to the ground.

The picture shows the Holy of Holies *(debir)* of a Canaanite shrine from the Late Bronze Age (at the time of Joshua's conquest) found at Hazor. On the left stands a basalt statue of a god sitting on a throne and holding a cup in his hand. Beside the statue there is a row of rounded stelae (Heb. *mazzeboth),* one of which shows a pair of hands raised up in prayer under a representation of the moon's crescent and the sun's disc. When discovered, the temple was in ruins and the head of the statue was found severed; it is shown as replaced by the excavators (cf. the story about the Philistine god Dagon in 1 Sam. 5 : 4).

FOR the LORD your God is bringing you into a
good land, a land of brooks of water, of fountains
and springs, flowing forth in valleys and hills.

(Deut. 8 : 7)

Just before their entry into Canaan, the wandering Israelite tribes are told by Moses of the special attractions of
the Promised Land. By comparison with Egypt, where the Nile is the main source of water, and in contrast to the
parched and barren desert, Canaan might be considered as a land of rivers, springs and abundant water. The
rain-water infiltrates through the limestone of the Palestine hills, till it reaches a layer of impervious rock above
which it percolates to the foot of the hills where it issues at the surface in springs. These springs are more plentiful
in some regions than in others. In Judah, there are two or three to every 40 sq. miles; in Samaria, seven or eight;
and in Galilee about nine. The most copious of the Galilean springs are those which feed the headwaters of the
Jordan, above all the spring of Dan.
The photograph shows the Jordan after its exit from the Sea of Galilee, and the lush green vegetation of the
valley watered by the river.

A land of wheat and barley, of vines and fig trees and pomegranates, a land of olive trees and honey.

(Deut. 8 : 8)

This description of the Land of Israel is meant not only for nomads entering a region of permanent settlements from the desert. Canaan is described as a land rich in the seven main kinds of cultivated plants also by an Egyptian who spent some time there just before the patriarchal period. "It is a good land, containing figs and vines, and its wine is richly spiced. There is honey in abundance there and vast quantities of oil, all the fruit of its trees. It grows wheat and barley and has cattle without number" (from the *Story of Sinuhe* — the quoted portion of the papyrus is shown at bottom of page). The wheat (top left) that grew in the fertile regions of Canaan was of excellent quality and had won a name for itself even outside the borders of the country. For instance, the Egyptians used the Hebrew-Canaanite word *qemah* for the finest kind of wheat-flour. Barley (bottom left) was grown more frequently than wheat and provided food for both man and beast. The vine (top middle) was known in Canaan from the earliest times and supplied various products — wine, grapes and raisins. Canaanite wine was also known in Egypt; its different varieties were called "wine of Apiru" and "wine of Hurru" (i.e. from Canaan). Figs (bottom right) were eaten fresh, dried or preserved. The pomegranate (top right) was used as both food and drink. The olive (bottom right) flourished in ancient Palestine and, to this day, the numerous ancient olive-trees are a characteristic feature of the landscape. The honey meant here is a syrup made from fruit, hence its inclusion amongst the fruit-trees. It was usually made from dates, the products of the palm-tree (bottom middle). The Bible mentions corn, honey and oil among the products exported from Palestine to Egypt and Phoenicia. The prophet Ezekiel speaks of the sale of wheat, honey and oil from Palestine, all of which were well known in the markets of Tyre, the "merchant of the peoples on many coastlands" (ibid. 27 : 17); the prophet Hosea also mentions that "oil is carried to Egypt" (ibid. 12 : 2).

A land whose stones are iron, and out of whose hills you can dig copper.   (Deut. 8 : 9)

Until recently, it was thought that the author of these biblical verses had been induced to exaggerate by his great love for the Holy Land. To-day, however, we know that copper deposits are actually found all along the Arabah, from Punon in the north to Tabah and Wadi Merah (south-west of Elath) in the south. Moreover, there are iron deposits in Trans-Jordan in the mountains of Gilead and near the Jabbok river, not far from the point in the Jordan plain where Solomon had the Temple vessels cast (1 Kings 7 : 46). Both Josephus and the Mishnah (*Sukkah,* 3 : 1) mention a "mountain of iron" in these regions. Unmistakable traces of copper and iron working going back to biblical times — such as slag, crucibles and miners' dwellings — have been found in Trans-Jordan, the Arabah and Edom. The powerful kings of Israel and Judah — Solomon, Jehoshaphat and Uzziah — organized the extraction of the metal on a commercial scale as a national enterprise. The most striking testimony to the thoroughness of their efforts is provided by the remarkable metallurgical establishment at Ezion-geber which is unique amongst finds in the ancient Orient.

Shown in the illustration here are the so-called 'Mines of Solomon' in the Timna Valley. Here, copper was extracted in biblical times and sent to Ezion-geber for smelting. The composition of the slag at Timnah indicates that apparently iron, too, was once mined there. Despite the heat and extreme dryness of the place and the lack of suitable fuel, the royal slaves managed to extract and to smelt the metal which was then exported partly by way of the Red Sea.

WHO led you through the great and terrible wilderness . . . who brought you
water out of the flinty rock.   (Deut. 8 : 15)

The Book of the Law here intends to fix the wandering in the desert ineradicably in the people's memory. Hence, even after they are established in their own land, they are forbidden to forget their former sufferings in the desert. Unlike the Prophetic Books (Jer. 2 : 2; Hos. 11 : 1-5), the Law does not idealize the long trek through the desert, but gives a realistic picture of the terrors of that barren desolation: the endless distances, the thirst, the hunger, and the menace of snake and scorpion.

In such a desert, the might of God is more powerfully revealed than in a cultivated and populated land. The people see with their own eyes that the leader who caused abundant water to flow from the rock by striking it with his staff (Nu. 20 : 11) is the emissary of a good, beneficent and merciful Deity. The Psalmist laid special stress on the grandeur of God and His loving-kindness to the wanderers in the desert: "Some wandered in desert wastes, finding no way to a city to dwell in; hungry and thirsty, their soul fainted within them. Then they cried to the LORD in their trouble, and He delivered them from their distress" (Ps. 107 : 4-6).

The illustration shows the spring of Kadesh (Ain Qudeirat), the waters of which burst forth from the rock.

H EAR, O Israel; you are to . . . go in to dispossess nations greater than yourselves, cities great and fortified up to heaven.

(Deut. 9 : 1)

For security reasons, the cities of Canaan were built on hilltops, on ravine-girt mountain-spurs, or on natural hillocks in the plains. To the Israelites, wandering in the desert, there was something amazing and terrifying about these fortified Canaanite cities (see p. 210). During the time of the Hyksos, the cities of Canaan were further strengthened. In several places — Jericho, Lachish, Gezer, Megiddo, Beth-shean and Hazor — huge ramparts of stamped earth were discovered. They engirdled the cities with a glacis that gave them the appearance of being "fortified up to heaven".

The upper picture shows one of these cities — Tell el Fara — probably biblical Sharuhen (Josh. 19 : 6). It was protected on the east by the ravine of the Besor Valley and on the west by a deep moat. In the other picture, we see the glacis excavated at Tell Jerisheh (perhaps the Gath Rimmon mentioned in Josh. 19 : 45) near Tel Aviv. The glacis consists of alternate layers of sand and beaten earth, on a foundation of square bricks. These sloping layers lean at their top against a mud-brick wall.

We learn from the Book of Joshua that the Israelites had to use stratagems in order to capture these Canaanite fortresses.

Fᴏʀ the land which you are entering
to take possession of it is not like the land
of Egypt, from which you have come,
where you sowed your seed and watered
it with your feet, like a garden of vegetables.   (Deut. 11 : 10)

This verse brings out one of the major contrasts between the natural conditions of Egypt and those of Canaan.
The latter depends on the bounty of a seasonal rainfall (see following page), whereas the former is abundantly
supplied with water by the Nile. Egypt was famous for its irrigation system, its network of canals and water-
pumping installations, worked by hands and feet. For this reason, the ancients thought it "a garden of vegetables"
or "like the garden of the Lord, like the land of Egypt" (Gen. 13 : 10) which needed no rain.
Reproduced here is a painting from the tomb of Ipui, a high official of the time of Ramses II (thirteenth cent.
B.C.). It shows part of his palatial residence and a slave working an irrigation machine (of the type called by the
Arabs *shaduf*) in a garden on the bank of a river or pond where ornamental plants and trees grow luxuriantly.
The contraption consists of a post painted white on which is balanced a beam (the sweep). From the end of the
pole there is suspended a bucket which the slave is about to lower into the pond for filling. He will then raise it
again by means of the counterpoise weight at the right end of the sweep. By moving the sweep sideways he can
guide the full bucket exactly to the place to be irrigated.

A land of hills and valleys ...   (Deut. 11 : 11)

This verse emphasizes the main topographical characteristics of the Holy Land, a land of hills and valleys, in contrast to the uniform flatness of Egypt. It is thus unsuited to irrigation by means of canals; it only "drinks water by the rain from heaven" (ibid.). Topographically, the Holy Land is a patchwork of small natural units. The narrow strip of territory, about 120 miles wide, which separates the Mediterranean from the desert, can be divided into four different sections: the coastal plain, the western hill region, the Jordan valley and the Trans-Jordan plateau. From north to south, too, the country is intersected by alternations of "hills and valleys".

These topographical differences account for the regional variations of temperature, rainfall, agriculture and forms of settlement (see p. 211). The peculiar topography of the country also influenced its history and cultural development. From the dawn of history, Canaan had been split up into small political units, economically, politically and culturally distinguished from each other by their geographical characteristics. It was left to the Israelites to overcome these naturally centrifugal tendencies and to establish a well-organized united state embracing both hills and valleys.

The picture shows a landscape south-west of Jerusalem.

THESE are the statutes and ordinances which you shall be careful to do . . .   (Deut. 12 : 1)

The speeches of Moses in Deuteronomy (chapters 12-30) contain laws and statutes governing the relations between man and God and between man and man. They conclude with a blessing to those who keep these laws and a curse upon those who transgress them. The legislation incorporates laws and customs that had been observed by the forefathers of the nation for generations and which now were codified and given divine sanction in the Mosaic covenant. In some respects it also resembles the famous Code of Hammurabi, King of Babylon (18th cent. B.C.), which marks the culmination of a long period of development in legal matters in the ancient East. The Code of Hammurabi combines ancient Sumerian and Akkadian laws with elements of West Semitic legal practice which must already have been well-known in and about Canaan (see p. 156).
The two hundred and eighty eight sections of the Code were engraved on a diorite stele found at Susa, the capital of ancient Elam. This is the "official text" of the laws. At the top of the stele the king stands in the traditional Mesopotamian manner before Shamash, the god of righteousness, and prepares to receive from him the symbols of kingship and justice. The god's footstool is decorated with semi-circles (perhaps symbolizing mountains), and the rays of the sun issue from his shoulders. With his right hand he extends the ring and rod to the king who is raising his hand to his mouth in a gesture of subservience.

SOME of the gods of the peoples that are round
about you, whether near to you or far off from you,
from the one end of the earth to the other.

(Deut. 13 : 7)

The prohibition of idolatry was absolute, applying both to the gods of the Israelites' neighbours in and about Canaan and to the gods of more distant nations — the Assyrians, Babylonians, Hittites and Egyptians — who were renowned throughout the ancient world.

Two of the gods of the neighbouring peoples are represented here. The image on the left (from Ugarit, 13th cent. B.C.) is perhaps of El, the chief god of the Canaanite pantheon, who was apparently regarded as the creator of the universe and called "the fashioner of all creatures". He is shown in a relief, seated on a throne with his feet resting on a footstool; his right hand, in which there is a bowl, is stretched towards the man (a king or high priest) who is standing before him. The god's left hand is raised in a gesture of benediction.

The second reproduction is of a relief of the goddess Ishtar-Astarte of Arbela from the 8th cent. B.C. The relief was found at Til-Barsib on the Euphrates. The goddess is standing on the back of a lion and is holding reins in her right hand. Above her head is her symbol — an eight-pointed star. Her left hand is raised as if in benediction. One of the cult-centres of the goddess, who was venerated throughout Assyria, was in the city of Arbela to the east of the Tigris. It was in the name of Ishtar of Arbela that seers appeared who foretold the future to the great Assyrian kings of the 7th cent. B.C. Against prophets of this kind the Law utters a solemn warning in this section (Deut. 13 : 2-6) and threatens them with death.

YOU shall not plant any tree as an Asherah beside
the altar of the LORD your God which you shall
make.   (Deut. 16 : 21)

The Hebrew word *asherah* has two meanings in the Bible: a) a sacred tree (as in this verse; and sometimes in the
plural form *asherim*); b) the goddess Asherah, one of the principal deities of the Canaanite pantheon. In the
Ugaritic texts, this goddess is given the title "the creatress of the gods" as befits the consort of El, the father of
the gods (see previous page).
It was a common practice amongst the Hebrew tribes and the Canaanites to plant sacred trees beside places of
worship (springs, wells, pillars, and even altars); indeed it still is to a certain extent today amongst the simple
Moslem peasants. The prohibition of this practice in the Mosaic Law was extended by later interpretations to
include even the planting of trees in the Temple court.
There were places in Israel where this practice still survived in the time of the Judges and even during the period
of the First Temple. To the Canaanites, the *asherah* tree probably symbolized the divine power of reproduction
with which the earth was endowed by the graciousness of the goddess Asherah. Hence the tree was given
the same name as the goddess. The cult was widespread in the ancient East. From Cyprus, for example, comes
this pottery group representing three women dancing round a tree which is, no doubt, meant to be an *asherah*.
The group is contemporary with the Israelite Kingdom.

AND has gone and served other gods and worshipped them, or the sun or the moon or any of the host of heaven, which I have forbidden.

(Deut. 17 : 3)

The sun, the moon and the stars aroused potent religious feelings in most of the pagan peoples. In one passage in the Book of Deuteronomy (4 : 19) we are even told that the Lord "has allotted (them) to all the peoples under the whole heaven". The people of Israel, however, in its covenant with God, solemnly undertook to root out all such idolatrous practices from its midst.

In the heathen world, the most venerated and most sacred of the heavenly bodies was the sun. Even the Egyptian ruler Akhenaton (14th cent. B.C.), near-monotheist though he was and a determined opponent of the polytheism of his countrymen, fostered the cult of Aton, the sun-god, the creator of all things. In a relief from a temple at el-Amarna, reproduced above, Akhenaton and his queen are shown sacrificing to Aton who sheds his rays — which end in hands — over the royal household.

The moon was widely worshipped in Babylonia, especially at Ur and Haran, centres which feature in the wanderings of the patriarchs. The lower picture is a reproduction of a cylinder-seal from Ur of the Chaldees dating to the end of the third millennium B.C. At the right, the moon-god is sitting on a throne with his symbol, a crescent, above him. On the left a man, accompanied by two goddesses, is worshipping the moon-god.

WHEN you come to the land . . . and then say: "I will set a king over me, like all the nations . . ."

(Deut. 17 : 14)

Monarchy is essentially an institution of the gentile nations. However, the Law accedes to the people's desire to be ruled by a king — but only on condition that the king acts in accordance with its prescriptions. The Israelite king is forbidden to copy the behaviour of those oriental despots who considered themselves beings of a higher order than their subjects. The Law warns him to take care "that his heart may not be lifted up above his brethren" (Deut. 17: 20); and the prophet Samuel describes at length and in detail the "manner of the king" who subjects his people to serfdom (1 Sam. 8 : 10-11). The kings of antiquity prided themselves on their wealth, their numerous wives and their horses and silver and gold. The Israelite king, on the contrary, is forbidden to amass great wealth and strive after outward show, so that he should not be tempted to emulate the classic land of god-kings: "Only he must not multiply horses for himself, or cause the people to return to Egypt" (Deut. 17 : 16).

The luxurious splendour of royal life common in the Orient is demonstrated by the throne of Tutankhamon, the Egyptian king who reigned in the middle of the 14th cent. B.C. This is one of the most splendid artistic creations of antiquity. It is made of wood covered with gold and inlaid with faience, glass and precious stones. On the inside of the back there is a royal family scene. The king is sitting on a throne with his feet resting on a footstool. Beside him stands the queen holding a bowl in her left hand and touching the king with her right. Above them is the sun-disc with rays ending in hands — the symbol of the god Aton.

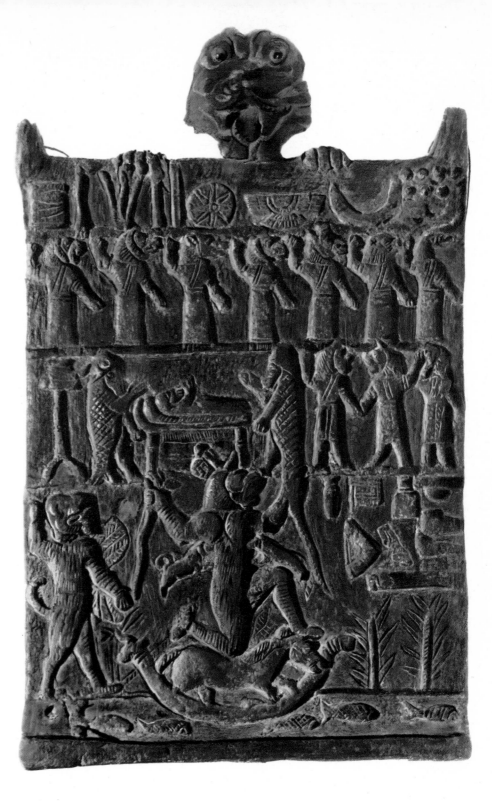

THERE shall not be found among you ... any one who practises divination, a soothsayer ... or a sorcerer ... or a charmer ... or a wizard, or a necromancer.

(Deut. 18 : 10-11)

The Mosaic Law forbids magic rites such as were commonly practised in the ancient East for medical and other purposes. In Assyria, it was customary to hang charm-plaques above the doorway of a sick man's house and above his bed, to exorcise the demons from his body.

One such plaque is reproduced here. It is made of bronze and is held by a lion-headed "good" spirit named Pazuzu. Each one of the four rows on the tablet portrays a different stage of the magic ceremonial. At the top are the emblems of the guardian deities (for explanation of emblems see p. 153). In the second row, there is a procession of seven demons, each with the head of an animal and its right hand raised in a menacing gesture. In the third row, the sick man is lying on his bed, at the ends of which stand two sorcerers whispering the incantation. They are both dressed in fish-shaped garments, as becomes the servants of Ea, the god of the ocean and of sorcery. Beside the bed there is a lamp, the emblem of the god Nusku. The fourth row shows the chief demon, Lamashtu, being carried away over the fish-filled ocean in the sacred bark of Ea. On the right there are various objects to be burned during the ritual.

IN the inheritance which you will hold in the land ... you shall not remove your neighbour's landmark, which the men of old have set.

(Deut. 19 : 14)

The primary object of this law was to preserve hereditary estates (cf. Prov. 22 : 28) and to protect the weak against the strong. The Bible elsewhere states: "Do not remove an ancient landmark; or enter the fields of the fatherless" (Prov. 23 : 10). Trespassing was a heinous sin and is mentioned as such in the solemn invocation of the blessing and the curse on Mount Gerizim and Mount Ebal: "Cursed be he who removes his neighbour's landmark" (Deut. 27 : 17).

The ancients believed that the gods, who had fixed the frontiers of nations (compare Deut. 32 : 8), were likewise responsible for the boundaries of landed properties. This belief was shared by the Greeks and Romans. In Mesopotamia, boundary-stones were first erected in the middle of the third millennium B.C. and their use became widespread from the middle of the second millennium onwards, during the rule of the Kassite peoples. Originally, they were inscribed with formulae concerning the defence of the boundaries and warnings to would-be trespassers; but later on, they began to serve as legal records in property transactions. The inscriptions on them were accompanied by the emblems of the gods invoked in the formula of the contractual oath.

The stone shown in our picture is one of the type called in Babylonian *kudurru* (i.e. boundary) from the reign of Marduk-nadin-ahi, King of Babylon (end of the 12th cent. B.C.). At the top of the stone are the emblems of the gods who protect the boundary (see the key on p. 153). Round the stone a snake is twined (on the right) and, on the front side, the king is holding a bow and two arrows for the protection of the boundary. The inscription records the transfer of the estate. It contains words of warning and imprecation against any would-be trespasser.

The purpose of the law prescribed here was to avoid as far as possible a long war, involving a siege. This was evidently regarded as a last resort; the enemy city was to be besieged only after it had rejected a peace offer. The capture of a fortified city was one of the most arduous operations of ancient warfare, since the defenders had the walls and the moat to protect them. The efforts of the attackers were directed either to starving out the inhabitants by a long siege, or to taking the city by storm by climbing, breaching the walls and gates, or by undermining the foundations of the walls. Which of these methods was adopted depended on the fighting quality and technical efficiency of the attacking army.

Our relief, which is from Medinet Habu, and belongs to the reign of Ramses III (12th cent. B.C.), portrays the capture of a Canaanite city in Syria. It illustrates some of the tactics employed in overcoming the resistance of a fortified and besieged city. Some soldiers are trying, under the protective covering of the large shields hung from their shoulders, to batter down the gate with axes. Others are storming the city with the help of ladders; while the bowmen (at right) provide them with long-range covering 'fire' aimed at the defenders standing on top of the wall. Still others are hard at work cutting down trees (see p. 277).

275

BUT the women and the little ones, the cattle, and everything else in the city, all its spoil, you shall take as booty for yourselves...

(Deut. 20 : 14)

The savage usages of ancient warfare gave the victor the disposal of all the possessions of the vanquished, including the women and children (see p. 233). As part of its mitigation of the horrors of war, the Mosaic Law prescribes more humane conduct in such cases, such as good treatment of female captives (Deut. 21 : 10-14).

Booty, in all its various forms, is frequently represented in ancient art, as for example in the Egyptian wall-painting reproduced here from the tomb of Rekhmire (15th cent. B.C.). It shows captives being led by Egyptian soldiers to the scribe who is registering them. On the left are the bearded male captives and behind them the females, wearing dresses that hang in numerous folds, after the Syrian fashion. They are leading their older children by the hand and carrying their infants in their arms, on their shoulders, or in baskets strapped to their backs (see the females in the centre of the picture).

WHEN you besiege a city
for a long time ... you shall
not destroy its trees by wield-
ing an axe against them. Only
the trees which you know are
not trees for food you may
destroy ... (Deut. 20 : 19-20)

The law against the destruction of food-producing trees
is intended to reduce the damage done by the army in a
siege. The besieging forces needed large quantities of
wood for various military purposes: building bridges
across the moat, underpinning the earthworks required
for the propulsion of the battering-rams, erecting towers for the bowmen, constructing booths and various
other field-works.

The felling of trees in war-time is implied in the passage
about the siege of Megiddo in the records of the Egyptian
king Thutmose III: "They measured this city surrounding
it with an inclosure, walled about with green timber of
all their pleasant (= "sweet") trees".

In Assyrian and Egyptian war-scenes we sometimes see
the besiegers cutting down the trees around the fortified
city. The relief reproduced here, from the reign of
Ramses II (13th cent. B.C.), shows the felled trees around
a conquered city. The city itself is in ruins, its gates
battered in, its windows dislodged, and bricks are
crumbling away from the walls.

For another representation of the cutting of trees, see
p. 275 (in the upper right corner of the illustration).

IF you chance to come upon a bird's nest, in any tree or on the ground, with young ones or eggs, and the mother sitting upon the young or upon the eggs, you shall not take the mother with the young. (Deut. 22 : 6)

The Law forbids the taking of a mother-bird with its young from the nest. There might be several reasons for this commandment: prevention of cruelty to animals; and concern that whole families should not be exterminated (cf. Lev. 22 : 27-28).

Since the nest is the place where most birds lay their eggs and hatch and rear their young, it serves as a symbol of the family life of the whole species. Only a few birds lay their eggs on the ground or between stones and rocks, while a few more dig holes in the earth, or line a hidden natural cavity to receive them. The nests that most birds build are of intricate design. The building is usually done just before each breeding season. In some species, such as the white stork, the same nest is used season after season for many years and is even inherited by successive generations.

In the Bible, the word for 'nest' is used either in a general sense, or specially for the nest of certain species (the pigeon, the swallow, etc.). The following examples of nesting-places are given: the edges of a ravine, rocks, barren wastes, branches, cedars. The "home" of the sparrow in Ps. 84 : 3 and the "home" of the stork (Ps. 104 : 17) are also nests.

This photograph of a fledgeling in a bird's nest was taken in the region of Lake Huleh.

YOU shall not plough with an ox and an ass together.   (Deut. 22 : 10)

This law is analogous to the prohibited sowing of two kinds of seed in the vineyard (Deut. 22 : 9); the wearing of mixed weaves (ibid. 11), and the cross-breeding of cattle (Lev. 19 : 19). Possibly the intention of the Lawgiver here, as elsewhere, was to set Israel apart from other nations and prevent it from following the ways of the pagan peoples. Or he may have wished to hint at the necessity of keeping separate the various species of plants and animals as made by the Creator. Ploughing with a team consisting of an ox and an ass — the commonest animals in Palestine — must have been usual enough in ancient times, just as it is still today (see the photograph which was taken in an Arab village in Galilee).

It may be that, in addition to the general intention of the Law against the mixing of different species, the Lawgiver also had in mind the prevention of cruelty to animals. Two animals of different species were not to be yoked together in order to prevent the discomfort ensuing to both from the difference in their natural manner of pulling the plough.

Y<small>OU</small> shall make yourself tassels on the four corners of your cloak with which you cover yourself.

(Deut. 22 : 12)

The tassels (Heb. *gedilim*) mentioned here were made of twisted and plaited threads. They are the same as the *tsitsit* of Nu. 15 : 37–41. The latter passage also gives the reason for this injunction: the tassels are a visible reminder of the commandments of the Law and, as such, help their wearer to subdue his own evil impulses and to perform the will of God — "and you shall . . . be holy to your God" (ibid. 39–40).

Other peoples of the ancient East, besides the Israelites, were in the habit of adorning the hem of their garments with fringes and tassels of various kinds. Threads of several colours were twined together at the end of the garment and plaited into separate tassels. The fringes thus formed served the dual purpose of strengthening and ornamentation.

Though very few actual garments have been preserved from antiquity, it is possible to reconstruct the details of the clothing from the representations found in contemporary paintings and sculpture. The wall-painting from Thebes reproduced in the lower figure and belonging to the 15th cent. B.C. depicts the governor of Tunip in Syria wearing a robe decorated with coloured bands with two tassels at each corner.

In the upper figure we see Puzur-Ishtar, governor of Mari in the 20th cent. B.C., enveloped in a flowing robe that reaches to his ankles. Along the edge there are tassels made of plaited threads.

No man shall take a mill or an upper millstone
in pledge; for he would be taking a life in pledge.
(Deut. 24 : 6)

This law, the purpose of which is to protect the debtor from the extortionate demands of the creditor, is one of
several laws restricting the rights of the latter. He is not to go to the debtor's house to fetch his pledge; he
is not to sleep in a cloak taken in pledge from a poor man, but restore it to its owner at sunset (Deut. 24 : 10-13).
Elsewhere, too, the Bible sternly rebukes those creditors who demand vital necessities in pledge, who take away
their fellow-man's bed from under him (Prov. 22 : 27) and have "stripped the naked of their clothing" (Job 22 : 6).
Here, the Mosaic Law forbids the taking of the mill-stone with which the housewife every morning grinds the
grain for bread — the staple food of her household (for the usual form of such millstones see pp. 138, 209). This
prohibition is applied even to one part of the mill, the *rekheb,* i.e. the upper millstone which was moved with a
grinding motion over the *shekheb,* or lower millstone. Apparently, the creditor preferred taking the upper stone,
because it was easier to carry; yet without it the mill was completely useless.
The mill shown here is the type used to this day by Arab women.

YOU shall not pervert the justice due to the sojourner or to the fatherless, or take a widow's garment in pledge. (Deut. 24 : 17)

One of the mainsprings of the biblical law is a humane concern for the fate of the weak and the helpless. The widow and the orphan belong to those who need help and protection; sometimes they are mentioned with the poor and the needy (Isa. 10 : 2; Job 31 : 16-17; etc.). These, together with the resident foreigner (Heb. *ger*), are often referred to as under-privileged members of biblical society (Ex. 22 : 21-22; Deut. 10 : 18; 14 : 29; etc.).

This anxiety to ensure just treatment for the poor, the widow and the orphan is also found in the writings of the other peoples of the ancient East. Thus, the Sumerian ruler of Lagash, Gudea (end of the third millennium B.C.), in his description of the ideal conditions that prevailed at the time of the inauguration of his temple, says: "The rich did not oppress the orphan and the widow was not oppressed". Similarly, his contemporary, Urnammu the King of Ur, declares, in the preamble to his laws, that the king will not abandon the orphan to the mercies of the rich, nor the widow to the mercies of a despotic lord. In the Ugaritic texts, Danel, the ruler and righteous judge, likewise guarantees the rights of the widow and the orphan.

In addition, the Bible recognizes the special rights of the *ger*. Moreover, unlike all these legislators, the Bible does not leave this concern for the widow and the orphan to the law-courts' or the king's responsibility, but imposes it as a moral duty upon every individual citizen.

Reproduced here is a relief representing Hammurabi, King of Babylon, who is shown praying to the goddess Ishtar. Hammurabi was one of the most important eastern rulers who concerned himself with the fate of the weak and the oppressed. In the concluding section of his laws (see p. 268), he proudly avers that those laws were given only for the protection of the weak: "Lest the strong might oppress the weak, lest justice might be withheld from the orphan or the widow . . . I wrote these precious words on my stele and I set it up in the presence of the statue of myself, I, the King of Justice . . ."

IF there is a dispute be-
tween men, and they
come into court ... then
if the guilty man deserves
to be beaten, the judge
shall cause him to lie
down and be beaten in
his presence ...

(Deut. 25 : 1-2)

The verse shows that flogging was a customary punishment in Israel. However, to preserve some feeling of respect for the culprit as a human being, the Law set a limit to the permissible number of strokes — "forty stripes may be given him, but not more" (Deut. 25 : 3). This number was characteristically reduced by the Jewish sages: "How many stripes do they inflict on a man? Forty save one ..." (Mishnah, Makkoth 3 : 10). Israelite justice, though distinguished by the special character of Israelite society, still had several points in common with the general legal practices of antiquity.

The Egyptian wall-painting reproduced above, from the tomb of Rekhmire (15th cent. B.C.), depicts the court over which the deceased had presided in his lifetime. At the sides of the court-room stand forty of the nobles of Upper Egypt, holding writing implements. In the entrance, the bowed accused are being forcibly dragged by 'policemen' before the vizier to be tried on a criminal charge. The accompanying inscription instructs the vizier how to conduct the trial. Beside the inscription lie forty scrolls of law which may be royal rulings.

The second picture, found at Beni Hasan and belonging to the Twelfth Dynasty, shows a prostrate culprit being flogged. He is held down by three men, while a fourth administers the strokes. The court overseer is standing by. On the right, youths are brought before judges who deliver their verdict.

YOU shall not muzzle an ox when it treads out the grain.

(Deut. 25 : 4)

The early rabbis extended the meaning of this verse to cover any animal engaged in treading out corn or any similar task. They explained that the Bible took this example of an ox, because it was the animal most usually employed for such a purpose (cf. Hos. 10 : 11). This method of threshing crops is still used in the Middle East. The corn is spread over the threshing-floor and the oxen (or other animals) separate the grain from the chaff by trampling alone or by dragging heavy wooden boards behind them. Sometimes the animals are tied to a central pivot and left to walk round and round by themselves; sometimes the farmer drives them.

The Mosaic law against muzzling an ox engaged in treading out corn was presumably prompted by that humane attitude to animals which also found expression in the law against taking a bird with its young (see p. 278). The modern *fellahin* do not follow any consistent rule in this matter; sometimes they muzzle their threshing animals, sometimes they do not.

The photograph shows a team of muzzled mules on a threshing floor in the village of Naim at the foot of the hill of Moreh in Lower Galilee.

Y<small>OU</small> shall not have in your bag two kinds of weights, a
large and a small. You shall not have in your house two kinds
of measures, a large and a small.   (Deut. 25 : 13-14)

The Law utters a warning against double-dealing in the use of weights — large ones for buying and small ones
for selling; it insists on "a full and just weight" (Deut. 25 : 15; cf. p. 194), i.e. a fixed standard. This refers to the
commercial sharp-practice castigated by the prophet Amos: "That we may make the ephah small and the shekel
great, and deal deceitfully with false balances" (Amos 8 : 5). The Book of Proverbs repeats the Mosaic warning
in the same terms: "Diverse weights and diverse measures are both alike an abomination to the LORD" (Prov.
20 : 10).

It is worth remarking that hardly any two of the extant weights from the biblical period are absolutely identical.
This is no doubt to be explained, in the main, by local differences, chronological variation and the technical
inability to produce absolutely accurate weights. Such objective difficulties opened the door to commercial
dishonesty.

In the picture we see bronze scales with weights of haematite from the Late Bronze Age which were found at
Ugarit. The weight on the top left is shaped like a human head. The weights found at Ugarit represent Egyptian,
Babylonian and Canaanite metrological systems, as was appropriate to this centre of international trade.

AND behold, now I bring the
first of the fruit of the ground, which
You, O LORD have given me. And
you shall set it down before the
LORD your God . . . (Deut. 26 : 10)

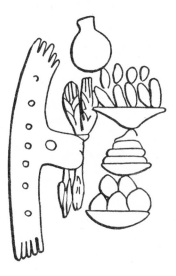

In biblical times, the first-fruits of the earth's produce formed one of the principal sacrifices. They consisted of a relatively limited assortment of the agricultural crops grown by the Israelite farmer, all of which belonged to "the seven kinds mentioned in the praise of the Land, viz.: wheat, barley, vines, figs, pomegranates, olives and honey" (Sifre to Deuteronomy, 297; cf. Deut. 8 : 8). The first-fruits were not placed on the altar, but handed over to the priest in a special rite described in detail in Deut. 26 : 1-11. This presentation of the earth's first products to the priest was a widespread practice which seems to have been observed by most peoples of the ancient East. The rites varied according to their different levels of material and spiritual development. In Egypt, the first-fruits were brought to the temple of the local god. They were also offered to the goddess of the harvest, Renenet (or Thermuthis), either in the field or in the temple.

The painting reproduced in the upper picture is from the tomb of Nakht at Thebes and belongs to the 15th cent. B.C. It portrays agricultural produce offered to the goddess of the harvest. On the left is the emblem of the goddess and a sheaf of corn. On the right are dishes containing vegetables and, apparently, loaves of bread.

In the lower picture, from a tomb of the New Kingdom, men are winnowing corn on a threshing-floor. Above them is the same emblem that appears in the upper picture.

O R offered any of it to the dead...
(Deut. 26 : 14)

This may be a reference to the widespread ancient practice of preparing food and drink for the dead and placing it on their graves. To judge from contemporary references, this practice was widespread amongst the Jewish masses at the time of the Second Temple. Thus we find in the Book of Tobit (4 : 17): "Cast thy bread upon the grave of the righteous and do not give it to the sinful"; and in the Syriac Book of Ahikar (2 : 10): "Pour out thy wine upon the graves of the righteous"; cf. also Eccles. 30 : 18. In Egypt, which provides the classic example of the cult of the dead, it was the task of a special priestly caste to see that the deceased continued to receive sustenance in the after-life.

The wall-painting reproduced here from the tomb of Ptahsekhemankh (Fifth Dynasty) depicts the preparation of a meal for the deceased. In the top row, men are carrying various kinds of food and vessels which appear to contain drink. At the right, a servant is carrying a tray on which there are dishes. The second man from the right is carrying a pigeon and the third a goose. On the table at the left of the row there are grapes, lettuce and spring onions. In the bottom row, oxen are being carved into joints.

YOU shall set up large stones, and plaster them with plaster. And you shall write upon them all the words of this law . . .

(Deut. 27 : 2-3)

The custom of inscribing events and laws on memorial stones was universal in the ancient East. Hammurabi, King of Babylonia, had his code engraved in its entirety on a stele about 7 ft. high (see p. 268).

Whitewashing the stone before the inscription was an Egyptian practice. The whitewashed stone was then written on or painted on in black ink or in other contrasting colours. Not only is it less difficult to write on a stone than to engrave it, but it is also easier to read a written script than to decipher letters cut into stone. To ensure the preservation of the inscriptions, the writing was renewed from time to time. If the Lawgiver intended the numerous laws contained in the Book of Deuteronomy or even the whole law of Moses (Josh. 8 : 32) to be inscribed on stone, we can well understand why it was specified that the stones erected were to be large ones.

The stelae reproduced here are from the temple precinct at Gebal (Byblos) and belong to the Middle Bronze Age. They are up to 8 ft. high, whitewashed and may have been prepared for inscriptions.

THESE shall stand upon Mount Gerizim to bless the people . . .
And these shall stand upon Mount Ebal for the curse . . .

(Deut. 27 : 12-13)

The tribes of Israel were bidden to stand on the two peaks that rise on either side of Shechem — Mount Gerizim
and Mount Ebal — and there solemnize their acceptance of God's commandments with a blessing and a curse.
According to the Bible, this symbolic ceremony marked the choice of Israel as the People of God (Deut. 27 : 9).
Mount Gerizim (rising to a height of 2849 ft. and called by the Arabs Jebel et-Tur) lies to the south of Shechem
while Mount Ebal (Jebel Islamiya, height 3077 ft.) is north of the town. The choice of these two peaks for the
symbolic blessing and curse (Deut. 11 : 29) may have been suggested by an old tradition going back to the
patriarchs (Gen. 12 : 6-7; 33 : 18-19). Gerizim, as the more fertile of the two and on account of the numerous
springs at its foot, was chosen for the blessing (hence its Samaritan name — *Tura Berikha* "Mount of Blessing").
On Ebal, Joshua built an altar to the Lord and inscribed on the stones there a copy of the Mosaic Law (Josh.
8 : 30-33). In the Samaritan creed, Gerizim occupied a position of special importance, being venerated as "The
Chosen Mountain", surpassing the Temple Mount at Jerusalem in sanctity.
In the view above, Mount Gerizim is on the left and Mount Ebal on the right. They are separated by the Valley
of Shechem in which is situated Tell Balata, the site of the biblical Shechem (see p. 90).

Cursed be the man who makes a
graven or molten image, an abomination
to the Lord, a thing made by the hands
of a craftsman ...   (Deut. 27 : 15)

The making of statues and graven images is the
first act forbidden to the tribes of Israel in the
solemn blessing and curse (see previous page). In
antiquity, metal idols were made in one of two
ways: in the first — and more ancient — the metal
was shaped with a hammer and chisel; in the
second, it was melted in a crucible and poured into
moulds; thus were made the "molten gods" of
Ex. 34 : 17. Bronze idols cast in a mould have been
found in Canaanite temples: they are mostly
small, and some of them are overlaid with gold-
leaf.

Illustrated here is a stone mould found in the
excavations at Nahariya on a *bamah,* or open place
of worship (probably from the 17th cent. B.C.).
The mould, which was apparently used for casting
the idol of the goddess — perhaps Asherath-Yam
(Asherah of the Sea) — still contains traces of the
metal poured into it. Two horns protrude from
under the conical headdress. Fragments of two
silver horns were found on the site which fit
exactly into the grooves of the mould. Beside the
mould is a modern cast made from it.

AND the LORD will bring you back in ships to
Egypt, . . . and there you shall offer yourselves for
sale to your enemies as male and female slaves, but
no man will buy you. (Deut. 28 : 68)

The preceding threatening verses list the sequence of dire punishments in store for a disobedient Israel — siege,
sack, famine, plague, exile and wandering — and they culminate here in the direst of them all: slavery in Egypt.
We can feel the indelible impression made on the people by the first Egyptian enslavement: "That you were a
servant in the land of Egypt" (Deut. 5 : 15; etc.). The Egyptian practice of acquiring male and female slaves from
Asia, either by capture or purchase, is frequently illustrated in Egyptian art. Here we reproduce one of the earliest
representations of Asiatics being brought captive to Egypt.
From the evidence of their dress and hair-style, the captives — men, women and children — may be Semites
from Canaan. They are being taken to Egypt in ships, exactly as described in our verse. Their hands are upraised
in a gesture of submissive greeting to Sahure, an Egyptian Pharaoh of the Fifth Dynasty (second half of the third
millennium B.C.). The ships have already reached port; the mast has been lowered and lashed to the ship, and
the rudder (i.e. the three oars tied to the stern) lifted out of the water.

LIKE an eagle that
stirs up its nest . . .
(Deut. 32 : 11)

Moses depicts the feeling of God for His people Israel in poetic imagery taken from the animal and vegetable world. In the wilderness, God found Israel and made it into a nation; He stretched His protective wings over it, even as the vulture gently wakes its young, watches over them, teaches them to fly and carries them on its back till they are full grown.

The vulture (Heb. *nesher* — usually translated "eagle"), "with great wings and long pinions" (Ezek. 17 : 3), is the largest of all Palestinian birds. It is almost about four feet in length and measures ten feet from wing-tip to wing-tip. Its bald head and legs look as if they had been plucked. This keen-sighted bird (see also p. 190) hovers at a great height searching for the carrion that forms its principal food, and once found, swoops upon it at great speed (Job. 39 : 29-30; Hab. 1 : 8). It nests on cliff-tops (Ob. 1 : 3; Job. 39 : 27-28). In this lofty and exposed position the feeble fledgelings require devoted parental care for fifty days. The vultures have almost entirely disappeared from Palestine. Today, only a few isolated pairs remain amongst the crags of Mount Carmel, Mount Gilboa and the Galilee mountains.

Here is one of the few photographs ever taken of a vulture's nest in the north of the country.

AND He made him suck honey out of the rock and oil out of the flinty rock.

(Deut. 32 : 13)

The Song of Moses enumerates, one by one, most of the blessings that God has plentifully bestowed upon Israel in his land: rich crops, plantations, fruit. Even the lifeless barren rocks of the country produced honey and oil. The reference here is to the honey that literally flows from the rock of the caves, from the fissures of limestone crags, and above all from the banks of valleys where the bees find shelter for their hives. The verse also refers to the oil of the olive-trees which grow in thin soil and even amongst rocks, as in Galilee, and which were famed in antiquity for the excellent quality of their fruit.

The wild olive is still found in Palestine, especially on Mount Carmel and in Galilee. The cultivated olive *(Olea europaea)* has been grown there from the earliest times, and especially in the mountains of Ephraim and Judaea. This tree has roots that go deep into the ground, a thick trunk, thick and gnarled branches and leaves that are green above and silvered on their underside. Its fruit ripens five to six months after the appearance of the blossom at the beginning of summer. Since earliest times, the olive has played an important part in the economy of the country, so much so that in antiquity it was known as "the land of olive-trees" (see pp. 260-261).

WITH fat of lambs and rams, herds of Bashan . . .   (Deut. 32 : 14)

The land of Canaan was richly blessed with cattle and sheep. Here the Bible includes the rams of Bashan in its enumeration of choice livestock. Bashan was famous for its pastures and forests (Jer. 50 : 19; Mi. 7 : 14; Zech. 11 : 2) and its thoroughbred cattle. "The cows of Bashan" and "the bulls of Bashan" are expressions used in the Bible to symbolize abundance and power (Am. 4 : 1; Ps. 22 : 1). The flesh of the fattened cattle of Bashan was considered rich, tender meat, fit to be served up at "a great sacrificial feast" (Ezek. 39 : 17-18). The almost full-grown ram, with horns already showing, is frequently mentioned in the Bible as a sacrificial animal (see p. 182). In the picture from Nimrud (8th cent. B.C.) reproduced here, the troops of the Assyrian king are seen carrying off into exile the inhabitants of a conquered city of Palestine. Amongst the sheep taken as booty by the Assyrians there are fat rams. (For a similar picture showing spoils of rams, the produce of Bashan's rich pastures, cf. vol. II, to Josh. 12 : 31.)

THEY shall be wasted with hunger, and devoured with burning heat ... (Deut. 32:24)

The plenty of Canaan (see previous page) had a demoralizing effect on the Israelites: "But Jeshurun waxed fat, and kicked" (Deut. 32 : 15). The "perverse generation" (ibid. 20) turned its back on God and sacrificed "to demons which were no gods" (ibid. 17). For this it will be severely punished. The dire punishments, frequently referred to by the Prophets, are: sword, famine and plague. The author of the Song of Moses poetically describes the Israelites as "wasted with hunger" — exhausted and emaciated by starvation — and "devoured with burning heat" — consumed by a wasting fever. Starvation was one of the grimmest of the disasters that afflicted the countries of the ancient East and is often described in contemporary literature and official records (see p. 108).

The Egyptian relief from the Twelfth Dynasty (first part of the second millennium B.C.) reproduced here is an artistic portrayal of a man so weakened by hunger that he has to lean on his staff for support. He is a herdsman from the Libyan desert.

THE LORD came
from Sinai, and dawn-
ed from Seir upon us;
He shone forth from
Mount Paran, He came
from the ten thousands
of holy ones, with
flaming fire at His right
hand.   (Deut. 33 : 2)

Here the Bible describes afresh the awesome revelations of the Divine Presence in the deserts of Sinai and the Negeb (cf. Judges 5 : 4-5; Ps. 68 : 7-10; Hab. 3 : 3-5), the primary purpose of which was to give guidance to the tribes of Israel. The revelations were not confined to Mount Horeb, but accompanied the Israelites throughout their journeyings; thus, God revealed Himself at the oasis of Kadesh Barnea.
Some scholars hold that, since Mount Sinai is mentioned here apparently together with Kadesh Barnea (referred to in our verse in the word *kodesh* "holy ones"), it must be in the northern part of the peninsula; they identify it with Jebel Hilal, about 30 miles west of Kadesh (see lower picture). This mountain rises to a height of about 3000 ft. and towers above the surrounding barrenness of the desert.
In the Bible, the name Mount Seir (i.e. the wooded mountain) is applied to an extensive region stretching from the eastern edge of Sinai to the mountains of Edom on the east of the Arabah (cf. the upper figure which was taken in the vicinity of Petra).

YOUR enemies shall come fawning to you; and
you shall tread upon their high places.

(Deut. 33 : 29)

The blessing of Moses ends with a eulogy of Israel's might: "And He thrust out the enemy before you, and said,
Destroy" (Deut. 33 : 27). With the terror of the Lord upon them, the enemy will surrender and deny their
enmity to Israel, while God treads victoriously upon their backs *(bamoth)* — a metaphorical description of the
enemy's rout and unconditional surrender. The Hebrew word *bamah* appears here to have the early meaning of
"back" or "body", as in Ugaritic, and not the usual later meaning of "high place" as translated above. In the
ancient East, the trampling of the vanquished by the victor symbolized abject submission.
Here, for example, we see one of the reliefs from Medinet Habu (12th cent. B.C.) in which Ramses III is shown
treading upon the bodies of the defeated Sea Peoples.

AND Moses went up from the plains of Moab to Mount Nebo, to the top of Pisgah, which is opposite Jericho. And the LORD showed him all the land . . .

(Deut. 34 : 1)

Moses goes up to the top of Mount Nebo to look out over the Promised Land before he dies: "I let you see it with your eyes, but you shall not go over there" (Deut. 34 : 4). The highest point on the ridge of Mount Nebo, near Heshbon, has been identified with the peak today called Ras Siyagha which commands a magnificent panorama of the Holy Land, embracing Gilead, Judah and the hills of Ephraim.

A modern author has described the view from the top of Mount Nebo in the following words: "The further south the eye travels, the clearer the picture and the richer the colours; at last, at the Dead Sea, everything looks so transparent and so near that you imagine you could leap down or even touch it with your hands."

As Moses surveys the Promised Land before his death, God reminds him of the oath whereby He swore to Abraham, Isaac and Jacob that He would give the Land to their seed (ibid.).

Our photograph shows the view of the Jordan Valley and the northern end of the Dead Sea from Mount Nebo.

INDEXES

OBJECTS AND MONUMENTS

37. Dodanim—British Museum, London
    Ashkenaz—Eremitage Museum, Leningrad
38. Philistine—Medinet Habu, Egypt
    Caphtor—Knossos Palace, Crete
    Canaan—Palestine Archaeological Museum, Jerusalem
    Het—Hittite Museum, Ankara,
40. Iraq Museum, Baghdad
42. Shem—Oriental Institute, University of Chicago
    Elam—Louvre, Paris
    Ashur—Louvre, Paris
43. Aram—Staatliche Museen, Berlin
    Eber—Louvre, Paris
44. Brick—Staatliche Museen, Berlin
45. Model—Iraq Museum, Baghdad
    Seal—Collection A. Moortgart, Berlin
51. British Museum, London
54. Metropolitan Museum of Arts, New-York
56. British Museum, London
57. Sakkarah, Egypt
58. Palestine Archaeological Museum, Jerusalem
59. Sakkarah, Egypt
67. University Museum, University of Pennsylvania, Philadelphia
68. Staatliche Museen, Berlin
73. National Museum, Beirut
74. Sculpture—National Museum, Aleppo
    Relief—British Museum, London
76. Louvre, Paris
77. Hittite Museum, Ankara
85. Relief—Walters Art Gallery, Baltimore
    Figurine—Babylonian Collection, Yale University
88. Stele—Egyptian Museum, Cairo
91. Bronze figurine—Clark Collection, Y.M.C.A., Jerusalem
    Pottery figurine—Department of Antiquities, Jerusalem (Israel)
95. Sakkarah, Egypt
98. British Museum, London
99. Staatliche Museen, Berlin
101. Papyrus—British Museum, London
103. Staatliche Museen, Berlin
105. Head of Semite—Egyptian Museum, Cairo
106. Relief—Rijksmuseum v. Oudheden, Leiden
107. Model—Ashmolean Museum, Oxford
108. Sakkarah, Egypt
109. Metropolitan Museum of Arts, New York
111. Oriental Institute, University of Chicago
112. Cup—Egyptian Museum, Cairo
112—3. Scarabs of Anat-her and Samqan—v. Bissing Collection, Munich
    Scarabs of Jacob-her and Khiyan—British Museum, London
    Dagger handle—Egyptian Museum, Cairo
117. Metropolitan Museum of Arts, New York
118. Metropolitan Museum of Arts, New York
120. Boat—Palestine Archaeological Museum, Jerusalem
    Deer—Tomb in Alfasi Rd., Jerusalem
    Wolf—National Museum, Aleppo, Syria
122. Coffin—Egyptian Museum, Cairo
123. Embalming materials—Metropolitan Museum of Arts, New-York

EXODUS

127. Museum of Turin, Italy
131. Basket—Metropolitan Museum of Arts, New York
132. Medinet Habu, Egypt
135. Metropolitan Museum of Arts, New York
138. Statue—Museum of Fine Arts, Boston
139. Tutankhamon—Egyptian Museum, Cairo
    Akhenaton—Staatliche Museen, Berlin
    Amenophis III, Thutmosis III—British Museum, London
    Hatshepsut—Metropolitan Museum of Arts, New York
140—1. Karnak, Egypt
145. Karnak, Egypt
146. Sakkarah, Egypt
153. Louvre, Paris
154. University Museum, University of Pennsylvania, Philadelphia
155. Relief—Louvre, Paris

156. University Museum, University of Pennsylvania, Philadelphia
157. Palestine Archaeological Museum, Jerusalem
158. Egyptian Museum, Cairo
163. Arch of Titus, Rome
    Cast and Coin—Archaeological Department, Hebrew University, Jerusalem
164. Vessel—Byblos Excavations
167. Collection Dr. N. Shalem, Jerusalem
168. Louvre, Paris
169. Department of Antiquities, Jerusalem (Israel)
170. Palestine Archaeological Museum, Jerusalem
171. Ny-Carlsberg Glyptothek, Copenhagen
173. Egyptian Museum, Cairo
175. Mastaba of Mereruka, Sakkarah, Egypt

LEVITICUS

179. Louvre, Paris
180. Offering dish—Egyptian Museum, Cairo
    Baking tray—Palestine Archaeological Museum, Jerusalem
182. Relief—Hittite Museum, Ankara
183. Egyptian Museum, Cairo
184. Model—Metropolitan Museum of Arts, New York
186. Camels—British Museum, London
    Hare—Tomb of Meten, Egypt
192. Ivory relief—Louvre, Paris
194. Vessel—Museum of the Ancient Orient, Istanbul
195. Louvre, Paris
198. Museum of the Ancient Orient, Istanbul

NUMBERS

202. Standard-bearer from Mari—Louvre, Paris
209. Stone vessels—Department of Antiquities, Jerusalem (Israel)
    Pottery vessel—Hazor Expedition, Israel
210. Karnak, Egypt
213. Egyptian Museum, Cairo
218. Hazor Expedition, Israel
221. Bronze snake — Department of Antiquities, Jerusalem (Israel)
    Standard—Hazor Expedition, Israel
225. Palestine Archaeological Museum, Jerusalem
228. Aurochs—Staatliche Museen, Berlin
    Baal relief—Louvre, Paris
229. Staatliche Museen, Berlin
231. Louvre, Paris
232—3. British Museum, London
234. Palestine Archaeological Museum, Jerusalem

DEUTERONOMY

252. Knossos Palace, Crete
256. Stone statue—Museum of the Ancient Orient, Istanbul
    Wooden statue—Brooklyn Museum, New York
268. Louvre, Paris
269. Ishtar stele—Louvre, Paris
    El stele—National Museum, Aleppo
271. Relief—Metropolitan Museum of Arts, New York
    Seal—British Museum, London
272. Egyptian Museum, Cairo
273. Collection de Clercq, Paris
274. British Museum, London
275. Medinet Habu, Egypt
277. Karnak, Egypt
280. Statue: Body—Museum of the Ancient Orient, Istanbul
    Head—Staatliche Museen, Berlin
282. British Museum, London
285. Louvre, Paris
287. Museum of Fine Arts, Boston
290. Department of Antiquities, Jerusalem (Israel)
291. Cast—Staatliche Museen, Berlin
294. British Museum, London
295. Meir, Egypt

301

REPRODUCTIONS

GENESIS

19. Schocken Library, Jerusalem
22. Ivory casket—after R.D. Barnett: *Catalogue of Nimrud Ivories*
26. N. de G. Davies and A.H. Gardiner: *Ancient Egyptian Paintings*
36. M. Pallottino: *Etruscan Painting*
38—9. Below—R. Lepsius: *Denkmäler aus Ägypten und Äthiopien*
41. H. Schmöckel: *Ur, Assur und Babylon*
43. Maadkarib—W. Phillips: *Qataban and Sheba*
44. Seal—After H. Frankfort: *The Art and Architecture of the Ancient Orient*
46. Plan—L. Woolley: *The Antiquaries Journal*, XI, 1931
    Street—after P. Lemaire & D. Baldi: *Atlante biblico*
    Ziggurat—after L. Woolley: *Ur Excavations*, V.
63. Line drawing—A.M. Blackman: *The Rock Tombs of Meir*
    Fresco—as Nos. 38—9 above
64. As No. 63 above (line-drawing)
66. After E. Peet and A.H. Gardiner: *Inscriptions of Sinai*, II
69. A. Lhote-Hassia: *Les Chefs-d'oeuvre de la Peinture Egyptienne*
75. N.de G. Davies and A.H. Gardiner: *Tomb of Kenamun*
80. E. Chiera: *Excavations at Nuzi*, I (*Harvard Semitic Studies*, V)
84. N. de G. Davies and A.H. Gardiner: *Tomb of the Two Sculptors*
85. Figurine—E. Douglas van Buren: *Clay Figurines*
88. Mesha inscription—after *Corpus Inscriptionum Semiticarum*
90. Drawing—G. Welter: *Forschungen und Fortschritte*
94. As No. 26
100. Fresco—N. de G. Davies and A.H. Gardiner: *Tomb of Nakht*
    Drawing—courtesy J. Leibovitch, Jerusalem
102. N. de G. Davies and A.H. Gardiner: *Tomb of Nakht*
104. As No. 69
105. Barber—courtesy of Metropolitan Museum of Arts, New York
    Egyptian Noble—as Nos. 38—9
106. Line drawing—P.E. Newberry: *Scarabs*
107. Line drawing—A. Erman & H. Ranke: *Ägypten und Ägyptisches Leben im Altertum*
110. As No. 26
114. Chariot—A. Mekhitarian: *Egyptian Painting*
    Semitic caravan—as Nos. 38—9
115. A.C.Th.E. Prisse d'Avennes: *Histoire de l'Art Egyptien*
116. As No. 69
120—1. Donkey—as No. 115
    Lions, Archer, Repast—G. Loud: *The Megiddo Ivories*
122—3. Mummification—W. Dawson: *Journal of Egyptian Archaeology*, XIII, 1927
124. N. de G. Davies and A.H. Gardiner: *Tomb of Neferhotep*

EXODUS

128. As Nos. 38—9
129. A. Gayet: *Le temple de Louxor*
130. As No. 26
131. Reeds—as No. 75
136. As No. 26
137. Frog—W. Smith: *Egyptian Painting*
    Locust—as No. 114 (Chariot)
138. Fresco—as No. 69
143. As No. 26
149. Below—water-colour R. Koppel—courtesy Prof. S.F. Bodenheimer, Jerusalem
150. As No. 26
152. After E.L. Sukenik: *Otsar ha-Megillot ha-Genuzot*
155. Fresco—courtesy Metropolitan Museum of Arts, New York
152. Above - H. Grimme: *Inschriften vom Sinai*
    Below—J. Leibovitch: *Inscriptions Proto-sinaïtiques*

164. Forks—R.A.S. Macalister: *The Excavation of Gezer*
172. Courtesy Metropolitan Museum of Arts, New York
174. As No. 84
176. Seal-maker—P.E. Newberry: *Proceedings of the Society of Biblical Archaeology*, XXVII

LEVITICUS

181. Fresco—as No. 114 (Chariot)
185. As Nos. 38-9
187. Line-drawing—as No. 107
190. Kermes—as No. 149

191. P.E. Newberry: *Beni Hasan*
192. Line drawing—H. Bonnet: *Reallexikon der Ägyptischen Religionsgeschichte*
193. Above—H. Zimmern: *Beiträge zur Babyl. Religion*
    Below—A. E. Wallis: *The Book of the Dead*

NUMBERS

202. Fresco—as No. 114 (Chariot)
202. W. Wrzeszinski: *Atlas zur Altägyptischen Kulturgeschichte*, II
207. Above—as No. 152
    Line drawing below—N. de G. Davies: *Tell el Amarna*
208. As No. 102
216. As No. 84
232. G.A. Reisner, C.S. Fisher, C.D. Lyon: *Harvard Excavations at Samaria*, II
235. After Y. Yadin: *Israel Exploration Journal*, III

DEUTERONOMY

261. Sinuhe text—A.H. Gardiner: *Notes on the Story of Sinuhe*
266. N. de G. Davies and A.H. Gardiner: *Two Ramesside Tombs*
270. K. Galling: *Biblisches Reallexikon*
276. Line drawing—N. de G. Davies and A.H. Gardiner: *Tomb of Rekhmire*
280. Courtesy Metropolitan Museum of Arts, New York
283. Above—as No. 276
    Below—B. Ubach: *La Biblia*
286. Above—as No. 102
    Below—as No. 26
289. After Foto W. van de Poll: *Nelson Atlas of the Bible*
297. As No. 203

MAPS (Drawn by Eng. Pinhas Yoeli)
Nos. 20, 33, 37, 39, 42, 47, 87, 141, 201, 212, 223, 236, 239

RECONSTRUCTIONS (by Eva Avi-Yonah)

133. After N. de G. Davies and A.H. Gardiner: *Tomb of Puyemre*, I
160. After Dr. M. Haran, Jerusalem
162. Mari—after A. Parrot: *Studia Mariana*
    Megiddo—after a photograph of the Palestine Archaeological Museum, Jerusalem
165. As No. 160
166. As No. 160
176. After W. Wrzeszinski: *Atlas zur Altägyptischen Kulturgeschichte* I
194. After A.E. Wallis Budge: *The Book of the Dead*
204. After A. Lhote-Hassia: *Les Chefs-d'oeuvre de la Peinture Egyptienne*
205. As No. 176

PHOTOGRAPHS